To Pluto

The most wonderful little dog in the world.
He was my mate and very best friend.

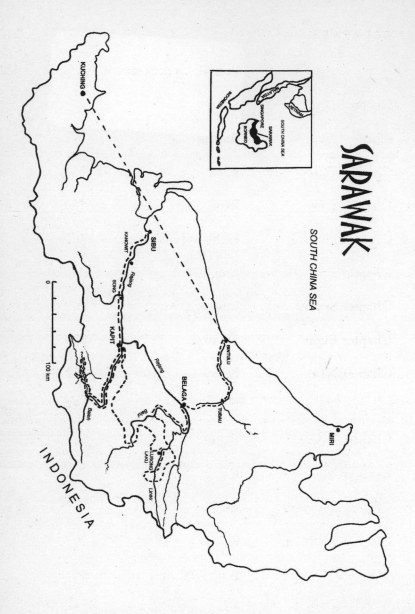

espresso with the

HEADHUNTERS

A journey through the jungles of Borneo

John Wassner

SUMMERSDALE

Summersdale Publishers Ltd
46 West Street
Chichester
West Sussex
PO19 1RP
UK

www.summersdale.com

Printed and bound in Great Britain.

ISBN 1 84024 137 3

contents

prelude to disaster

Among some of the most remarkable drunks I've encountered in my life are headhunters. Not just the kind that take you out to a boozy lunch in anticipation of a fat commission once they've placed you in a six-figure job, but more so the ones who live deep in the jungles of Borneo. I had first come across one of these 'wild men' of Borneo in Kuala Lumpur. A short stocky man, decked out in feathers and sporting incredibly stretched earlobes, was making a call from a public phone. The sight of a tribesman in traditional dress amidst the office towers and chic designer boutiques of modern KL was startling, to say the least.

Later that afternoon, as I was about to enjoy a double espresso (my third cup since lunch) in the lush tropical gardens of the Hilton, I saw the man's picture on the front page of *The Star*: his name was Jampang and he belonged to a group of Ibans visiting the capital to protest against new logging concessions that threatened their forest. Until that day I had never heard of the Ibans, or indeed the State of Sarawak, their homeland which was originally ruled by a dynasty of 'White Rajas' but is now part of Malaysia. I briefly pondered the existence of such tribes just an hour's flight away from where I was relaxing in air-conditioned comfort, when my next espresso arrived, instantly shifting my attention to the aroma emanating from the tiny cup.

Two days later, as I was killing time at Singapore Airport waiting for my connecting flight to Australia, I came across a book entitled *Sarawak*. Curiosity took hold and I started leafing through page after glossy page of photographs that could have been taken straight out of *National Geographic*: breathtaking aerial shots of mighty rivers flowing through the jungle; hunters with blowpipes and poisoned darts; spectacular flora and fauna; and a few bleached skulls hanging from the rafters of longhouses. I bought the book, and by the time I arrived in Sydney I had made up my mind: I was going to Borneo. The decision was probably not quite as spontaneous as it appears: like most people in the advertising business, I was starting to feel a degree of 'burn-out' – a state of mind suggesting that it was time to do something radical. Some folks in the business take this as a signal to throw in the towel in the big smoke and relocate to some peaceful rural setting – preferably in tropical Queensland – to grow avocados or macadamia nuts and revert to a total state of seventies bliss, filled with peace, love and copious amounts of grass. I opted for the jungle instead.

After a year of gathering information, poring over maps, making detailed travel arrangements and buying all the necessary equipment that would see me through just about any conceivable eventuality in the jungle, I finally did what I had rehearsed in my mind over many a cup of coffee – I hung up a shingle on the office door saying 'GONE TO SEE THE HEADHUNTERS'. Which no doubt raised a few eyebrows among my poor stressed-out colleagues.

Postscript

Some names of people and longhouses have been changed to protect the guilty and to discourage tour groups from descending upon their homes.

chapter one

sibu

From the air Borneo looks like an advertisement for New Zealand wool carpets: deep, lush piles of greenery, interrupted only by the occasional river that looks like a giant snake winding its way through a landscape frozen in time. The island itself is gigantic – the second largest in the world after Greenland. Anchored halfway between Singapore and the island of Java, its southern province of Kalimantan belongs to Indonesia, while the north is made up of Sabah and Sarawak, both part of Malaysia. The tiny oil-rich sultanate of Brunei is wedged somewhere between these two provinces.

I had often seen Borneo from the air on some of my frequent trips to Asia, and the almost mystical appearance of the island with its jungles and volcanic peaks shrouded in mist seldom failed to evoke a feeling of adventure in what must be one of the world's last few unspoiled places. There are virtually no roads other than one major highway running along the coast and the occasional logging track deep in the interior. Transport is largely by air (weather permitting) or river (depth permitting). The isolation created by the island's rugged geography is, one assumes, in no small measure responsible for the incredible diversity of tribal life that can be found deep in the interior: some two hundred indigenous groups, each with their own dialects or languages – many of which are mutually unintelligible. In many ways the people of Borneo seem to have evolved like those of the

Amazon: the use of blowpipes, headhunting, the haircuts, the body decorations, rituals and religious beliefs, all bear a striking resemblance to cultures found on the opposite side of the globe, yet nowhere else on Earth. Is there a connection? The thought had intrigued me for the best part of a year, and perhaps now I was about to find out.

As if on cue, the captain's voice comes over the PA system, interrupting my reveries. 'Good morning ladies and gentlemen. We're on our final approach to Sibu, and after hanging a left over the bay we should have you on the ground in just a couple of shakes of the wings.' The distinct Australian accent and sense of humour came as somewhat of a surprise, to say the least, on a domestic Malaysian Airlines flight.

'The temperature in Sibu is a pleasant 39 degrees. Your crew and I trust you'll have a nice day!'

Thank you for that, skipper. Shortly after the announcement, the tiny Fokker Friendship touched down, throwing up clouds of dust and the smell of burning rubber as the aircraft comes to a screeching halt in front of the terminal on the hot, shimmering tarmac. As the exit door hinges up, a blast of hot air, similar to that when opening an oven door, hits the cabin interior. Welcome to the equator.

'Flight to Kapit, sir?'

'Yes, that's right.' I hand my ticket to the check-in clerk.

'Please stand on the scales.'

'You mean my luggage?'

'Yes, please.'

My carefully packed army backpack goes on the scales: 9.2 kilos. (I could have told him that, after packing and re-packing the damned thing countless times to keep the weight down in anticipation of some heavy going in the jungle.)

'Now you, please,' the clerk says with a broad smile, pointing once more at the scales.

'Me?'

'Yes, please.'

I do as the man asks, realising that we are dealing with some very small aircraft where every bit of weight counts.

'Please wait for your boarding call – the flight is a little delayed.'

'How long?'

'Soon.'

'Like what – an hour, two?'

'Yes.'

'Which one?'

'Yes. Very soon, sir.'

OK, then, coffee time. I search the terminal for the *restoran* and find it by following the smell of fried chilli and exotic spices wafting through the terminal. It's a pretty basic sort of affair, but with a very long counter full of wonderful local dishes. There is no espresso machine, causing some serious complications in my decision-making process. I opt for the *nasi kampong* (a local version of neighbouring Indonesia's famous rice dish *nasi goreng*) and a chilled guava juice instead.

The place is packed with hundreds of Malays decked out in their pilgrim's best: it's Ramadan, the Muslim holy month and a bonanza for Malaysian Airlines who are about to ferry a large chunk of Sibu's population to Mecca for the annual *hadj*. 'Mind if we join you, *lah*?'

I've always loved the Malay speech mannerism of adding '*lah*' to just about any word worth emphasising. I look up from my plate of rice, but with a piece of red-hot chilli stuck in my throat I am temporarily left speechless. Eyes watering, I gesture towards the empty chairs. The parents and several children install themselves at the table, their trays laden with a wondrous array of foods.

'*Silakan makan,*' the father invites me, pointing at the plates that are being neatly arranged in the centre of the table in anticipation of the communal feasting about to take place.

'Please help yourself.' I gratefully acknowledge their generosity by taking a few morsels from the tempting selection.

'You going up-river?' the father asks, looking up and down my newly acquired photo-journalist's jacket featuring 14 zip pockets (including three waterproof ones) plus one hidden compartment inside the back lining.

'Yes, for a couple of weeks.'

'Aha. Nice.'

'Have you been there?'

He looks at me, almost incredulously. 'No. Never.'

His response does not really surprise me. Although Malays make up nearly 20 per cent of Sarawak's coastal population, few of them ever venture into the interior of the country. Maybe it's the headhunting stories that occasionally make the rounds. Or a simple fear of the unknown. Or even, perhaps, a genuine lack of interest.

Whatever the reasons, for me there's a whole new world of excitement waiting, and a plane on the tarmac ready to take me there. Over the din of the airport, the PA system comes alive with a burst of crackles and sounds fading in and out in quick succession. I failed to pick up anything I may have understood from the garbled message, so I asked my new friends for a translation.

'I don't know. My English is not so good.'

I wish my host and his family a happy pilgrimage and a safe return as I make my way back to the check-in counter. The clerk greets me with a broad smile.

'Ah, sir, there you are. I'm afraid your flight has been cancelled. Bad weather in Kapit. Cannot land.' A shrug of the shoulders as if to say that's that.

I had been warned of this. Weather in this part of the world can play havoc with schedules. Sudden tropical downpours will turn a landing strip into knee-deep mud within minutes, and pilots will cancel flights at the slightest hint of rain.

'You can catch the Express Boat to Kapit tomorrow morning,' says the still smiling clerk. Thanking him for his thoughtfulness, I head straight for the taxi stand. Just in front of me is a sun-tanned and obviously very happy pilot, his arms around two giggling hostesses. They take the last taxi in the queue. As I am about to set down my backpack, a *bas mini* (mini bus) pulls up at the kerbside.

'Looking for a hotel, sir?'

Indeed. A few questions and answers later, we're off through the chaos of traffic weaving in and out of lanes, traffic lights largely ignored and a basket of produce falling off the back of a bike, scattering its contents across the road surface to the delight of local school children on their way home. The town is only small. But its location at the mouth of the Rajang River, some 60 kilometres upstream from the sea, has turned this once sleepy village into a major port city, handling rubber, timber, pepper and even oil for trans-shipment to other parts of Malaysia and the rest of the world.

It's a busy place with a bustling waterfront, noisy markets and a motley population made up of Chinese traders, oil workers, loggers and a fair mix of tribal people who come here to seek their fortunes. The *bas mini* rounds a corner and proceeds slowly down a narrow lane where hawkers are starting to set up their stalls for the night market. Right at the end of the lane a large neon sign proclaims 'Premier Hotel' – my destination. I dump my backpack in the room and return to the lobby where a real espresso machine promises a welcome break before I head out to discover the delights or otherwise of downtown Sibu. Refreshed after my double espresso, several cigarettes and a phone call to find out departure times for the Express Boats in the morning, I step out of the hotel and straight into the sauna-like humidity. As usual, my glasses fog up instantly.

The place is really bumping and jumping, but in a slow, tropical sort of way. People amble down the streets, some holding hands, a fairly common Asian expression of friendship. The air is thick and blue from the exhaust fumes created by the seemingly endless cavalcade of motorcycles, buses and overloaded trucks. At intersections the noise can be deafening as hundreds of engines rev up for the race to be first off the mark when the lights turn green. Scattered amidst the organised chaos and in the most unlikely places are little havens of rest and tranquillity: the ubiquitous coffee shops and hawker stalls where the cacophony of sounds suddenly becomes a secondary background as the mental focus shifts towards an icy cold drink or plates laden with food.

As I wander down the narrow lanes leading to the waterfront, the area suddenly opens up into a large market, crammed with stalls selling everything from fresh produce to plastic wares, clothes and an incredible variety of live animals, most of which no doubt are destined for the cooking pot. On the far side of the square the market takes on a tribal character, with groups of Ibans squatting on the floor selling jungle produce, baskets, rattan mats, brass gongs and the odd bits of local craft.

As if to mark the exit of this exotic enclave, a lone musician, his body tattooed from head to toe, occupies the very last mat, playing his *sape* – a string instrument that emits haunting, almost plaintive melodies, and a sound that I would become familiar with during many a magical longhouse night.

Another few minutes walk and I emerged from of the maze of streets into the grandly named Esplanade, Sibu's waterfront. Crossing the road towards the jetties I catch my first glimpse of the mighty Rajang, my pathway to adventure. Although a hub of frantic activity during the day, the jetties are now deserted, save a couple of fishermen dangling their lines in the water and chatting quietly as if anxious not to disturb the peace of the night. Right next to them, bobbing in the water with gentle waves lapping at their hulls, are several of Borneo's famed Express Boats, tied up one against another to form a gigantic raft that reaches at least fifty metres out into the river. Express Boats are unlike anything that floats or plies the waters elsewhere in the world. According to (unconfirmed) stories, the boats were first built after World War II using aircraft fuselages with the wings chopped off and a large engine mounted at the back. Their speed (up to 70 km per hour) made them an instant hit with the population by cutting travelling time to remote towns such as Kapit or Belaga down to hours, instead of days. They looked impressive and slightly scary. But just how scary they could be I wouldn't find out until the morning.

chapter two

rajang

The phone wakes me from a deep sleep.

'Good morning, this is the reception. You asked us to wake you. But it is late already, I am sorry Sir.'

I look at the clock. Holy shit! It's five twenty-five and I'm supposed to be at the wharf in twenty minutes! As if struck by a bolt of lightning I jump out of bed, turn on the shower and have a thirty-second splash. There's no time to shave. I asked for a five o'clock wake-up call, but someone goofed down there. I dress in less than a minute. Lacing up the canvas jungle boots takes another two minutes. Back to the bathroom for a glass of water to pop my weekly malaria tablet, and I'm off, slinging my pack over one shoulder.

The waterfront is not all that far, but with the humidity, my fogged-up glasses and the weight of my pack, it seems to be miles away. As I approach the jetty, the boats start sounding their horns impatiently, one by one announcing their imminent departure to stragglers like myself. There's a flurry of last-minute activity as baskets, cardboard boxes and all manner of merchandise are being piled on the boats and secured to the roof. Some passengers have already settled on top of the hot roof, ready for a wild ride in the wind.

The gangplanks are about the width of a paperback novel, conjuring up images of people like myself who suffer from chronic balance problems being crushed between the bumping hulls of adjoining vessels. A toothless wrinkled face pops up in front of me, pointing at my backpack and indicating an offer of help. Glad for any assistance I can get, I pass the pack to the old man and he takes off at a light trot. Someone else takes my hand and guides me firmly across the plank to the safety of the deck.

But that was only number one: there are six more boat-to-boat crossings to negotiate until I reach the Kapit Express, right at the end of the line. Bathed in sweat and adrenalin pumping from the early morning onslaught of rapid-fire activities, I take a sip from my water bottle and collapse into the first seat available below deck, momentarily closing my eyes. My newly-found state of bliss, however, is short-lived. With an almighty roar, the powerful turbo-charged V-12 twin engines explode into life, sending a shudder down the length of the boat. Outside, deckhands untie the lines and the boats start peeling from the jetty one by one, briefly floating sideways before taking off at full-throttle towards the centre of the river.

I sit back in my seat, light a cigarette and take in my new surroundings. The cabin seems comfortable enough. In fact, it's no different to that of any ordinary small aircraft: reclining seats, headrests and even films (predominantly kung-fu action) played out at a deafening 10,000 decibels on large screens mounted on the bulkheads.

The pilot sits in the cockpit, guided by hand signals from a 'pointman' who perches cross-legged at the bow, watching out for ever-present logs and all manner of debris floating down the gigantic river. Although the skills of the pilots (mostly the Chinese boat owners themselves) are admirable, semi-submerged logs regularly mangle propellers, and other more serious accidents do happen. The notorious Pelagus

Rapids – a seething, two kilometre stretch of wild, foaming waters between Kapit and Belaga – have claimed many lives over the years, as the bullet-shaped boats try to navigate their way around treacherous bends, listing dangerously with engines screaming in reverse thrust to avoid the next obstacle. In 1990 two boats collided head-on, just off Kapit in early-morning fog. One of them rolled and sank instantly with serious loss of life.

Looking around the cabin, it quickly becomes evident that, in spite of new regulations introduced recently, safety codes remain largely ignored. There are only two bottleneck exits at the front, adjoining the cockpit. Windows are firmly sealed and the one solitary 'emergency exit' at the back of the cabin opens outwards, making it impossible to open under pressure of water. Life jackets are strewn haphazardly around various locations, in numbers nowhere sufficient to cover all the passengers on board.

'*Makan! Makan!*' The magic words promising breakfast after my somewhat hasty departure from Sibu turn my head away from the lifejacket with the missing straps and to the direction of the food wallah who is making his way slowly up the aisle. Some fried noodles with chicken and copious amounts of chilli, a hard-boiled egg and a Foochow bun fill the empty spot in my stomach. I feel a lot better now and start to wake up. Getting up before sunrise is not something I cherish. There are many other things I'd rather do. Like sleep, sleep and sleep.

Holding on to my can of warm Coke, I decide to venture outside to take in some of the activity on the river. Although it's still early, the sun is already burning down without mercy, creating dazzling reflections on the water. The Rajang is Malaysia's equivalent of the Amazon – the main thoroughfare into the interior. Its sheer size is impressive, to say the least, with some stretches over a kilometre wide, giving it more the appearance of a lake than a river. Along the banks, sleepy Malaysian villages with houses precariously perched on stilts appear and disappear back into their idyllic jungle setting as the boat plies the silt-laden brown waters at full speed.

A tap on my shoulder. I turn around and, just above me on the roof, a smiling face invites me to share a small space with apparently grand river views. (He must have noticed how I tend to hang on like grim death to the doorframe every time the vessel swerved to avoid oncoming logs.) But there's no way he is going to get me up there. I decline politely and offer him a cigarette instead, which he takes gratefully with a nod of his head.

'You going to Belaga?' he shouts into the wind.

'No, I get off at Kapit.' I shout back.

'Ah, nice place. You visit longhouse maybe?'

'Yes, I hope so.'

'You have guide, already?'

'Yes, I'm meeting him in Kapit.'

At least I hope so, assuming the guide worked out that yesterday's flight was cancelled and that I'd be coming up by boat instead. An ear-piercing blast (right next to me) from the boat's air-horns is answered in turn by a blast from a second Express Boat that has come alongside. Both slow down and almost come to a halt, floating a short distance in the current. Suddenly an almighty blast from boat number two and we take off at full-throttle, side by side, with passengers cheering, yelping and whooping the pilots on to go faster.

'Express Boat Race,' says the man on the roof, as if replying to what must have been quite a puzzled expression on my face.

'Ah, I see. How far do they race?'

'Maybe to Kanowit.'

Right. That's at least half an hour away. The boats are now head-to-head, racing at a steady speed, seemingly oblivious to the tug-boat pulling an enormous raft of logs and heading straight towards us. The tug sounds its horn. Number one expresses a reply, followed by number two. Then, as the logs are almost upon our bows, both boats swerve in opposite directions, leaving tug, logs and everything else to slide into the huge wake they created.

More whooping and yelping from the passengers on the roof as they take obvious delight in the sights of the tug and its appendages bobbing up and down in the resulting surf-like conditions. As we approach the Kanowit jetty, both boats slow down and number two waves us in. It appears that the race resulted in a tie, as none of the roof-dwellers seem to be able to agree on an outright winner. Never mind, *lah*. The consensus seems to be that it was a good race.

The stop in Kanowit is only short – just enough to unload a few passengers and their chattels. Heading upstream, the landscape starts to change as the river narrows and the first longhouses start to appear, high up on its banks. In their most basic interpretation, longhouses are really entire villages, contained in one single, very long building that accommodates anywhere between twenty and sometimes up to fifty or more families under the one roof. A veranda that runs along the entire length of the house is the equivalent of the village main street, with day-to-day activities taking place there under the watchful eye of the headman and his senior cronies.

It is communal living in its most fundamental form – an early forerunner, perhaps, of the hippy communes that emerged in the seventies, but based on highly complex cultural and religious traditions, firmly enshrined in age-old tribal laws. Closer to the major population centres near the coast, most longhouses are of the 'modern' type: constructed by the government in an effort to resettle communities and put them in closer touch with what is loosely called the 'twentieth century'. These dwellings are ugly affairs, with tin roofs (that soon turn rusty), plywood interior walls, fluorescent lights and weather-board exteriors. However, like all longhouses, they are built high up on riverbanks, on elevated platforms to minimise the risk of flooding and to keep out snakes, crocodiles and other kinds of unwanted visitors.

As we approach lunchtime, the midday sun is starting to make itself felt on my neck and arms and I retreat back into the cabin, where the air-conditioning is working overtime: it's freezing in here, and I retrieve my lightweight sweater from the backpack. About to re-fasten the straps on the pack, I notice one of the outside pockets, containing my first aid kit, is still open. I must have forgotten to do it up after taking my malaria tablets out in the morning.

The malaria tablets!

My heart stops beating for a moment as I frantically search the kit. Nothing. I must have left them back in the hotel. Slumping into my seat, I contemplate the situation. Malaria is one of the real risks one encounters in this part of the world, especially out in the jungle where hordes of eager mosquitoes descend from the sky at sunset in search of some tasty drops of 'whitefella' blood.

Cerebral malaria is the worst kind, and statistics of annual fatalities among the local population are not encouraging. Worse still, I am allergic to the most common kind of malaria tablets, something I found out when I collapsed a couple of years ago. I was dining with my partner Nerida at the terrace restaurant of the plush Oriental Hotel in Bangkok. To complete a good meal, I was enjoying the dessert I had been eyeing all night. All I remember is taking my first spoonful of the tempting treat when suddenly all the tables around me started spinning and my mind went blank.

The next thing I saw was a crowd of people around me, with the maître d' and a select entourage of managers, assistant managers and waiters, all in their formal best, asking me questions, proffering glasses of water and trying to get me up from under the table.

'I am sorry,' I said, trying to smile. 'What happened?'

'I think you passed out, sir. May we take you to your room? We have already notified the doctor.'

No, it couldn't have been the dessert, I'd barely touched it. The tuxedoed procession accompanied me through the lobby to a lift already waiting. I don't know how I got into bed, but I didn't wake up until the next morning. Nerida sat next to me on the bed, cooling my burning forehead with cold compresses.

'Hi.' I said.

'Hi.'

'What's up?'

'Looks like you got yourself a bout of malaria.'

It appears that the hotel doctor had been and diagnosed an allergic reaction to the malaria tablets I had bought over the counter in Singapore. Allergies of this kind can apparently manifest themselves by artificially recreating the symptoms of a disease. And if that's what malaria is like – burning fever, hotel furniture spinning around inside your head, unpredictable bowel movements and a host of other unpleasant ways of spending a couple of days in bed – I'd really rather not know about it.

Stuck on an Express Boat in the middle of Borneo I consider my options, lighting a cigarette under the pretext of relaxing the mind. There is a (very slight) chance that I could replenish my supplies in Kapit – the last outpost of 'civilisation' before I venture deep into the interior. Or I could try and ring the hotel to see if someone had found the tablets. This would require getting them up-river somehow. Perhaps with the skipper of the next Express Boat? And if all else fails I may have to return to Sibu, get a new prescription and go through another Express Boat racing challenge on the way back.

The latter option would mean a delay in my trip, and in all likelihood changes of schedule all along the way. But I've waited twelve months for this, so I'm not going to let a couple of lousy tablets spoil it for me. Kapit, here we come!

chapter three

kapit

The concrete steps leading up the steep riverbank to the tiny town look daunting. Having survived another set of narrow gangplanks and clambered ashore with many a helping hand, I now face this 'stairway to heaven' – some hundred steps, perhaps – in the midday heat.

Puffing and panting I make it to the top and deposit my backpack on the ground. Across the road I spot a welcoming '*Kedai Kopi*' sign, promising respite over a cup of coffee while I catch my breath. A young Chinese lady makes her way slowly to the front of the coffee shop, dragging her sandals noisily over the floor. I order *kopi susu* – an ultra-sweet strong coffee topped up with at least half a can of sweetened condensed milk. I feel rather light-headed from the stair-climbing experience and start seriously wondering how on earth I am going to make it through the jungle with my pack, which seems to be weighing a tonne. But the coffee and cold Coke quickly restore my faith, and I suddenly feel on top of the world as I take in the colourful procession of characters disgorging from the latest Express Boat.

A group of Ibans emerge, balancing precariously over the slippery wooden mooring logs and making their way up the embankment, carrying pepper, jungle ferns, chickens, pigs and a host of other goods to trade or sell at Kapit's wooden bazaar. Some of the women carry babies on their backs in beautifully embroidered baskets. A couple of men have *parangs* – a sort of sword once used to lop off heads, but nowadays put to much more mundane tasks such as chopping bamboo, clearing jungle paths, carving wood or threatening mothers-in-law.

My camera doesn't stop clicking as I zoom in on the passing parade of up-river folk who have come to town for their once-a-month 'big time'. As I snap away, I notice an old man with earlobes stretched under the weight of two massive silver balls, standing at a discreet (and safe) distance and looking at me in as much amazement as I have been eyeing him through my lens. I call out '*Selamat pagi!*' and he returns the greeting with a broad smile and a wave of his hand. Opening my packet of cigarettes, I point its contents at him in a universal invitation that crosses all language barriers. He comes over to the table, takes a cigarette, smiles politely and sits down.

'*Kopi?*' I ask.

He nods and leans back in his chair, depositing his basket of goodies next to him. This is going to be interesting. Here I am, just five minutes in town and sharing a table with someone from a world that is so different from mine that he may as well have come from Mars.

In spite of his small stature, he looks impressive. Tattoos in intricate swirl designs cover his throat, arms and thighs. (There may be others but he is wearing a bleached-out T-shirt and shorts, so I can't tell.) He's a wiry fellow, with sinews protruding from his arms and legs, and taut muscles which, used to the harsh life in the wilderness, would have mastered the steep steps up from the river as if they were a child's hopscotch game.

His coffee arrives and he slurps it with a great deal of gusto and matching sound effects.

We make several attempts at communicating, but his Malay is even worse than mine, judging by his nods, smiles and hand signals. So we resort to discreet glances at one another, followed by lots of smiles and polite gestures. (Sugar? Another cigarette? Coke?)

His coffee finished, he burps, gets up, retrieves an orange from his basket and hands it to me.

'Thank you,' I say in English, returning his compliment with a gift of Australian cigarettes which he eagerly accepts with a sincere and very agitated handshake. He wanders off, turning back periodically with a friendly wave, and mighty proud of his gift: wait till the others see this.

Malaria tablets. I should try to get them before I check in at the hotel, which I am told is just a couple of blocks up the road.

The waitress with the shuffling feet points across the street in response to my enquiry about a doctor. I look at her quizzically. All I can see is a half dozen stalls, some with vegetables spread on rattan mats on the ground, and lots of locals squatting around.

'Klinik Sia!' the lady says, emphatically pointing at a door just behind the chickens. Yes, indeed, there it is. How could I miss it, I think, having expected a more traditional doctor's surgery instead of a shop front with chickens in the doorway.

The waiting room is full. But not everyone expects to see the doctor because the reception desk doubles up as a dispensary and attending nurses administer first aid on the spot, dressing wounds and handing out pills in bulk from a vast array of containers lined up on the shelves like cookie jars. One rather bulky woman removes her child from a chair and beckons me to sit down. I do as I am told. The room is totally devoid of reading matter; not one *Reader's Digest* or *Country Homes* magazine in sight. The only distraction is a whirring ceiling fan, which I watch for a while. But I don't have to wait too long.

'Mr John?' The man in the freshly starched white coat looks around the room and his eyes stop at me. (An obvious choice, I would have thought.)

'Please come in.'

I take the seat offered to me and explain my predicament. Dr Sia 'ums' and 'ahs', looks up a bulky pharmacopoeia and shakes his head.

'I'm sorry, Mr John, I don't have any malaria tablets that are not sulphur based. But you can try the other *Klinik*, only three doors up. They may be able to help you.'

There is no charge for the consultation. I try my luck three doors up. The scene is the same, minus the ceiling fan. But I'm in luck. The doctor prescribes the correct pills and I get a stash, neatly piled into a small plastic bag, from the dispensary on the way out. Again there's no charge for the consultation, but I have to pay for the pills – a grand total of two ringgit – about one-tenth of the going price back home. Much relieved, I start making my way to the hotel, but I barely reach the top of the lane when I hear someone calling out.

'Mr John! Mr John!'

It's the nurse from the dispensary, a small satchel in her hand, chasing me up the street.

'I am sorry, Mr John. I make a mistake – you have the wrong pills. I give you the sulphur – not good for you. I am sorry. But these are OK, *lah*.'

Before I can thank her for her attentiveness, she's off down the lane, ready to tackle anew the challenges of the waiting room without ceiling fan.

Little did I know that I was in for another surprise when I approached the hotel reception.

'Ah, Mr Wassner, welcome to the Meligai Hotel. We have a message for you.' He hands me a little yellow slip: 'Call Josephine on extension 361.'

'Josephine? Are you sure this is for me? I don't know anybody here.'

'Yes, sir. Miss Josephine, your guide. She has been expecting you yesterday.'

I was floored. Josephine? Miss? As the thought sinks in, my images of a tough tribal (male) warrior, ready to wrestle crocodiles and cut up king cobras with his *parang* as he guides me through the jungle, start to vanish. Female guides aren't uncommon anywhere, it's just that it was the last thing I expected in Borneo. I ring the number from my room. No answer. She's probably out about town, buying up provisions for the trip.

After a leisurely shower (the continuation of my early-morning attempt at it), I turn the air-conditioning up to supersonic and sit back on the bed, reflecting on the day's events. Before long, the idea of a little nap becomes increasingly appealing. It doesn't last long, however. After about half an hour I wake up and the adrenalin is pumping once more: there's a whole fascinating world out there, waiting to be discovered.

I dress and set out to explore the town – all eight blocks of it. Built up high on the riverbank, Kapit is situated at the confluence of the Rajang and Baleh rivers and was strategically selected by the 'White Raja' Charles Brooke late last century to keep warring tribes apart.

The town is dominated by Fort Sylvia, which affords sweeping views and, most importantly in its heyday, advance warnings of approaching raiding parties from the up-river Kayans or Kenyahs, out to score a few heads from the local Iban – and vice versa. It is the last government outpost before heading into the *ulu*, the tribal areas of Borneo. From here on there is nothing but jungle, mist-shrouded mountains and rivers, with the odd logging camp breaking up nature here and there.

In many respects, Kapit has the feel of a real frontier town, alive with markets, traders and all manner of activities during the day; prostitutes, pool halls, discos and karaoke bars complement the scene at night. It takes me all of ten minutes to see the place, passing a tiny Chinese temple overgrown with bamboo and ferns, countless shops selling jeans, sarongs, kitchen utensils, Rambo-style knives with matching battle fatigues and innumerable types of plastic containers. It's not exactly a shopper's paradise, but for the locals it's Manhattan, complete with a bitumen road that runs south for about thirty kilometres and then stops abruptly in the middle of nowhere. At the other end of town is Fort Sylvia, which now houses government offices and sports several 'high water' markers, one of them halfway up the door and some eighteen metres above the river.

Ahead of me are just a couple of concrete administrative buildings, so I return to the town square in search of the lady with the shuffling slippers. However, the rickety metal tables scattered on the footpath outside the Kah Ping Restaurant seem to offer a better vantage point for observing the goings-on around me, so I settle for a table in the shade.

'*Kopi? Teh? Guinness?*'

The menu at this time of day is obviously limited but a cold bottle of Carlsberg would make an appealing companion while I jot down some entries in my pocket diary. I linger a while and thoroughly enjoy my surroundings. Coffee shops are a way of life in this part of the world, something I can readily identify with, having grown up in Europe. The only difference is that we drink our coffee in tiny cups and call it 'espresso'. My thoughts are interrupted by a young man approaching the table.

'Hello. Are you Mr John from Australia?' and almost in the same breath, as he spots the packet on the table, 'can I have a cigarette?'

He sits down.

'I'm Jo's cousin.'

Ah, the famous Josephine, my guide. Still slightly puzzled, I ask him how he knew who I was. With an almost embarrassed chuckle he says, 'You're the only *orang putih* – er, the only white man in town. Not too hard to find, *lah!*'

We chat about the heat, Kapit, Australia, my trip, and get along famously. As suddenly as he appeared, he gets up, shakes my hand and tells me that Josephine will meet me in the Meligai lobby at seven o'clock. Which leaves me time for one more coffee.

The lift bell rings. Finding it hard to hold back my curiosity, I glance over my shoulder. A pretty young Malaysian girl steps out, followed by three children. I return to yesterday's copy of the *Borneo Post*.

Again the lift bell rings. The doors open. Empty. Doors close again. Back to the newspaper.

At the third ring, a young woman steps out, looks in my direction and waves.

'Hi, Mr John. I am Josephine.'

She's nothing like what I expected. Short and slightly on the plump side, she does not give the impression of someone who has made a career of traipsing around in the wilderness.

'Maybe later we go for some dinner, yes? We can eat some local food at the night markets.'

Sounds good to me. For now, however, it's obviously 'getting to know you time' as we retire to the bar. Josephine is a Kayan, and very proud of it. The Kayans regard themselves as the 'aristocrats' of the *ulu,* and many of their longhouses have taken up Christianity with an almost unmatched fervour. Her first question, as we settle at the bar, is, 'Mr John, are you a Christian?' Sorry, sweetheart, I'm Jewish and right out of hymns.

'No,' I say, not wanting to immerse myself into a potentially deep and meaningful theological debate at the end of an exhausting day.

'Never mind, *lah*!' She quickly changes the topic by pulling a map out of her Hello Kitty backpack and outlining our plans for the next few days. (Not that we really need to do this – I had spent the best part of a year researching and planning this trip down to the smallest detail. But it's nice to see it all finally become reality.)

'This will be a nice change for me,' says Josephine, sipping on an over-sized daiquiri complete with paper umbrellas and multi-coloured straws. 'Usually I take small tour groups to some of the more accessible longhouses, but I rarely get the chance to go into the kind of remote areas you are planning to visit. Should be an interesting experience for both of us!'

Indeed. I know exactly how the lady feels: the area further up-river is teeming with rarely visited longhouses and our trip has all the makings of a journey into the unknown. It will be pot luck all the way. But Josephine's knowledge of several tribal languages and local customs, together with her ability to take care of logistics such as transportation and provisions, should see us through the worst, as we take on the numerous rivers and little-visited tributaries, most of which aren't even shown on her maps. So she folds them up, tucks them away in her bag, and concentrates on her tiny folding umbrellas instead.

Later, over dinner, we make arrangements for the morning. Another early start: breakfast at the markets, obtaining permits for travel beyond Kapit, a longboat ride down to Song where we'll stop over for lunch, and then up the Katibas river for an overnight stay at a traditional Iban longhouse. The thought of getting up with the roosters brings on one of the discreet yawns I used to specialise in during drawn-out client meetings (mouth shut, nostrils flaring, eyes watering – a pretty passable disguise of boredom). I politely decline Josephine's invitation to party on at the Karaoke bar and head straight for the starched white sheets in my room.

In the morning I find fog hanging over the river like a suspended feather quilt, with puffs of white climbing up here and there towards the top of the trees. Down near the Shell jetty (a sort of floating petrol station) Iban families are already unloading longboats, the women hauling their wares up to the market while the men tie up their canoes and catch up on the latest gossip.

The Express Boats, too, are starting to come alive, with skippers testing their air-horns and the idling engines of the boats gurgling away amidst the confusion of people boarding or haggling over fares. Josephine is already waiting at the café, and so is a huge enamel pot of strong local coffee, a welcome sight at sunrise.

'Good morning! Did you sleep well?' she enquires.

'Yes, thank you. So what's for breakfast?'

'Sit down,' she gestures towards the plastic chairs, 'I order already.'

Fine by me. I love all types of local food and especially the spicy south-east Asian variety which is starting to arrive now, one-by-one, in individual dishes: a plate of fried noodles liberally sprinkled with slivers of hot chilli, a bowl of flavourful beef *rendang*, hard-boiled eggs, several steaming hot Chinese buns and my first taste of real jungle food: fern tips served on a banana leaf.

I start with the coffee, which is excellent, and wonder whether I will really need the mini espresso maker I packed 'just in case' together with a kilo of my favourite Italian roast. Most local coffee comes from nearby Sumatra, where the fabled 'Aged Mandheling' blend is produced from beans grown at high altitude.

This isn't Mandheling, but it does the trick of waking me up rather nicely. We both eat in silence, focusing on the food before us. More coffee.

'How much time do we have?' I ask.

She reclines in her chair, slowly picks up her cup of coffee and smiles, '*Jalan, jalan*,' meaning take it easy, we have plenty of time. I'm starting to like this lady.

The Government offices don't open until eight o'clock, giving us time for a leisurely stroll through the colourful markets. It's a fascinating place, brimming with exotic fruit, vegetables, plants, livestock and just about anything that can be sold or traded at a modest profit.

A small crowd has gathered around one of the rattan mats spread out on the floor. The attraction turns out to be a huge python, freshly killed and ready for the cooking pot. It can be bought by the metre or by the slice. Next to the snake-man someone is selling a fresh pangolin – a type of armoured anteater that bears a resemblance to an armadillo with feathers. And then there are the pigs: pigs everywhere, rooting, squealing, wallowing, blissfully oblivious to their imminent fate. Right at the end of the stretch is the chicken place with its very own adjoining *klinik*.

Josephine doesn't like the smells. She suggests we start making our way to the Resident's Office, as it must be getting close to opening time.

The Permits section is on the first floor of the low-rise concrete building. We fill in the required forms and hand them back to the clerk behind the counter, who asks for my passport, stamps the forms and puts them in a tray.

'Please take a seat.'

We sit and wait. The ceiling fans whirr above us. A few minutes pass and we're called up, this time to a desk. The questions come rapid-fire: Where are we going? Why are we going? With whom are we going? How long do we plan to stay? Next of kin? Although the questioning seems excessive, in a way it is not unreasonable. The Malaysian government is somewhat sensitive about its tribal people and (officially, at least) wants to afford them a measure of protection from the outside world. On the practical side, keeping track of wayward wanderers has its benefits; should an emergency arise, the police can quickly organise a search party.

The crunch comes with the final question: 'Do you have invitations to longhouses?' Procedure requires any up-river travellers to have such invitations in order to obtain a permit. (Although this may be a little hard to police, as none of the tribes have developed a written language and not all of them have been educated in Malay. Furthermore, invitations can be obtained quite easily, usually for a small fee, from any of the tribal visitors down at the Shell jetty.)

This is where Josephine comes into her own: Yes, we have an invitation to her family's longhouse. Yes, she has cousins, nephews, uncles, aunts and in-laws in all the remaining longhouses along the way. And yes, all this can be verified by her uncle, who is a Member of Sarawak's Parliament. The latter comment seems to strike a note with the official. He stamps the permit and hands it to us with a smile.

'Now you must take it to the *polis* for stamping, and then bring it back to counter eight.'

Another concrete building, just down the road. It's hot. Very hot. The police permit office is, predictably, on the first floor. We climb up the stairs and are in luck as the sergeant is present and turns out to be a jovial sort of fellow. There is much chit-chat, we are offered a cold drink and he signs the original of the forms together with the six carbon copies (which he retains). The permit is issued subject to the condition that I report back to Belaga Police at the end of my trip, and copies are forwarded to the District Officer, Kapit, the Divisional Superintendent of Police, Kapit, the District Officer, Belaga, and Officer Commanding District, Belaga Police Station. Hey, I'm famous! All these people concerned for the well-being of one little Australian traveller! Back to the Resident's office for the final stamping of the stamped permit and we're free to go.

Coffee. Definitely. Halfway down the road two motorcycles come to a screeching halt right next to us, throwing up a cloud of dust. Jo's cousin and friend. We hop on the back and enjoy the brief but hair-raising ride back into town.

The coffee shop is abuzz with people, all of whom seem to know Jo. There's lots of back-slapping as we enter, followed by the predictable questions: How long have you been in town, Jo? Where are you off to? Come have some coffee. One of the entourage is our boatman, and he tells us that there's been a change of plan: the water level at the upper reaches of the Katibas river has dropped dramatically and its tributaries cannot be navigated.

'Never mind,' says Jo, 'we'll go up the Baleh instead.' Just like that.

Pondering the fact that I've been here for less than 48 hours and already experienced two major changes in schedule (that's an average of one per day, as the statisticians would tell us), I come to the conclusion that in a place like this, one simply cannot plan ahead with any degree of precision. Nature plays havoc with schedules; rivers can rise or fall several metres in a matter of hours, driving rain or fog will bring most activities to a grinding halt, knee-deep mud can bog down an all-terrain vehicle hopelessly.

Under the circumstances, the Baleh looks like a pretty good option. We shoulder our gear – I my rugged US army backpack, Josephine her Hello Kitty satchel – and proceed down to the slippery logs awaiting us at the jetty. Our boatman is already there, ready to lend a helping hand as we clamber aboard. Balancing ourselves carefully as the boat bobs about in the water, we take our respective places. Josephine will act as 'point-man' (or point-person in today's politically correct language), warning the boatman of oncoming logs or debris via subtle or frantic hand signals, depending on the size of the log.

I sit in a puddle of water in the middle, with the boatman making up the rear, mainly in a standing position and looking like an out-of-place Venetian gondolier. (I hope he doesn't sing!) My backpack is stowed safely behind me, providing an almost comfortable backrest. Camera around my neck and a big grin of anticipation on my face, we take off and head towards the centre of the Baleh, dodging Express Boats, logging rafts, a variety of flotsam and tribal longboats heading home.

The river is brown and flows at a rapid pace. Large, slow tugboats pass us, pulling rafts of several hundred logs behind them. On the opposite bank a logging camp appears, rising out of the mud, with few signs of life. As we progress upstream past several longhouses, a school and a fuel depot, the sky suddenly turns dark and within seconds opens up to shower us with a massive tropical downpour, giving us barely time to extract the rain ponchos from our packs. Visibility is almost nil, and the boatman pulls up under a couple of trees overhanging the river. He looks at us and smiles. Josephine smiles. I smile. There's no point in talking – the noise is deafening. We sit and watch the rain as it hits the water's surface, its pounding droplets transforming the foaming river into a surreal palm-fringed Jacuzzi. Only minutes after it started to unleash its fury, the sky turns blue and the sun resumes its merciless frying of earth and longboat passengers alike.

The heat is unbelievable and I can feel the sun burning right through my clothes. For the first time I can actually experience the benefits of well-designed 'adventure travel' clothing, and I am glad that I listened to the expert advice of the salesman back in the Sydney trekking shop as I roll down my shirtsleeves for added protection, and zip the full-length trouser sleeves on to my 'convertible' shorts, much to the amusement of the boatman who has been watching the proceedings with great interest.

The scenery around us doesn't change much until we make a sharp turn to the right and enter a small tributary. The transformation is instant and startling. Thick vegetation closes in on us as the river narrows. The quiet is almost unsettling. In many parts, branches of trees overhang the river, forming a dark, leafy tunnel through which we glide as we proceed upstream. Thick vines covered in wild orchids reach down to the surface of the water. Gigantic butterflies in vibrant colours flit through the blossoms of exotic-looking flowers, and periodically a bird takes flight on our approach, screeching all the way up to the forest canopy. It's nature gone berserk – a riot of growth, colours and lush vegetation set in thick jungle. This is it, the real thing. This is what I came for: scenery so unbelievable it's almost like living a dream. Overawed by the experience, I even neglect my ever-present camera. It's as if this majestic beauty was meant to be experienced live – and in a way I'm sure it is, because it would be near impossible to try and capture all of this grandeur in a mere photograph.

The boatman eases the throttle on the small outboard engine and Josephine plunges a long paddle into the river, gauging its depth. We've reached some shallow parts of the river, and ahead of us a set of small rapids bubbles away. I am amazed at the boatman's skills, as he zigzags his way from one small current to the next, constantly keeping an eye open for tell-tale signs of submerged rocks or sandbanks. We cross the rapids with apparent ease and the boat speeds up, ready for its next obstacle; this time it's a small waterfall, which means we all have to get out and carry the boat past it.

It sounds easy enough to me and I eagerly jump over the side, into the cooling water. Completely into the cooling water, because in my enthusiasm I did not anticipate the slippery boulders beneath me. Emerging from my unplanned dip, I am greeted with a burst of uproarious laughter – the first of many to follow. City slicker.

Back on deck, and dripping from yet more water after struggling over the falls,

I resume my position of honour amidships and try to ignore what appear to be shrieks of delight from a bunch of monkeys who have been observing my escapades from the safety of the riverbank.

The belongings in my pockets are dry (including the cigarettes) thanks to the innumerable waterproof pouches I have brought along for just such occasions. The ever-narrowing river now snakes its way through, twisting and turning. Huge cliffs surround us on both sides and the longhouses become fewer and fewer.

It is getting late in the afternoon and time to look for a friendly place to stay. The longhouse in which we had planned to spend the night had a white flag flying from a bamboo pole at the jetty, a sign indicating a taboo and warning visitors to stay away. Usually such taboos are put in place when someone has died, making the entire settlement off-limits to strangers.

Just an hour further up-river, however, we round a bend and another longhouse appears. Our boatman makes his way towards the large logs used as a substitute jetty and warns me not to leave the boat until we have been invited by the headman to step ashore. Our arrival causes a controlled commotion as children, women and one or two men appear, forming a silent semi-circle around the boat.

Once more, Josephine comes into her own, because she speaks Iban (beside four other local languages) and now starts cheerfully to address the assembly with a few pleasantries and, apparently, a selection of jokes which delight our welcome committee and cause the chief to emerge from his afternoon nap. One man detaches himself from the crowd and walks over to the old man. After a brief exchange, he comes running down towards us, relaying the chief's invitation to join him on the longhouse veranda. We've got our invitation and a roof over our heads!

chapter four

iban

The mooring logs look pretty slippery, so I shoulder my backpack and decide to take a shortcut by walking up towards the steps via the pleasant-looking beach instead. I jump ashore and straight into knee-deep mud, my arms searching frantically for something to hold on to. This is a signal for the silent crowd to erupt into a chorus of wild laughter, led by shrieking children who are now running down the banks to come to my rescue.

Thoroughly covered in grey slime, I climb up the steep, rickety bamboo steps to join the others at the bottom of the longhouse where yet another obstacle awaits me: a huge log leading from the ground to the platform. I am expected to walk up the log, using the notches as steps. No way.

But there's no choice, mainly because I am reluctant to give yet another bad impression. So I bravely face the challenge head-on and start climbing, following the example of the kids in front of me. One step. Two steps. And that's it – I feel that I can't find my balance, especially with the weight of my backpack shifting alarmingly from one side to the other. Stuck part of the way, I take off my pack, drop it to the ground and proceed to climb up the trunk, monkey-fashion, on all fours.

There are cheers from the impromptu spectator gallery on the longhouse open veranda, where the chief awaits me on a floor mat together with his entourage of distinguished elders. Protocol: first, take off shoes. The calf-high canvas jungle boots (Malaysian army regulation issue) may be useful to keep snakes and leeches at bay, but when it comes to visiting longhouses they're a cumbersome affair. It takes an eternity to undo the one-and-a-half metre long laces. (Longer when they're covered in mud.) Everyone watches me in deadly silence, including some kids with open mouths and some others who are starting to get the giggles.

Boots off, I adopt the best stately composure I can muster under the circumstances and walk straight over to the official welcoming party. Josephine has already joined them, looking very relaxed and smoking what looks like a gigantic joint of locally-grown tobacco.

The headman, or *tuai rumah*, extends his hand, bids me welcome (at least that's what I think, mainly because he's smiling), and motions me to sit down. I thank him, pull out my magic icebreakers and everyone takes a cigarette, including the women who sit at a respectful distance from the 'official party'. The conversation starts in earnest, with the chief asking questions in a language I don't understand, but which Josephine obligingly translates for me in much abbreviated form: Where did we come from? Where are we heading? How was the trip? What are the water levels like downstream?

She explains that this type of small-talk is traditional, culminating in most cases in an invitation to stay. To bring up the subject of accommodation before then would be a serious breach of longhouse etiquette, and is usually quite unnecessary as the Ibans pride themselves in their hospitality towards strangers.

So the party merrily chatters on in a strange flow of guttural, clicking sounds that would challenge even the most accomplished ventriloquist. I try to follow the gist of the conversation through observation of facial expressions and occasional hand movements. One man in particular has me fascinated: he is diminutive in size, but has a vibrant personality, a delightfully infectious laugh and sparkling, mischievous eyes just below the straight fringe of his 'basin' haircut. The holes in his stretched earlobes are quite large and his thighs, arms, shoulder blades and chest are covered in intricate, circular floral-design tattoos. There's even one on his throat. (Ouch!)

Whenever he talks, he either has his audience spellbound or rolling with laughter. He is obviously the resident version of the village storyteller-cum-clown, and I instantly take to him. He sits on the mat with one leg tucked under his buttocks, the other one drawn up to his chest and one hand resting on the knee. I mentally nickname him The Little One.

The chief's wife and daughters now join the party, bearing platters of cracker biscuits (longhouse favourites throughout Sarawak) and huge mugs of coffee. The coffee is good. More clicking and clacking sounds from the chief, and a bunch of kids, following his instructions, clamber down the log to fetch my pack. Looks like we've been invited to stay.

The inseparable duo – Josephine and her Hello Kitty bag – follow the chief's wife inside. I gather my muddy boots and backpack and proceed to catch up with them, ahead of a procession of Iban kids, panting dogs, toothless grandmothers and various assorted onlookers who follow my every move with great interest.

The inside is surprisingly dark and the floor (bamboo poles held together with cross straps) creaks, rattles and bounces with every step. Running parallel to the outside platform, the *ruai,* or main veranda, is essentially a long, wide corridor that stretches from one end of the building to the other, with doors all along one side leading to individual family living areas. The whole thing looks like a stretched-out country motel along a highway. Except that here the highway has a roof.

The chief's wife stops in front of her family's apartment – their *bilik*, which is right in the centre of the longhouse – and ushers us inside. (Our boots and loyal procession of onlookers remain outside.) It's quite a spacious living area, with a slightly raised platform on one side and rattan mats spread out on the floor on the other. Towards the back there is a small kitchen space with an open fireplace on the ground, and above it a roof flap activated by a bamboo pole. The walls are covered with all sorts of everyday items: *parangs* (the traditional all-purpose machetes), brass gongs, blowpipes, a decorative head-dress made from hornbill feathers, two Yamaha outboard engines, several wooden carvings and a faded magazine cover of Queen Elizabeth II at her coronation.

Lined up against one wall are gigantic glazed Chinese jars used to store rice, cracker biscuits and other staple items of a typical longhouse household. Adjoining them are several chests containing sarongs, T-shirts, denim shorts and assorted 'his and hers' jewellery worn on festive occasions.

But I can't see any human skulls hanging from the rafters. Perhaps they are kept upstairs in the loft. There's a rickety bamboo ladder – the thought is tempting but I chicken out. Josephine is busy talking with the ladies of the house (the Chief's wife and her two teenage daughters) and I find myself a small space in the corner where I can deposit my belongings.

'Do you want to have a bath with us, Mr John?'

'Excuse me?'

'We all go and wash now.' says Josephine, and I notice that she has changed into a sarong. There's no bathroom, but plenty of running water right outside the longhouse. As I clamber down the slippery riverbank, keenly watched by my intrepid band of followers, Josephine points out the bathing areas: up-river for women, down-river for men.

Resigned to my down-river fate, I join the men who are frolicking in the water. Cleanliness is an important aspect of Iban life, and the daily dips in the river are as much a time for personal hygiene as they are for socialising. Splashing about in the river, I can feel a sort of 'bonding' happening with the longhouse men. There's much fun and laughter, especially after my friend, The Little One, sneaks up from behind and pulls my legs off the rock that I had used to stabilise myself against the fast-running current.

About a hundred metres further down the river is the official 'toilet'. The procedure is simple: pick a spot in the water, immerse yourself and do what you came to do. (No flushing necessary.) Toilets of this kind are commonplace in Borneo, and while the locations may vary from secluded spots to quite open areas, they all have one thing in common:

they are, for obvious reasons, invariably located down-river from the bathing areas.

Refreshed and clean, I once more climb up the bamboo steps, the 'monkey log', and back in the *bilik* manage to get changed into a fresh set of clothes under my all-purpose sarong. Outside the door, the troops are starting to gather on a big mat, emerging one-by-one out of the various apartments. This is pre-dinner discussion time, a sort of longhouse happy hour.

First item on the agenda: a glass of *tuak*. Made from rice wine and a concoction of secret herbs and spices, this milky-white liquid packs a punch! I had heard many stories about wild *tuak*-infused longhouse nights, well before I had even set foot on the shores of Borneo. And one thing I remember in particular is that refusing to accept it will cause serious offence.

My full-size tumbler of this jungle apéritif is filled to the brim. All eyes are on me and I down it in one go, as custom prescribes. Cheers from the gallery and the chief's daughter immediately proceeds to fill my glass again. Thank you for that, ma'am. But I'll treat this refill with a little more respect, because the night is young and I've just proven my manhood.

There are a few disappointed looks, but the conversation resumes and someone is starting to pluck the strings of a beautifully decorated *sape*, providing a gentle but fitting musical background to this strange cocktail bar in the forest.

Sitting back with my legs crossed, I come to the conclusion that this is a very civilised way to relax after a hot day's travel. A glass of *tuak* in my hand (not too bad, actually, once you get used to it) and some convivial conversation around me (even if I don't understand a word) provide a perfect framework for observing longhouse life.

The tattoos fascinate me most; intricate swirly designs that have been applied over extended periods of time by the resident longhouse artist. The process is quite elaborate, with a traditional motif being traced on to the skin with black dye made from soot. The artist then punctures the skin with a sharpened piece of bamboo and a hammer. It is a series of dots progressively applied until the design is complete. While most designs have purely decorative purposes, some can signify specific achievements such as special hunting skills or the number of heads taken in battle.

Just a little distance from us, another group starts to form, made up of several old women with saggy breasts hanging over their sarongs, and a few young girls wearing T-shirts (damn it!). The old ladies either chew betel nuts or smoke enormous cigars of locally-grown tobacco wrapped in banana leaves. One of them calls out and invites me to share some of the tobacco, which she keeps in a small, carved wooden box. I take a banana leaf and start rolling it, almost expertly, into a smoke. Obviously impressed by my capabilities, the old lady starts chatting to me.

I have no clue what she is saying. Trying to turn the conversation into a dialogue, I reply in kind with a few words of Malay. She doesn't have a clue what I am saying, either. But we get on famously just the same, gesturing and laughing a lot.

The noise from our group attracts the attention of several young men who have just emerged from their *biliks*. They come bearing offerings of *tuak*, each one made to a different, proudly-kept recipe. Proper longhouse manners prescribe that I have to try them all.

'You come from Australia, yah?' says one of them while he sidles up next to me. His English is very good, having just returned from a logging camp assignment in Papua New Guinea.

'I work with many Australians in Niugini. He tell me about Opera House and Kangaroo.' A cue for his colleague to jump up and perform an impromptu hopping dance, calling out, 'Kangaroo! Kangaroo!'

One of the elderly ladies fills a tumbler of *tuak* and the performer downs it.

'Now you!' my neighbour prompts me with a nudge in the ribs. I have the feeling that refusing won't get me anywhere, so I get up, ready to jump. But the old lady beats me to it and like a flash of lightning stands in front of me, proffering another glass of *tuak*.

'Drink!' my friend calls out.

'Drink! Drink! Drink!' the others chant in chorus.

OK, here we go. I down the drink and start jumping around the room in a passable imitation of Skippy the Bush Kangaroo. Someone starts urging me on with cries of 'Kangaroo!' and is soon joined by others, until the entire longhouse resounds to a wild chant.

'Kangaroo! Kangaroo! Kangaroo!'

Exhausted, I collapse back on to my spot on the mat, only to be pulled up by the old lady holding another shot of *tuak*.

'Drink! Drink! Drink!' It's surprising how quickly these guys pick up English. I down the evil brew once more and am rescued by Josephine who announces that dinner is ready. Without further prompting I retire to the headman's *bilik* and realise that I am quite hungry and in dire need of something to line my *tuak*-unaccustomed stomach.

The food has been laid out in a row of dishes on a big mat. This is the 'first sitting', reserved exclusively for the men. (The women eat later, after the men have finished.) We take our seats and the chief washes his hands in a small brass bowl, which he passes on to me. There are no utensils as food is traditionally eaten with the fingers, using the right hand only (the left hand, as in much of Asia, is considered unclean).

Invited to help myself, I immediately reach for the bowl of fern tips, the very dish I so much enjoyed in Kapit. Spiced up with a little chilli, these ferns taste wonderful and fresh. The rice, too, is unlike any I have ever tasted before. Grown by the Ibans on small farm plots in the jungle, it is slightly brownish in colour and more akin to wild rice than the traditional white varieties. As topping for the rice, our hostess has prepared a selection of stir-fried wild boar, stewed monkey and chicken cooked in a bamboo tube.

The latter is particularly interesting because of its simplicity: pieces of diced chicken are marinated and inserted into a section of bamboo, which is sealed with a bunch of herbs stuffed tightly into the opening. The tube is then simply placed into an open fire and steamed. The result is sensational: the meat is moist and tender and the herbs provide just a hint of added fragrance.

The final dish was prepared by the headman's youngest daughter, and she presents it to us with a great deal of pride: fresh river fish, marinated in lemon and lime juice spiced with ginger, chillies, shallots and coriander, and served on a banana leaf with wild tapioca as an accompaniment.

'Mmm. *Bagus!*' I call out as a show of sincere appreciation. I'm sure the young daughter is blushing behind the flicker of the oil lamp, but I can't really tell.

'Do they eat like this everyday?' I ask Jo, who has been watching the proceedings from behind her cigar.

'I don't think so. This was all prepared in your honour. And I have another surprise for you: the *tuai rumah* just told me that they are putting on a *gawai* for you tonight, so you can experience some traditional longhouse dances.'

Outside, the preparations have started in earnest: several men are carrying large brass gongs to 'centre-stage', that is, the large mat in front of the *tuai rumah*'s door. The *sape* player is tuning his instrument. And the chief is straightening the hornbill feathers on his head-dress, his elaborately carved headhunter's sword resting on the lap of his youngest son who is guarding it with an expression that matches the importance of the honour bestowed upon him.

Our boatman, Lupak, has already settled on the floor. Surrounded by packets of cigarettes, a box of tobacco and a jug of *tuak*, he seems ready for the night. The moment he spots me he calls out, 'Mr John! *Tuak!*' pointing at the full jug. How can one refuse? I sit down next to him and the two loggers, who have returned with fame and brand-new jeans from their recent stint in New Guinea, join us.

While venturing as far afield as New Guinea is perhaps somewhat unusual for longhouse men, the Iban custom of *bejalai* has seen generations of young men seeking fortune and adventure by undertaking journeys ranging from three months to three years. Often travelling in groups, their explorations in the past took them to far-ranging mountains, remote valleys and sometimes even into enemy territory. It was a sort of 'test of manhood', teaching them self-reliance as part of their transition into adulthood. Today *bejalai* is still practised, but the destinations are more likely to be cities like Sibu, Miri, Kuching or even Singapore.

Curious to find out how these cross-cultural experiences affect their views of traditional tribal life, I question the loggers about their future plans. They tell me that they just came back for the big end-of-harvest *gawai*, a kind of annual holiday. After that, they plan to go to Brunei to work in the oil fields and save up some more money so that they can come back to their longhouse and get married. Do they plan to live with their community or are they likely to succumb to the temptations of the city? They both answer simultaneously and emphatically, 'In the longhouse.'

In spite of the government's efforts to 'bring the modern world' to the longhouse communities, it seems that many of Sarawak's native peoples have found their own way of coping with change by selectively accepting what they perceive to be useful from our society, and at the same time rejecting what is likely to interfere with their own traditional values and way of life.

The muffled sound of a brass gong reverberates through the building, resulting in an instant hush. The *tuai rumah*, resplendent in his feathers and sitting cross-legged on the floor, begins to address the assembly, his body swaying back and forth as he speaks. It is a welcome speech for me, I am told, recited in verses the chief composes as he speaks. Such songs could take anything from fifteen minutes to over an hour, depending upon the skills of the performer. Finally he gets up and walks in our direction. Although small in stature, decked out in his headdress, with a longhaired monkey coat draped around his shoulders and his *parang* strapped around the waist, he cuts an imposing warrior figure. I sure would hate to meet him in the jungle on a dark night. But his sincere handshake and the warm, welcoming look in his eyes create a feeling that transcends all language barriers. I am now part of his little community and a friend who may return any time.

The *tuai rumah* releases my hand and, turning around, suddenly jumps into the air, emitting a blood-curdling cry. The gongs start beating frantically and the headman begins to dance with a fierce expression on his face. His feet move in measured, widesweeping semi-circles around the floor. Momentarily his movements freeze, as he shields his eyes with one hand, scanning the imaginary treetops of the forest. A sound behind him; he ducks low and readies his sword. Total quiet, only the sound of the gongs, accompanied now by occasional, gentle *sape* notes. The dancer turns around and moves silently, in a crouched position, towards his enemy. A leap forward, followed by a prolonged scream, and the warrior returns triumphantly, holding a head in his open palm. The gongs are now beating in a feverish frenzy, but their sound is almost drowned out by the tumultuous cheers of the audience, many of whom would have partaken in the 'real thing' in days gone by.

The origins of headhunting are somewhat obscure, but it is said to have been introduced to Sarawak by the Kayans when they migrated across the watershed from Indonesia, and the practice was subsequently taken up (with a great deal of enthusiasm) by the Ibans. According to one popular folk tale, the practice was started when a famous Kenyah chief called Tokong, set out with a group of warriors on a retaliatory raid against a neighbouring longhouse. Along the way the party was intercepted by a frog, who advised Tokong to take their enemies' heads back home. Elaborating on his theory, he told the warriors that the spirit, or *toh*, residing in such heads would ensure good harvests, health for everyone and prosperity for the community in general.

The chief pondered this advice before going to sleep, but ended up dismissing it as the type of foolish thing a frog would say. During the night, however, Tokong dreamed of fields that yielded an abundance of rice, of gigantic jars filled with sweet potatoes, and sugar cane piled up to the longhouse rafters. He related his dream to the rest of the raiding party in the morning, and the decision was made to try out the frog's advice. The raid was swift and deadly: seven heads were taken and when the warriors returned to the river they found their canoe pointing in the right direction and the currents reversed to offer them a quick escape. On their way home they passed their rice fields and found that a plentiful new harvest had sprung up overnight. But the biggest surprise awaited them back home, where they were greeted with war whoops and gongs beating. Everyone came out to welcome them, even those who had been sick for years; the lame were dancing and the infirm fetched water from the river. To celebrate the power of *toh*, the heads were suspended above a fire to keep them warm. And the party was on.

Whatever the origins of headhunting, the custom has been alive and well for several hundred years and has become associated with almost every major longhouse event. The death of a chief required the taking of heads, whose original owners became his slaves during the long journey into the afterworld. This was followed by yet another head when the official period of mourning came to an end. Childbirth, too – especially the arrival of a male – required the taking of heads in order to properly conduct the name-giving ceremony. But by far the most important aspect of the custom was during courtship, for no young suitor was considered a man until his *parang* had drawn blood by severing someone's head. In fact, headhunting was so much ingrained in the mind that grandmothers would urge their grandsons, still in the cradle, to avenge their grandfather whose head was roasting somewhere above an enemy's fireplace.

Even the humble *parang* was subject to the rules, for it could not be carried as part of everyday equipment until it had drawn blood in the course of taking someone's head. But no matter how intricately the concept of headhunting was woven into the fabric of these communities, it still required more than just bravado to properly plan and execute a foray into enemy territory, especially as the potential executioners, by nature, tend to be a kind and tolerant people.

To build up the required steam, a succession of feasts was held where, over several months, the beat of the gongs turned the warriors' dances into a frenzy to a point where they were champing at the bit to be let loose. Quite often new war canoes were built to transport a hundred or more men. To do this required the selection of suitable trees which, predictably, had to be blessed with human blood. Bird-flight omens were consulted and pigs' livers dissected in search for propitious signs. By the time the designated day arrived, the warriors were raring to go: they would paddle furiously and run the rest of the way at breakneck speed until they reached their unsuspecting victims and swiftly executed the task they had come to complete. Most commonly, this involved lighting a fire under the longhouse and pouncing upon the victims as they tried to flee the inferno. Other times, however, when the occupants outnumbered the raiders, a great deal of stealth was required in order to minimise casualties in the war party.

Tuak time. The chief gulps down the offering and holds out his glass for more, which causes the crowd to erupt into a chorus of wild catcalls and cheers. Looking around the room, he spots Josephine in a corner and hands her his headdress, a longhouse invitation to dance. Kayans are renowned for their graceful dances and Jo doesn't disappoint. She performs a slow and hauntingly beautiful hornbill dance, mimicking the sacred bird's movements with incredible precision. The crowd falls silent, enthralled by the skilful performance before them. But even the grace and beauty of Jo's hornbill rendition doesn't save her from her drinking fate after she finishes the dance. She empties the glass, asks for a refill and hands it to me, together with the feathers.

This sets the crowd off once more, with one clown starting to chant 'Kangaroo!' and, inevitably, everyone else joining in the fray.

The *tuak* gives me courage. But I don't know how to do the 'Hornbill' and I've already done the 'Kangaroo'. So I opt for another Australian icon – the ostrich-like emu which I figure would be easy enough to imitate.

I ask Josephine to translate my description of the bird, but she just waves her hand.

'Never mind, they don't care. Just dance for them, they'll love it!'

So here goes the emu – long strutting steps, the head alternately looking left and right. I stop, shield my eyes (just like the chief did) and jump in the air with a scream. The crowd is delighted at my imitation of the old warrior. Back to the emu: I stretch my neck and look around. I retract my neck and move my head between my legs, looking back at the revellers through my knees. And as a grand finale, I squat down and pretend to lay an egg, accompanied by a few clucking chicken sounds. The crowd goes wild, the *tuak* flows and the room starts spinning around me.

'Kangaroo! Kangaroo! Kangaroo!' they chant, asking for an encore. At this stage I am virtually beyond caring and start hopping about wildly until I trip over a pair of stretched-out legs and fall right into the basket of party snacks, sending the biscuits flying in all directions. Obviously satisfied with my performance, the laughing crowd calls for more *tuak* and I oblige. (Purely to conform with custom, of course).

Back in my own little social circle, Lupak raises his glass questioningly towards me. I tell him that I intend to have a little break, as after a dozen or so glasses I am starting to lose count. He agrees. 'Five minutes,' he says, pointing at his fake Rolex watch. I ignore the ultimatum and offer him a cigarette. He lights it and puts his arm around my shoulder.

'Mr John, he OK,' he says to his friends who reply with thumbs-up signs. To emphasise the point, the logger next to me now also puts his arm around my shoulder. Sandwiched between my two new friends, I find it difficult to stop The Little One from replenishing my glass as he settles down in front of us, in search of new drinking partners.

Meanwhile the dancers, who have been performing in a seemingly endless succession, are starting to become a blur. I think I need some fresh air. But I don't find much relief outside. The night is stifling.

'We go for swim.' It's the boatman. And his friends.

Before I know it, I find myself in the river, splashing and yahooing with the others.

The entire scene is almost surreal: the night noises of the jungle, gigantic palm trees overhanging the moonlit river, the distant sound of *sape* and gongs from the longhouse, and a bunch of drunken Ibans frolicking next to me.

Having temporarily exhausted our energies, we return to the party and find Josephine on the balcony. '*Kopi!*' she calls out to us, as we approach the carved log steps, and never has this magic word for coffee sounded so sweet to me. The party seems to have died down a little, and, taking advantage of the lull, the vertically-challenged storyteller is entertaining a group of ladies with some obviously wild tales.

I join a group of elderly warriors on the floor, who immediately welcome me with a glass of *tuak*. A polite sip and I return to my coffee. One of the men hands me a biscuit and I notice the tattoos on his knuckles; each one represents a head he has taken. Hopefully, a long time ago.

Refreshed from the swim and revived by the coffee, I am ready to re-join the festivities, which are starting to pulsate once more to the beat of the gongs. Boy, can these guys boogie! Lupak, too, has found his second wind, judging by the jug he is carrying around.

'Mr John! *Tuak*!'

Too late. He saw me. Perhaps one more glass before I turn in. A sort of nightcap. But he seems to have unilaterally entered me in an unofficial *tuak* drinking challenge. He's now even calling me 'brother'.

It's one o'clock. It's two o'clock. It's three o'clock. At four, the party is still going (although the number of young kids on the ground has thinned out). Daylight appears suddenly in the tropics. Time to get some sleep.

Machine-gun fire. I wake up with a jolt and try to find my bearings. Longhouse. Party. Rain pelting the roof with the sort of fury only a tropical downpour could muster.

Relieved that it is nature rather than some mad local Rambo causing the noise, I slide back into my sleeping bag. Next to me, the young daughters, their mother and two dogs are fast asleep. The chief is snoring away in his own corner, his small son snugly moulded against his side. They all seem to be oblivious to the noise of the rain and the incredible din outside: dogs fighting and yelping, roosters crowing, pigs grunting and squealing under the house. Floors creaking with the endless procession of people wandering in and out of their *biliks*.

The longhouse is stirring into life – it's almost nine o'clock. In the far corner of the room I suddenly notice Josephine, pointing at a mug and mouthing the word '*Kopi*?'

I nod enthusiastically and quietly step over the sleeping bodies on the floor, lured by the aroma and the steam coming out of the cups. We sit on a mat, silently enjoying our coffee, and Josephine rolls her first cigar of the day.

There's movement on the floor. The daughters wake up and smile at us. Outside on the veranda, there's laughter and lots of excitement. We step over the remaining bodies to go and have a look. It appears that during the night a rather large python had found its way into one of the chicken coops, in search of a midnight snack. Having swallowed the chicken, it is now too big to make its way back through the fence, much to the delight of the ex-chicken's owner, who has suddenly traded a potential bowl of chicken soup for a much larger meal. This, no doubt, calls for a celebration and the proud new owner of a very long python invites us all to partake in a toast. With *tuak*. Naturally. I can't believe these guys. But they all settle happily on the mat, while I quietly sneak outside.

The rain is hammering the outer platform relentlessly. Far too wet and slippery to go down to the river. Fortunately this longhouse features a few special creature-comforts including an outhouse-style toilet, perched precariously over the edge of the platform. I make a run for it. There's no toilet bowl or 'can', just a hole in the floor, with pigs waiting in eager anticipation a long distance below.

Back in the house, the girls are cooking up a storm – breakfast! Strangely, I feel quite rested and there's no trace of a hangover. I offer to give the ladies a hand with their preparations, but am met with blank stares: a longhouse kitchen is women's domain.

Feeling unwanted, I go back out in the rain and proceed to have a leisurely shave instead, splashing my face with the fresh rain water. A few kids, looking like drowned rats, eye me in total amazement as I spread shaving foam over my face. They obviously want a share of the fun and push each other around until one brave young warrior steps forward and holds out his hand. They all line up and, half a can later, everyone is lathered-up and looking like miniature issues of Santa Claus.

'*Kopi*!' We are being summoned to breakfast; fried rice with *ikan bilis* (tiny dried and rather pungent fish), a mound of spicy local vegetables, coffee and the inevitable cracker biscuits.

The *tuai rumah*, having crawled out of his corner, now emerges somewhat bleary-eyed. He stops in front of the mat, points at me and with a broad grin says, 'Kangaroo!' We linger a while over our breakfast as the rain persists. The chief produces a gigantic yawn, stretches and goes outside to confer with the men: the river has swollen to a dangerous level and it is not safe to go to the farms. He decrees a 'day at home'.

Pity. I had looked forward to visiting the rice paddies. But most family farms are located over an hour's boat travel away and the river is a raging torrent, having risen an incredible six metres in just a few hours.

I check the kitchen for more coffee and I'm in luck. A fresh pot has just been put on the fire and is starting to bubble away. Mug in hand, I walk back outside and start exploring the surroundings. The rain has eased off and a few rays of sunshine are starting to break through the dark clouds, bathing the landscape in an eerie light. Everything is still, other than the rushing, brown water below. The longboats, tied securely against a large palm tree, are straining against their ropes in the fast-moving river. Two young men methodically bail water from the hulls.

On the bamboo platform, several men are checking their fishing nets, and in the far corner someone is repairing a section of the floor with lengths of split bamboo. The whole outdoor veranda has a somewhat ramshackle look about it, with piles of wood, tools, baskets, farm implements, rusted oil canisters and miscellaneous bits of debris strewn everywhere. But in spite of its messy appearance, the place is kept immaculately clean: it seems as if there's hardly a moment when one woman or another is not wandering about, broom in hand, sweeping the platform, the *ruai*, or a *bilik*.

The 'lay day' at home gives the longhouse occupants an opportunity to catch up on some chores, and inside little groups have formed, attending to their various tasks. One section of the *ruai* has turned into an efficient little assembly line: three men are splitting some rattan into very thin, long strips; and next to them a group of women weave the strips into new floormats, while another is making hats. Further along, an old lady is putting her finishing touches to a *selabit*, the universal carry basket used by men and women alike. Fitted with shoulder and forehead straps, properly loaded such baskets can hold up to 60 kilograms of unhusked rice.

The self-sufficiency of these people is astonishing. Despite the fact that many everyday objects can readily be bought at the markets in Kapit, longhouse communities throughout Sarawak still pride themselves in making their own tools, clothing, baskets – in fact, just about anything they require for day-to-day living.

'Hello, John.'

It's Josephine, and she's dropped the 'Mr' bit at last.

'Enjoying yourself?'

Affirmative, ma'am.

'Would you like to see a *pua kumbu* being made?'

'A *pua*-what?'

'A *pua-kumbu*. It's a very special form of wall hanging that requires much skill. The chief's daughter is weaving one right now. Come and watch.'

I follow Josephine to the end of the longhouse, where we find the pretty young daughter sitting on the floor, leaning hard against a backstrap which supports a long frame. The warp is firmly tied to one of the main support pillars of the veranda. Watching her nimble fingers fly across, around and underneath her work is a delight to the eye. But what really strikes me is the intricate design of crocodiles, human spirit figures and decorative patterns that are starting to emerge from her masterpiece. Skilled weavers take great pride in finishing a *pua kumbu* with intricate designs. In fact, their standing in the community is much enhanced with each new piece created, and their worth as a woman is often judged by their performance at the loom.

Out of courtesy, I ask the artist whether I may take a photograph, pointing at my camera. She smiles and waves a very definite 'no' with her hands. Turning to Josephine, she explains that the motifs used are sacred and that she would prefer that I didn't capture their spirits on film. But she invites me to sit down and watch. All around her are natural materials gathered from the jungle: fibres, wild cotton and dyes in rich deep tones of ochre, indigo, black and brown. The colours, extracted from earth, lime or soot, are pounded and mixed with different grasses, leaves, bark or fruit and then boiled until the desired shade for each colour is obtained.

Noticing my interest, the headman's wife approaches, and lovingly looking at her daughter begins to sing a gentle, lilting melody.

'When they heard my work was completed
so soon, my darling,
All the women of the longhouse gathered
Saying how very fine was the design I had woven
With green-blue thread, saying that I, beloved
Was clever to the tips of my fingers
And they asked how I had progressed to
difficult patterns so quickly.'

Josephine explains that this is a traditional Iban love song[1] that illustrates the high esteem that a masterful weaver is held in. I am deeply moved by its simple beauty and suddenly find myself reflecting upon the obvious paradox that somehow manages to reconcile headhunting with poetry. The Iban are a gentle people. They are warm and friendly, overflowing with hospitality towards strangers, and they love to laugh and party whenever the slightest opportunity presents itself.

Despite their reputation as fierce warriors (which they no doubt are), the Ibans lead very ordered lives, governed by strict rules of expected behaviour and social interaction which are observed scrupulously in order to maintain harmony in their closely-knit longhouse communities. Dishonesty and lies are frowned upon and the ancient custom of erecting 'liar's piles' still survives in many parts of Sarawak. Offenders are taken to a place near the longhouse, where the headman describes the transgression and invites the assembled members of his community to throw sticks – not at the liar, but at a designated spot next to him. The offender experiences shame with every stick thrown in his presence.

As an interesting addendum, the liar's pile often remains in place for years and keeps on growing as people add sticks to it, long after the original reason for its existence has been forgotten. It thus becomes a permanent reminder to everyone that lies are not part of the longhouse way of life.

'Hurry up, brother!'

It's Lupak, the boatman, wearing his favourite Kapit Football Club T-shirt and obviously recovered from his world record attempt at synchronised *tuak* drinking.

'We're going to the farm with the ladies,' he says, while I'm still struggling, trying to lace up my boots. Water bottle, camera, cigarettes and I'm all set for the afternoon's outing. Josephine, the chief's two daughters and an elderly lady are already down at the mooring logs, depositing their baskets, *parangs* and miscellaneous other objects into the hull of the longboat. Lupak and I follow them, treading carefully on the slippery steps, when the bamboo suddenly gives way under my feet, sending me on a non-stop bumpy ride all the way down to the boats where, predictably, I come to an abrupt stop in the mud. Cause for renewed laughter. The chief's daughters are at their giggling best this afternoon.

We cast off and head straight upstream against the torrential currents of the water.

The jungle has come alive once more after the downpour, with butterflies the size of dinner plates flitting around magnificent orchid blossoms, and birds that defy classification screeching in the treetops.

As the vegetation closes in around us, the landscape takes on an almost surreal appearance, reminiscent of a Tunnel of Love ride in a 1950s amusement park. The quiet of the surroundings is eerie, punctuated only occasionally by the soft gurgling of a small waterfall on the riverbank. I sit back, using one of the carry baskets as a prop, and take in the majesty of the landscape. Inevitably, my thoughts wander towards man's insistence on destroying such beauty – all in the interest of a few bucks and an intangible excuse commonly labelled 'progress'.

Chief's daughter number one calls out and points towards the shore. All eyes turn to the indicated spot and daughter number two pulls the *parang* out of her basket. I can't see a thing and wonder what all the excitement is about when Lupak veers the boat sharply and steers the bow straight into the mud of a small beach. Everyone gets out and I follow the little procession into the overgrown vegetation.

'Dinner,' says Lupak, noticing the quizzical look on my face. The *parangs* come out and, led by the daughters, everyone starts chopping away at a clump of bamboo, carefully cutting off the juicy tips. Fresh bamboo shoots. So that's what's on the menu for tonight. The baskets fill very quickly and we merrily return to the boat, picking a few wild chillies from a bush on the way back. Lupak is first to hit the beach and sounds the alarm: '*Ular*!'

Everyone freezes at the sight of a gigantic snake exploring the strange wooden intruder on its beach. It's a king cobra, the deadliest snake in Borneo, and this one must be well over four metres long.

Lupak is fairly close to it, but he is motionless and seems very calm. The snake rears its head slightly, senses the air with a few flickers of the tongue, and returns to its exploration of the boat, seemingly unaware of our presence. Josephine squeezes my arm in a silent expression of extreme fear. The wait seems endless and the cobra is in no apparent hurry to go away, sniffing here and there, slithering in and out of the mud, until it finally decides to go for a swim and takes off towards the centre of the river, leaving a rather large wake behind it.

'Very dangerous,' says Lupak, the first one to come back alive from the group's frozen state.

'Yeach,' says Josephine, 'I hate snakes.'

And we all return to the boat. Travelling further upstream, the river is getting narrower and some gigantic cliff faces are closing in on us as we head further towards the Indonesian border. The shallow-water rapids are becoming more frequent now and the routine is always the same: get out of the boat, carry it over the slippery rocks, fall into the water a couple of times and climb back into the boat.

The rice fields are not far from here, I am told, and I can't help thinking about the hardships these people face every day in order to eke out a meagre living from just a few clearings in the jungle. Although longhouses are traditionally built near land that can easily be cleared, the slash-and-burn methods used by the Ibans means that plots only stay fertile for a few years, after which they must be given time to recover and new land has to be found further afield. This form of shifting agriculture requires new 'farms' to be established further and further away from the longhouse, until daily travel becomes too difficult. When that happens, it's time to move on and a reconnaissance party is sent out to find a suitable location for a new longhouse. Provided that all the omens are right and the *tuai burong* (the longhouse chief-birdwatcher) has carefully studied the flight of the hornbill, the selected spot is marked amidst elaborate rituals and the explorers return to the community, ready to start preparations for a celebratory *gawai*.

As our boat rounds another bend, we're within sight of the rice fields and the eldest daughter proudly points them out to me. The landing spot looks idyllic: a perfect little beach surrounded by palm trees and nestled between two rather large rocks. But just as we start heading for it, there's a commotion; it's a bunch of monkeys running about, jumping from rock to rock and screaming in panic, with our friend king cobra lurking just below them.

Lupak takes it all as a bad omen and informs us that we should return home instantly. He turns the boat around and heads straight back into the rapids, while Josephine keeps a wary eye on the snake in the distance. We stop once more, closer to the longhouse, to pick some fresh fern tips for dinner, and arrive back just in time for another tropical downpour to drench us to the skin before we manage to reach shelter on the veranda.

In stark contrast to the previous night, the mood around the longhouse seems rather subdued. People are wandering about slowly, carrying out little chores and obviously nursing some hefty hangovers. The women are preparing dinner, and groups of men are sitting around chatting quietly among themselves. But above all not a single jug of *tuak* in sight! With the rain easing off, I take the opportunity to wash and shave in the river before dinner.

Refreshed and resplendent in my khaki shorts and a clean T-shirt, I join one of the groups on the floor. This is the best time of the day, when peace and quiet descends over the jungle and the sun disappears somewhere beyond the treetops. Night falls quickly at the equator – just a few minutes of transition between daylight and pitch-black night. It's a relaxing time, a sort of prelude to a well-earned rest.

Dinner is far less elaborate this second time around, and I am glad because I start to feel so much more part of the community than when I first arrived. Some rice topped with chillies, the freshly-picked bamboo shoots and fern tips, and a small platter of deliciously juicy catfish caught just hours ago.

Josephine makes some coffee and we all retire to a mat in one corner of the chief's apartment. Tonight is 'story time' (at Josephine's request) and the headman proceeds to recount experiences with ghosts, ancestral spirits and mythical animals of the forest. In a slow and deliberate voice he relates one of the events that has left a deep impression on him – the story of the old aunt who disappeared in the jungle with her little girl. No one saw them leave, yet there was a certain 'presence' in the house that said 'they're alive'.

Despite this spectral reassurance, however, their sudden disappearance proved quite unsettling and search parties were sent out. The area was combed for three days and three nights, to no avail. Finally, the community resigned itself to the fact that they would never see their friends again.

So the mystery remained, until several months later when the *tuai rumah*, returning from a hunt, was startled by an appearance: it was the little girl, standing between two large trees some distance away. The headman called out to her excitedly, but she only smiled and said, 'It's nice here, they're treating me well,' and then vanished back into the jungle without a trace.

To add another twist to the story, the aunt had also left a baby behind which was now in the care of the headman's family. When the chief returned to the longhouse after his encounter with the little girl, the baby started to cry inconsolably, and went on crying for days. The *tuai burong* suggested that a small bush of a specific kind of leaves be suspended from the rafter in the corner of the *bilik* in order to keep out the spirits. This seemed to work, because the baby stopped crying instantly. The dried-out leaves are still there, in the corner right behind the door, and the chief proudly points them out to us.

But obviously the bush doesn't keep out every kind of spirit because, right on cue, The Little One, with two of his cronies in tow, burst through the door carrying a large jug.

'*Tuak*!'

Looks like they're about to join us for the story-telling session. Has the bush been working in keeping out spirits? Josephine translates my question into Iban. Oh yes, says the chief, except for one incident when there was a gentle but persistent knock in the middle of the night. When he opened the door, he saw an old, white-haired ghost which, on seeing the suspended leaves, let out a piercing cry and disappeared back into the night. The chief looks at me and stares straight into my eyes, mumbling a few words as if an after-thought. Everyone breaks up with laughter and Josephine obliges once more with the translation, 'He says the ghost looked just like you!'

Sorry about that, Chief. Next time I'll dye my hair. The Little One starts pouring the *tuak*. As the residential storyteller, he naturally feels obliged to contribute to the entertainment. Sitting cross-legged on the floor, with the flickering oil lamp casting shadows on his face, he proceeds to talk about the giant crocodile that ate only members of one particular family.

Describing the demise of each family member over three generations in gruesome detail, he suddenly stops and looks around the room – just like a stand-up comedian waiting for someone to ask the obvious question that ultimately produces the punch line. I fall for it, asking why the croc only ate members of the one family.

'Because the family always called the crocodile by its name, something our tradition tells us not to do. That family violated the *adat* – our tribal laws – and paid the price.'

Time to top up the glasses. While the *tuak* is being poured The Little One, obviously relishing the limelight of his small oil lamp, seizes the opportunity to throw in a few jokes. The party is starting to get merrier by the minute and the little resident sit-down comedian has us all in stitches. Even though I don't understand the words, his body language and facial expressions make for outstanding entertainment and I enjoy every bit of his spontaneous performance.

Josephine fills the chief's glass and whispers a few words to him. Instantly there's a hush, and everyone looks at the old man in anticipation: the subject of headhunting has just been broached by my guide, a topic that has been painstakingly avoided so far. But the headman appears to be in an obliging mood, and slowly starts to talk.

'We don't do it any more. The government is too strict about it. It's now very difficult to get fresh heads.'

Apparently, in order for heads to maintain their spiritual power, they have to be fed fresh blood on a regular basis. How many heads has the chief taken in his youth? He looks at his hands and shows me the tattoos at his knuckles. Then he turns around and proudly points at several more on his shoulders. Can we see his headhunting *parang*? Sure thing. He gets up and unhooks an elaborately carved sword from the wall. Taking the blade out of its sheath, he lovingly glides a finger over the sharp edge.

'Many heads,' he repeats, with obviously a great deal of nostalgia as he passes the *parang* around for personal inspections. When was the last time he used it?

'Ah, during the big war when we attacked the Japanese with our canoes.' Then he adds matter-of-factly, 'The Japanese won.'

Gradually, and with the help of some additional *tuak*, the chief warms to the topic and starts talking about the headless victims found around the town of Miri as recently as last year.

'We think it was the flying ghost from Brunei – a very large bird with a beak like a giant pair of scissors. He flies very low and snaps off heads while people are working in the fields.'

The Little One demonstrates the scissors' action with his arms, which earns him another round of laughs. Josephine decides to push her luck a little further and asks whether there have been any 'head' incidents in the area. There's a moment of awkward silence as the headman ponders the question. Finally he decides to reply.

'Well, yes. Only two weeks ago we found two headless bodies not far from here, in the forest, and another one, that of a woman cut in half, in the river. Whoever did this could have been working in the logging camps. But then again, it may have been the ghost from Brunei.'

Silence all round. The events have evidently left their mark on the longhouse inhabitants.

The story also explains the chief's reluctance to let us go into the jungle yesterday, when we enquired about suitable walking tracks. Suddenly it all starts to make sense: the entire community is living in fear and no hunting or fishing party ventures further afield from the house than necessary, and when they do it's always in well-armed groups of at least six people.

Josephine gets up to make some coffee, but for once I decide to forego the pleasure and opt for some sleep instead. It's been a long day, and tomorrow there will be an early start as we say farewell to our newly-found friends and head back to Kapit, ready to tackle the next stage of our journey. I bid a polite *'selamat malam'* to everyone and settle back on my sleeping mat in the corner.

Coffee is ready and Josephine hands out the mugs. Against the light of the flickering lamp, the group's shadows take on an eerie dimension, reminiscent of an Indonesian *wayang* shadow-puppet show. Barely awake, I can make out snippets of conversation in the background – about flying ghosts, crocodiles and headless bodies. Should make for some great dreams.

chapter five

hell road of borneo

I feel great, and as the first rays of sunshine emerge tentatively from behind the early morning clouds I'm up and raring to go. And so is everyone else, it seems.

There's much activity around the longhouse, as families are gathering their carry baskets, *parangs*, fishing nets, food, dogs and anything else they can think of for a typical day at their hillside farms. The farewells are brief and we clamber down the riverbank into the waiting boat. Lupak seems a little hung over and doesn't talk much. Come to think of it, I hardly saw him at all last night, other than for a brief moment when I spotted him chatting up an Iban girl near the little palm grove. Maybe things didn't work out and he had an early night.

The trip back is relatively uneventful and fast. Groups of locals doing their morning ablutions in the river, longboats heading out to farms, a herd of bearded pigs staring blankly at us from the muddy banks and looking like a bad impersonation of ZZ Top, and increasing river traffic as we approach Kapit.

As we tie up at the floating Shell station, I spot the concrete steps and my bones start to groan of their own accord. But, much to my surprise, I'm managing my pack a lot better and even succumb to a brisk pace, knowing that there's a coffee shop at the top.

The lady with the soft-slipper shuffle is still there and serves us slow-motion refreshments. We don't linger around much as it will be a long day travelling high up into the cloud-shrouded mountains on the other side of the river.

Provisions are bought and loaded in a precarious pile in the centre of the boat: bags of rice, baskets filled with vegetables, salted fish, bottled water and, of course, the ubiquitous biscuits. It looks as though we are catering for an entire logging camp, but according to Josephine we'll need all of it because there are no shops where we are going and any contribution visitors can make to a longhouse menu is much appreciated.

Lupak fires up his outboard engine and heads straight into the mêlée of floating logs, barges, longboats and miscellaneous jungle flotsam. The trip is only short as our point of departure to the interior is a logging camp, just a few miles up-river. When we arrive, the camp seems deserted in the midday heat. We unload our gear and make our way to a building with the word 'KANTIN' brightly splashed above the door.

As soon as Josephine opens the creaking fly-screen door, she lets out a shriek, which is answered with an equally strident noise from far inside. Before Lupak and I can recover, Josephine has charged towards the source of the second noise and thrown her arms around a body that could have been a twin version of herself – straight out of the latest sheep-cloning manual. There's much back-slapping and cheek-kissing, accompanied by yet more noises before the momentum of the initial reunion dies down.

'This is Lily, my cousin,' says Josephine, 'and this is Mr John and our boatman, Lupak.'

Handshakes all round. The occasion clearly calls for celebration, and Josephine walks up to the counter to buy Coke for everyone. There's no one there. In fact, the entire canteen is deserted and the only sounds of life come from the whirring ceiling fans and a low continuous buzz from the freezer. Somewhere in the distance there's the sound of an old ABBA recording. But there's a buzzer on the counter. Josephine hesitantly pushes it. We wait.

The fly-screen door creaks again and an old Chinese man appears, flashing a smile of gold-capped teeth. He doesn't speak any English or Malay, but is fluent in Iban. As he unlocks the big padlock on the fridge he casually assesses our motley group of travellers. Where are we from? Where are we going? Who's the white guy? What brings us here? The answers to which must provide him with sufficient gossip for a week. We ask him to join us and he buys himself a bottle of Guinness.

Now it's Josephine's turn to interrogate. She quickly establishes that there is a four-wheel drive vehicle scheduled to leave this afternoon, providing us with an opportunity of transport across the mountains. The manager can make the arrangements, but he's taking his siesta and can't be disturbed until two o'clock.

Another round of Coke to celebrate the good news. It's only just after midday and we have time to kill. The cousins catch up on news from home. It appears that Lily is on her way to a Penan settlement to do a little trading in sarongs, plastic cups, cheap watches, T-shirts, sweets for the kids, 3D stickers and a whole array of other wondrous innovations from the Western world.

Did we want something to eat? The canteen manager is eager to provide us with some sustenance at mildly exorbitant logging camp rates. But what the hell, it beats rummaging around in our provisions which are still stacked up high on the riverbank.

Out comes lunch: half-frozen slices of white bread sandwiches filled with tinned corned-beef, kernels of canned sweetcorn and peas on the side, followed by an orange each. We eat in silence. The heat is oppressive with the ceiling fans shifting the hot air from one corner of the room to the other and back again. I decide to check out the surroundings.

The camp is one huge quagmire, with loggers' huts built around the outskirts on the edge of the jungle. In the centre there are several administrative huts, workshops, mechanical repair facilities and a gigantic dump of truck tyres, each one the height of a fully-grown basketball player.

And then there are logs. Logs everywhere. Giant mahogany logs destined for furniture (in some cases) and lesser species to be processed into chopsticks for the Japanese market (in most cases). Looking down on it all is the tropical rainforest – silent and foreboding, a witness to its own destruction.

Although Malaysia is said to have better controls for sustainable logging in place than most Asian nations (and this includes satellite surveillance to spot illegal operations), the problem seems to be that the plans look good on paper but are not always enforced – or enforceable. One of the ironies is that Sarawak's Minister for Tourism and Environment is himself a partner in one of the major logging operations and the Chief Minister, who has the power to award or refuse concessions, holds, together with his allies, about one third of the state's logging concessions. According to most recent government claims, Sarawak will be cutting its log production to a sustainable level in the near future. But they'd better hurry. According to the International Tropical Timber Organisation, the state could be logged-out within a decade.

Another wail of the camp's siren tears me away from my thoughts. It's two o'clock and time for us to pay the camp manager a visit. As we trudge down the muddy road, Josephine explains the customary inland transport system: there are no public roads, but timber companies have four-wheel drive shuttle services between camps and logging sites, and if there's room they will give 'outsiders' a lift for a pre-arranged fee.

The camp manager's hut stands out from the rest, with its beach umbrella and plastic garden furniture sitting lop-sided in the mud. We knock, and after a short pause a young Iban woman answers the door, two children in her arms and a third one clinging to her sarong. She invites us in and apologises: her husband is just getting up, but would we please make ourselves comfortable on the veranda.

As quickly as she disappeared, she re-emerges with a plate full of food: corned-beef sandwiches, sweetcorn, peas and oranges. The kids stand around and watch us in silence.

Suddenly, the man himself appears, straight out of the shower and resplendent in his starched khaki shirt (standard Malaysian Government issue), complete with shiny name badge proudly pinned above his left breast pocket.

He makes the rounds, shaking hands with everyone and welcoming us to 'his' camp. The conversation continues in Malay and it appears that he is happy to organise our lift to Camp Larissa, some 350 kilometres up in the mountains. There's only one problem: the Toyota four-wheel drive is in the workshop and he doesn't know when it will be ready.

We all saunter down to see the mechanics. The workshop is a huge shed, more like an aircraft hangar. A dozen or so mechanics clamber all over a giant logging truck. Next to it is our diminutive Toyota 4WD, awaiting its turn. The manager speaks to the head mechanic who estimates that the job should only take about half an hour or so.

Back to the canteen for refreshments. An hour goes by, listening to Lily's exploits of travelling the countryside lugging her wares from one longhouse to another, with the occasional foray into the jungle to convince the nomadic Penan that they need aspirin tablets. She doesn't like these jungle dwellers and feels uncomfortable with them, but the money is good.

The manager appears. 'It's nearly ready. Maybe another half hour, *lah*.'

An hour passes. And another. At the third creak of the door, our driver appears and announces the immediate departure of the 4WD transport. We collect our gear and walk over to the waiting pick-up truck, where at least twenty people are already packed tightly on to the back of the truck, some with one leg hanging over the tailgate.

'You better come up front in the cabin with us,' says the driver, and Josephine, Lily, myself and the driver pile in.

The four of us don't really fit on to a three-seater bench and I end up with the gear stick between my legs, wondering how this arrangement would work out. Lupak apparently thinks it won't as he waves us goodbye and our Toyota starts spinning its wheels in mud that reaches halfway up its hubcaps. The driver eases off the accelerator and we slowly start our ascent up the narrow, slippery logging track.

The scenery is breathtaking as we climb ever higher into the mountains, heading for the very heart of Borneo – the watershed that separates Malaysian Sarawak from Indonesia's Kalimantan province. As far as the eye can see, there's jungle covering the undulating landscape, punctuated by jagged mountain peaks that protrude from the foliage here and there, reaching for the clouds that hang in motionless suspense over the island.

Our climb up the mountain is becoming increasingly terrifying as we slip down even the gentlest inclines and labour our way back up the next slope, only to start spinning wheels just as we think we made it to the top. The driver seems pretty nonchalant about it all, and at times I feel that he is even getting some enjoyment out of it, with regular sideways glances aimed at our panic-stricken faces.

To make matters worse, the girls are starting to anticipate every gear change, accentuating them with loud 'Oohs' every time the gear stick slams against my manhood and sends me recoiling deep into the padding of the backrest.

We keep climbing. Higher and higher and the landscape is beginning to change. The thick vegetation around us is starting to open up in patches, affording glimpses of the valleys below. A sudden stop. The driver calls out a single word, which I don't understand, and everyone piles out and moves to the side of the road, looking down into the valley. I follow suit and join the line-up, eager to find out what's happening.

The scene I encounter is not what I expected. It's what we used to call a 'piss parade' in the army – an opportunity for the merry bunch of travellers to relieve themselves, while taking in some of the most spectacular scenery one could hope to find in any toilet in the world. Mission accomplished, the men jump back on the truck. The girls emerge from the bushes on the opposite side of the road. And I take advantage of the unscheduled stop to snap a few shots.

We don't get very far. Just beyond the next bend the truck bogs down. Everyone off. Sticks and pieces of timber are gathered from the roadside, placed under the wheels and after much engine-whining and mud-splashing, the Toyota edges forward in small leaps and bounds.

I resume my place opposite the threatening gear stick and ready myself for more of the bone-jarring trip along the narrow track. Everything shakes and rattles as we travel along and the trip is punctuated by countless large holes and ravines in the middle of the track, each one lifting the truck's occupants high up from their seats, only to slam them back into their cramped positions with a sharp jolting of the spine.

Sitting there, with my hands between my legs (a protective measure), I am starting to wonder whether I would not have been better off opting for the river, where the journey would have been a far less bone-shaking experience. The Rajang flows virtually parallel to the road, several thousand feet below us. And somewhere down there must be the unofficial border between Iban country and the up-river territories of the *orang ulu* – a collective name given to numerous tribes who inhabit the heart of Borneo.

This section of the Rajang has been the setting for countless battles between Ibans and some of the up-river people, who regularly sent down raiding parties in their huge war canoes looking for a few head trophies to take back home as proof of their warrior prowess, and in particular to impress the womenfolk.

The fiercest of these tribes by reputation were the Kayan and the Kenyah who inhabit the upper reaches of the Rajang and its major tributary, the Balui, all within relatively easy reach by river. But going there directly would have deprived me of one of the main reasons for coming to this remote part of the country – the hope of a chance encounter with some of the elusive nomadic people who inhabit the jungles around the island's watershed. Two of these groups, the Punan and the Ukit, are known as the 'invisible' people and live in isolated pockets of forest, far removed from the outside world.

The third group, the Penan, are more widely-spread through the area but are equally fascinating survivors from times gone by, surrounded now by a material world that is relentlessly encroaching upon them with bulldozers, Coca-Cola and paper money.

Another skid and a stop. This time we're on top of a ridge where half the logging track has disappeared down the mountainside. On the left is a sheer drop of several hundred feet. On the right, a newly created landslide of mud, tree roots and rocks. We inch our way forward, ever so slowly. There's about a hand-width of space left on either side for the wheels to move along.

The driver takes it all in his stride, apparently used to these conditions. A sigh of relief. We're past the critical stretch and the Toyota picks up speed, only to slide sideways into the bushes. Everyone out again. This time the broken branches and rocks don't work. The driver attaches a steel cable to a tree-trunk and slowly winches us out of the morass. We're all covered in mud.

At re-boarding time I generously offer to move to the back of the truck under the pretext that this would make the crew in the front cabin more comfortable. In reality, I am desperately looking for an escape from the cramped conditions and, especially, the vicious gear stick attacks.

The conditions on the back of the truck are no less cramped, but there's a jovial crowd of fellow sufferers and, above all, lots of fresh air. As I settle down on the rim of the tailgate, holding on to the side like grim death, my eyes wander across the load of passengers and their belongings. Everyone is wearing denim jeans and almost every beer brand available in Malaysia is represented on a veritable fashion parade of the latest T-shirts.

Some of these passengers have obviously seen the world, at least as far as the coast. Others have probably never been beyond the Rajang. Their belongings are equally limited: baskets, carry nets, plastic bags, some vegetables, one dead monkey, an antique single-shot hunting rifle, several *parangs*, two or three blowpipes and a brand-new CD player safely stowed away in a corner and still in its original Panasonic packaging.

Most on board seem to be up-river people, judging by their somewhat stocky build and quite distinct facial features. But two of the men are slim and remarkably light-skinned, quite possibly local Penan. The odd man out is an Iban, easily recognisable by the swirl of tattoos so characteristic of his people, and I can't help wondering what he is doing here, so far away from his traditional lands. Iban rarely travel into the *ulu* – with one notable recorded exception, perhaps, which has gone down in the annals of Borneo's history as 'The War of the Penises'[2]. As legend has it, this war (in which not a single drop of blood was spilled) was started by a partially-blind boy from Batang Ai, who was sent on a errand to an up-river tribe. There, because of his handicap, he was teased by some of the other children and especially by one bold young girl who pulled up her sarong in front of him, much to the delight of all the bystanders. The day went by without any further incidents as the longhouse children diverted their attention to other things. But when two boys started bullying the messenger later that night, he retorted that he saw one of their girls' vaginas.

As far as local etiquette is concerned, he couldn't have said anything worse, as modesty is a much-valued quality among longhouse communities. His angry reply instantly drew a challenge from one of the older boys, but recognising the unfair advantage he had over the blind boy, he asked him to send his father to fight instead. And if the father didn't take up the challenge, word would be passed around the entire district that the men of Batang Ai didn't have penises. This insult called for vengeance, and almost immediately after the blind boy's return, a war party was assembled to restore the honour of the Iban. The offence, however, was not sufficiently serious to call for heads to be taken (much to the disappointment of some members of the raiding party) and thus it was decided to extract a fine from the offending tribe instead.

Decked out in their finest plumage and wielding their *parangs*, the members of the Batang Ai delegation arrived at the longhouse and challenged the occupants to come out and take a look at their penises. This caused a great deal of consternation inside the house, as the warriors had caught the community off-guard and none of its men were prepared for an impromptu battle. Losing patience with the protracted silence from inside, the blind boy's father fired a shot up through the longhouse floor, an act that was instantly interpreted by his friends as a signal to start a wild rampage.

They hacked down fruit trees, burned nearby storage huts, slaughtered livestock and generally laid waste to the land surrounding the longhouse with great gusto. Eventually the longhouse chief appeared on the veranda, waving a fighting cock over his head as a sign of surrender. Outside, the pandemonium stopped and negotiations were begun in earnest. An offering was made to the gods as part of the formal act of submission and the Batang Ai people walked away with a couple of brass gongs and two much coveted Chinese storage jars as compensation for the insult.

Although that should have been the end of the affair, there was a sequel. While the Batang Ai people made their way home, word of the incident got to the chief of the up-river tribes, who hastily assembled a thousand men to go off in hot pursuit of the raiders. A major battle was looming, with dire potential consequences, sending the British Colonial District Officer up to the scene of the conflict, arriving just in time for the two opposing groups to face each other, ready to take heads. The District Officer gave instructions for the gongs and jars to be returned to their rightful owners, but the Batang Ai chief would have none of it, baring his buttocks to the District Officers instead and walking away defiantly.

In the meantime, a hurriedly convened huddle of local Chinese shopkeepers, fearing the worst for their stores, resolved to pay off the injured party with cash and goods. The offer was eagerly accepted and everyone went home, pride restored. Except for the District Officer who was left standing in the middle of the small town's main street, wondering what to write on his report sheet.

The truck keeps on climbing up the mountainside and the sun is burning down relentlessly. I can feel its rays searing into my skin right under my shirt. Then suddenly the sky blackens, and without warning unleashes a torrent of rain, sending everyone scampering to their bags to retrieve plastic raincoats or large rubbish bags – the latest in local rainwear.

My army poncho is stowed in an easily accessible pocket of my pack, but the few seconds it takes to slip it over my head already sees me wet to the bone. Somehow it's all fun and I quite enjoy the change of pace from the burning sun. The jungle around us is steaming with the ascending moisture and the valleys below are filling up with pockets of fog that hang motionless above the canopy. A hornbill bird takes flight, leaving its roadside meal behind. The scenery here is very different from what I had seen in the lowlands, with brooding, cloud-shrouded mountain peaks breaking through the forest in the distance.

This is the country of the spirits, remote and inaccessible, where the dead go once their souls have left the longhouse. The soul's journey is an ardent one and many rivers and mountains have to be crossed to reach the final destination in this jungle Nirvana.

The centre of it all is located around Apo Laggan – a mountain that looms above the others in the far distance. According to legend, the area is divided into five districts of the dead. Those who die from disease or old age go directly to Apo Laggan where they live in much the same way they have lived on Earth. Brave warriors killed in battle go to the Lake of Blood (Long Julan) where they will become rich without having to do any work. (As a bonus, they can also take their pick of all the women who died in childbirth.) People who drowned inherit all valuables lost in water. There are even places for still-born children (who become fearless as they did not know pain), and a special spot for suicides who are banished to Tan Tekan where they live miserably on *sago*, jungle berries, herbs and roots.

I ask the old man perching on the tailgate next to me to confirm that the mountain is in fact Apo Laggan. He just nods and looks at me silently. Then he points his bony fingers at the mountain and simply utters '*Toh*', the name of the dangerous mountain spirits who reside there. Everyone seems to have gone quiet, and I must admit that there is some kind of unease about the place. You can feel the mysticism in the air, with the forest dark and foreboding, and small patches of fog floating slowly like large helium balloons between the trees.

The driver ups the ante as if trying to get this place behind him as quickly as possible. But there's a long way to go; the trip is supposed to take around seven hours and we have covered only about half the distance. Looks like we may not make Camp Larissa tonight as darkness will descend upon us in a couple of hours or so.

The rain has stopped, but the landscape is still steaming. It seems as if we are about to start a long descent, and the slips and slides of the wheels are becoming increasingly scary. Rounding a bend, we encounter three Penan returning from the hunt. They are picture-book examples of what I had seen in the Sarawak Museum displays, complete with blowpipes, panhandle haircuts, elongated earlobes and wearing no clothes other than their tiny loin cloths.

One of them is carrying a rather large monkey on his back which, other than for the horror of death expressed through its wide-open eyes and bared teeth, almost looks like one of those stuffed toy apes with velcro-clad hands that one occasionally sees wrapped around its owner's neck at a country fair. Not wanting to miss the photo opportunity, I zoom in on the trio, but just as I am about to start snapping away, several harsh bumps in the road send some mud splashing my way. By now the Penan have disappeared in the distance behind us, and I am left with the task of cleaning my glasses and the camera lens. My fellow passengers seem grateful for the amusement this little incident has just provided them with, and one of them is starting to recreate the entire scene in slow motion including the accompanying sound-effect of my zoom, much to the delight of the others. These guys just love to take the piss out of each other, and foreigners are not exempt from a generous roasting.

The truck stops next to a few logs on the roadside and three passengers get off, waving to us as they disappear into the forest and get swallowed up by the jungle. More room. But not for long; before us the track widens into a large expanse of mud criss-crossed with huge tyre marks, the tell-tale signs of yet another logging camp. Our stop is only brief – just enough for a quick cup of coffee.

As we return to the Toyota, we find that the composition of travellers has changed and it seems that we now have an entire family of Penan and several of their friends. Only two elderly ladies from the previous group remain. The Penan seem a rather subdued lot – none of the boisterous banter I enjoyed from their predecessors. And certainly none of the T-shirt fashions. Although they are wearing some Western clothes (torn jeans, shiny nylon training shorts), they look very much the part of jungle dwellers.

Darkness falls and the surrounding scenery vanishes before our eyes, to be replaced by gigantic dark shadows and the shiny wet track before our headlights. No one talks very much, huddling against each other instead to gain a little warmth. The night up in the high mountains has turned somewhat chilly. Another hour passes and finally there are a few lights ahead of us. Like a horse champing at the bit to get home, our truck accelerates into the final stretch and instantly finds itself sliding sideways into knee-deep mud. Welcome to Camp Larissa.

We're well and truly stuck, within sight of our destination. After several attempts to free the vehicle, the driver walks down the road and returns, a few minutes later, with a bulldozer ready to push the Toyota back on to terra firma. Weary, shaken and aching in every joint, I pick up my backpack and trudge down the last few hundred metres to the camp, following the rest of the passengers. The group disperses in all directions, but Josephine, Lily and I head straight for the mess hall to top up our last meal of corned-beef sandwiches and peas with something hopefully more substantial.

We're the only ones there and it seems that the locals have headed for the hills and the relative comfort of their wooden loggers' huts, ready for an early night after a day's hard work of wielding chainsaws, loading fallen trees and skidding down muddy tracks in their giant trucks.

Our meals arrive: large bowls of rice and vegetables with a variety of small plates full of wonderfully spicy meat dishes. The canteen operator, eager to please us, inserts a few tokens into the jukebox and programmes in his latest selection of ABBA tunes. He turns towards us and proudly calls out, 'Disco!' while gyrating around with a few samples of his best dancefloor moves.

But none of us are in the mood to dance on the tables. We order coffee instead. Disappointed, he walks back to his counter, sulking about our lack of enthusiasm. We don't linger. A very early start is scheduled for tomorrow when we will actually begin our trek through the jungle. So we gladly take up the camp manager's offer to show us to our accommodation – a wood-cutter's hut that is temporarily vacant while its usual occupants are visiting their friends in the jungle. After a quick wash from a huge wooden barrel filled with rainwater, I slip into my sleeping bag and almost instantly fall asleep.

chapter six

jungle

It's only just after four o'clock, but I'm wide-awake in anticipation of the day's excitement. This is it: the day I have been waiting for, ever since I saw my first Tarzan film as a child. What will the jungle really be like?

Thoughts of leeches, snakes, wild animals and hacking a path through the thick undergrowth flash past me as I get dressed in my jungle best (minus pith helmet) and check my equipment one last time. Clothes, first aid kit, emergency rations, water bottle, repair kit, mosquito net, torch, sarong, poncho, rope, insect repellent, sunscreen and lots of waterproof satchels containing passport, money, film, camera and anything else that could get damaged during the numerous river crossings we will be making. I do up the straps on the backpack and clip the handy ammunition pouches containing camera, energy bars and sunscreen to the belt. Ready to go.

Outside, the camp is stirring to life. Gigantic logging trucks are lined up in a neat row, engines warming up. Drivers stand around in small huddles, talking quietly. A couple of dogs chase each other through the mud. Behind some huts, the whine of a chainsaw as a logger tests his equipment. It almost feels like being on a military base, with everyone getting ready to do battle with the forest.

'Hello, John! Up already?'

A sleepy Josephine emerges from the veranda and drops Hello Kitty next to her on the floor.

'Come. We'll meet Patrick.'

'Sure. Who's he?'

'Your guide for the next few days. He's a Penan and knows this area. You'll like him.'

News to me. This is the first I hear of another guide. But fine. So far Jo's planning has been pretty good and I trust her judgement. As we enter the mess hall, Patrick is already there, beaming from ear to ear with a smile that instantly breaks the ice.

'Hello, John, I'm pleased to meet you indeed.'

His accent takes me aback: very British. Where did he learn to speak with a plum in his mouth – and how did he end up being a 'Patrick'?

Sensing my confusion, he explains that his native name is really 'Pati' and that he went to an English missionary school on the coast.

Over breakfast he outlines our plans for the next few days: a short trip up to the ridge of the mountain and then some solid trekking to Lusong Laku, a Penan settlement on the Linau River, where we will spend the night before venturing further afield, trying to make contact with some of the nomadic groups in the forest.

'Sounds good to me. I'm ready when you are.'

'Let's go!' he says, grabbing a steamed meat bun for the road.

I do the same. These hot, Chinese rolls are a perfect antidote to a chilly morning. Outside, daylight is starting to emerge and the scenery, which I couldn't see in last night's darkness, is sheer magic. We're high up near the mountain-top and the valleys below are covered in thick fog. It all looks like a promotional trailer for the film *Gorillas in the Mist*. The similarities are striking, except for the gorillas, of course. Here they call their big apes Orang utans.

The truck is ready. Two passengers are already installed in the back, eating rice and vegetables with their fingers from a small banana leaf parcel. Patrick chats to them in the Penan language and introduces me. They are from Lusong Laku and will accompany us all the way there. Great. A little local knowledge can't go astray.

The customary spinning of wheels in the mud, and we're off, up a long winding road to the ridge of the mountain, which is now becoming clearly visible through the canopy of trees. A few rays of sun are poking through the clouds and the day is starting to warm up.

Fifteen minutes later we arrive at the end of the logging track – our starting point for a long hike.

Several Penan are squatting by the side of the road, waiting for a lift back to Camp Larissa. One of our travel companions talks to them and returns with a worried expression that transcends all language barriers. He has just been told that his two-year-old son has suffered severe burn injuries from a pan of hot oil that had spilled over his legs. The sad news dampens my enthusiasm somewhat. My mood deepens when I look down at the route we're about to take; several hundred feet of sheer drop down a slippery, muddy mountainside.

'Holy shit! Are we going down there?'

Patrick puts on one of his beaming smiles. 'Sure. You'll be OK.'

Like hell I will. I expected to be walking through flat jungle, wielding a machete to hack my way through the foliage. No one mentioned rock-climbing to me.

'Come on, John, let's do it. We have a long hike ahead of us.'

I hurriedly finalise my leech-proofing by tightly tucking my trouser legs into my canvas boots, slipping rubber bands over my shirt sleeves, buttoning up my collar and spraying the most susceptible parts of my body with tropical strength insecticide. Here we go, then.

The two Penan lead the way, rapidly zig-zagging from tree to tree. Looks easy enough. I fire the starting pistol in my mind and hurl myself downhill towards tree number one, hand stretched out to grab it. But I miss, the tree goes right past me and I slip by trees number two, three and four before getting a foot caught in a large root right in front of tree number five.

Phew. That was a bad start. Collecting my thoughts (and my trapped foot) I get up again, ready to try and get the hang of this.

Patrick smiles. 'Are you OK?'

'Sure,' I lie.

This time I actually manage to grab hold of two trees, before ending up in the mud and sliding at least twenty feet downhill. This is not so bad. Maybe the bum slide is an option worth trying. Knees up, in perfect crab position, I clamber down a few feet. But it's a slow way to move. And it does hurt the ego in front of the locals. Machismo takes over. After all, I was in the Australian army once. I can do this. Famous last words. My hands are so covered in mud that I cannot hold on to the wet tree-trunks and go hurtling once more past several trees in fast-forward mode. Resigned to my fate, I keep alternating between tree hugs, bum crawls and playground slides until finally I reach level ground at the bottom of the mountain of horror.

The others are already there, casually sitting on a fallen tree-trunk smoking cigarettes.

The downhill race only took about fifteen minutes, but I'm already utterly exhausted and bathed in perspiration. I try hard to catch my breath, but to little avail. The humidity is oppressive and the air stagnant. Nothing stirs. The place feels like one gigantic Turkish bath, making it very difficult to breathe.

Sitting still helps a little and I slowly manage to compose myself. Patrick and his friends are picking leeches off their bare legs and arms. I inspect my legs and am mighty proud that there's not one single one of the little suckers in sight. Until I notice some bright red mud on my shirt. I roll up the sleeve and find two very bloated leeches deeply entrenched in my skin. My shirt is soaked in blood, but the two little fellows are obviously enjoying themselves.

Burning them off with a cigarette is one method I have heard of and I try it. But the pair won't budge. So I take a cue from the others and pick them off with my fingers. Patrick sees this as an opportunity to teach me a little jungle craft, and guides me towards a tree.

'Look at the lower branches' he says. And there, hanging upside down like trapeze artists in a five-ring circus, are several large specimens waiting to drop down on anyone walking past.

Things aren't any better on the ground either, where a whole army of the wriggling creatures awaits us, heads reared in anticipation of an early morning Bloody Mary.

'Tiger Leech,' he says, singling out one particular striped specimen. He bends down and places his finger close to him. Right on cue, the leech moves forward. Patrick retracts his finger and Mr Leech drops back to the ground.

'They can smell your blood from quite a distance, you know.'

I ask him about the effectiveness of my tropical strength insect repellent, but he just shrugs his shoulders.

'If the repellent has a strong fragrance, it may cover up the smell of blood. But you may as well use after-shave or chicken manure. The effect is the same.'

Lesson learned. I'll save the repellent for mosquitoes and resign myself to hand-picking my leeches. The others are ready to go, so I shoulder my pack and follow the leader. We're on flat ground now and the going should be a lot easier. At least that's what I'm thinking. There's very little ground cover and the forest is surprisingly open. In fact, the visual sensation is almost that of a pretty alpine forest somewhere in Europe.

'This is primary jungle,' explains Patrick, 'and most of the forest life happens way up top in the canopy where the sun promotes growth. As you get further down, there's less light and consequently less growth.'

But what he doesn't tell me is that all that wonderful life up top eventually dies and comes tumbling down to the ground where it decomposes in its own humidity.

Crash! My foot goes right through a rotten log, proving the point. I extract it carefully and simultaneously skid across some wet leaves. By now the leaders of the pack are way ahead of us, and I try to catch up. But the going is a lot harder than I expected; far from being level ground, the terrain is tricky in the extreme.

For over an hour we clamber over gigantic tree roots, through rotting vegetation and past impenetrable thorny bushes. Everything is out to get you, it seems: vines dangling down from the enormous trees, entangling head, arms and backpack, small roots waiting to grab you by the ankles and slippery wet leaves in between. I pant and puff my way through it all, finding it extremely difficult to breathe in the 98 per cent humidity. I have to stop every few metres to catch my breath and regain my composure. Suddenly I understand the true meaning of 'steaming jungles'.

The only thing that keeps me going is the prospect of a break, when we'll sit down on some logs and I'll have an opportunity to contemplate these magical surroundings. Patrick, ever looking out for my welfare, is in fact suggesting that right now. I don't argue. Just taking my pack off is a huge relief. My clothes are soaked. My glasses are fogged-up. Perspiration runs down my face in small rivulets, its salt stinging my eyes. Even my hair is wet as if I had just stepped away from my hairdresser's shampoo basin.

A couple of our travelling companions light a fire. (Where on earth did they find dry wood?) On goes a small metal pot of water and out comes the coffee. My eyes light up. Not just at the thought of coffee, but even more so because it signals an extended break. I stretch out on the log. Total bliss. High above me the canopy seems suspended in mid-air, with occasional patches of blue sky forming a backdrop to the riot of entangled vines, branches and wild orchids that sprout in every direction. I am told that all the action is up there, way up, about a hundred feet or more above the ground. That's where, under the life-giving rays of the sun, an abundance of fauna and flora can be found.

'See the monkeys?' Patrick points to the canopy.

'Where?'

I had been staring at the treetops for some time, without noticing them. But now they seem to have materialised from nowhere, a whole troupe of them, cavorting and leaping about between adjoining trees.

Strange how you don't notice things when you're on the move. But now that I'm sitting down I suddenly discover that there is a lot of activity on the ground floor after all, with a multitude of insects, caterpillars, worms, ants of all kinds, beetles and all manner of miniature life scurrying about, attending to their important business. Just behind me, a woodpecker noisily chips away at a tree-trunk. And not far from him, I suddenly spot a rather large and colourful lizard sitting motionless on a rock, contemplating us from afar.

In a way I am surprised just how little wildlife there is in a forest which is supposed to be the home of wild pigs, tapirs, monkeys, orang utans – not to mention the occasional elephant, the near-extinct Sumatran rhinoceros or even the elusive clouded leopard. Patrick, as usual, has the answers. There are five separate vertical tiers in the forest, each one making up a different living space for specific species.

The forest floor and the undergrowth, both of which are almost constantly under the shade of the upper layers, have the least vegetation, and therefore only offer sparse cover for the larger, ground-dwelling animals. Unable to escape into the treetops when danger looms, these animals have to rely on camouflage, stealth and speed to survive any predators. Often they also adopt nocturnal habits, all of which explain why the forest appears to be devoid of wildlife.

The third layer (known as the 'under-storey') is made up of narrow, spindly trees, shrubs and woody plants that often intertwine in one gigantic tangle. They don't need as much light as the 'upper-storey' and thrive in the twilight conditions. This layer houses many smaller animals, offering them a quiet refuge and the opportunity to step from one tree to another when the need arises, without having to return to the ground.

Between the under-storey and the canopy there is a gap, sometimes called the 'flying area' – a sort of freeway for larger birds, flying lizards and flying snakes (a Borneo peculiarity).

The sun-drenched canopy itself is the most crowded space, with an incredible diversity of plants, trees and wildlife. The trees, reaching up to 150 feet (some 45 metres) in height, form a sort of umbrella that absorbs a maximum amount of photosynthesis which, in turn, provides the abundant growth. Everything is tuned-in to the sun, with leaves positioned to absorb its rays – even to the point where some of them will re-adjust their position during the day, to follow the sun's path across the sky. So intricate is nature's relationship between growth and the sun's energy, that the vast majority of trees have leaves that are elongated, finishing with a pointed 'drip tip' that is angled down in order quickly to disperse rainwater that may otherwise accumulate and thus prevent loss of important nutrients.

Towering above the canopy is a final layer of trees that protrude from the thick umbrella, seeking their own space in the crowded environment.

Coming back to earth I notice how quiet and peaceful everything is. Even my companions have gone silent. Large butterflies flit around between trees, a small army of ants marches relentlessly over the tiny obstacles in its path, a shiny black scorpion emerges from its blanket of leaves, its tail curled up in anticipation of a tasty morsel of prey. The peace and tranquillity has an incredibly calming effect on me and my fellow hikers – the silence interrupted only by the loud slurping of the coffee obviously being enjoyed in this cathedral of nature. One of the Penan cuts a branch from a tree and proceeds to whittle away at it with his *parang*. I marvel at his dexterity as he confidently carves it into a straight stick and begins to cut a beautiful pattern into its surface.

'For you,' he says, handing it to me. 'Stick for walking – very easy now.'

'Yes, very good,' the others confirm with underscoring nods.

I am somewhat taken aback by this unexpected gesture of kindness and proceed immediately to try out the new toy. Bad idea. The others take my enthusiasm as a signal to move on and we're off once more to do battle with the awesome obstacle course nature has placed ahead of us. The stick proves to be an invaluable walking aid, but I can't help noticing how I go crashing through the thicket like an elephant, while the Penan seem to be gliding over the ground almost effortlessly, hardly making a sound.

A twenty-metre breathing stop. There's a rushing sound not far from here, a river. As we emerge on its banks, I know that my worst fears are about to be realised. We are some thirty feet above the gurgling, rapidly flowing water and the only way to cross it is along a large tree-trunk. The two lead Penan saunter over it as if they were taking a leisurely stroll along a country highway.

'Now you.'

I try to retrieve my heart, which has just sunk to the bottom of my trousers. Some years ago, I suffered rather badly from a rare inner-ear disease that seriously affected my balance, sending me into frequent violent spins without warning. Although treatment has managed to cure the worst of it, I am still thrown off-balance in the dark and find it hard to keep a straight line on narrow, precarious perches such as this one.

The rest of the group has by now crossed and is standing on the other side, watching me intently and wondering what the hell the delay is. I explain my predicament to Patrick, who translates for everyone else's benefit.

'Never mind, *lah,*' says Patrick, nudging me gently on to the log while balancing me by steadying the backpack.

But before I can even take the first step, one of the Penan has already reached me from the other side. He takes my hand and shows me how to plant my walking stick firmly into the centre of the trunk to stabilise myself. This seems to work and I maintain my balance. Now it's one foot forward. Slowly. Hesitantly. A slight wobble and I manage to steady myself again. Loud cheers from the opposite bank. Encouraged, I repeat my performance and slowly, with lots of adjustments, I make the crossing.

Phew. Time to collapse in a heap and have a cigarette. The others join me in celebration of my achievement.

'How many more of these rivers do we have to cross?' I ask, trying to prepare myself mentally for possible repeat ordeals. Patrick translates the question and the reply comes underscored by a wide-sweeping, upward-pointing arm movement, 'As many as there are stars in the sky.'

Thank you for that graphic interpretation, my friend. My new-found fans start to laugh. I join in, thinking that my facial expressions on receiving the good news must have triggered off that response.

But one of them points at something behind me, and as I turn around I am face-to-face with a tree snake, dangling down from a branch and flicking its tongue near my nose, most likely trying to establish whether I am a likely meal. I can move fast if I have to. In a lightning flash I carry out a long-jump my sports teacher at school would have been proud of. My fans, by now, are uncontrollable, laughing and whooping like canned recordings in a bad television comedy show.

'It's OK,' says Patrick, 'he's a python. Not dangerous.'

Relieved, I go back to the snake to have a closer look. But by now it has lost interest and starts to climb back up the tree to look for something more productive to explore. The event does not alarm me, as I am familiar with pythons from back home. (We occasionally see them in our garden back in Australia.) But Borneo is different, and I don't know whether this particular species is meant to be friend or foe.

Recovering from the morning's entertainment, we set out once more to face the seemingly never-ending trek.

More breathing stops. More slippery logs over rushing rivers, swollen from the rain. More thorns, tangled roots, vines and leeches. But surprisingly, I seem to be coping a little better. The backpack doesn't seem as heavy as it was when we first started out. And after my initial success, the logs across the rivers no longer appear to be quite as daunting, especially with someone's steady hand guiding me safely across the precipice.

We've been underway for over three hours by now, and the heavy going is starting to take its toll on me. How much further? How many more logs? Can someone get rid of these leeches? My mind starts to wander back to my army days, when forced marches, interspersed with occasional 10-kilometre runs in full battle gear, were the order of the day. I managed it then, and I'll manage now. But there is one difference: I was twenty at the time. Now I'm over fifty, unfit and overweight. And the cigarettes don't help either.

I can hear another river coming up. This one sounds a lot louder. As we arrive at its banks, I realise that this is a big one and no log would be long enough to span it.

At the bottom of a rather steep bank, a welcoming committee from Lusang Laku is waiting for us with canoes, ready to ferry us across. A huge fallen tree provides us with a pathway to the bottom, and one by one we make our way down to the water. The locals take the first boat. As Patrick and I are about to embark, a discussion ensues and becomes progressively more agitated as the arguments heat up. Finally, one of the boatmen motions us aboard and we start the crossing against a rather heavy current.

'What was that all about, Patrick?'

'It's a long story. But I had pre-arranged for the boats to meet us and agreed to a fee of twenty-five Malaysian ringgit. Now they want forty. I am really ashamed because these are my people. Since the government attempted to resettle them, some of these groups have acquired a taste for paper money and are becoming greedy. It is very sad; their lives have changed so much.'

His thoughts are interrupted by an almighty crash: the big log we had stood on just moments before comes thundering down the riverbank, ending its slide with a gigantic splash in the muddy river. Must have scared the hell out of any resident crocodiles. Patrick and I look at each other in horror. The boatman thinks it's funny, mimicking the splashing noise and repeating it several times for good measure.

Back on dry land, our party, now grown in numbers, sets forth for the last leg.

'How far to Lusang Laku?' I ask.

'Oh, maybe another hour. Not far now.'

This may be so, but for someone in my condition it's an eternity and I start to wonder whether I'll make it. My legs are feeling like lead. I just want to lie down and go to sleep. However, sheer determination takes over and I freshen up my pace, walking almost mechanically across the endless succession of obstacles. Suddenly, light at the end of the tunnel. I can see a clearing ahead of us, bathed in brilliant sunshine. As we step out of the forest, the bright light is almost blinding, and it takes me a few moments to adjust to the new surroundings. The clearing is overgrown with very tall grass that reaches past my waist. There is no path through it and as I watch our little party progressing single-file, I can't help thinking of Tarzan again, leading a group of 'bwanas' and their native carriers through the elephant grass. This is the sort of place that must be snake heaven and I am glad I'm wearing my canvas boots.

At the end of the clearing there is a small thatched roof hut, more like a platform, really, with a few bamboo poles holding up some loosely scattered palm leaves. Must be pretty leaky in the rain. But to me it's a sign of human life and I pick up my pace. Can't be far now.

Wrong again. We keep on moving towards the crest of a hill, only to descend into a small valley and up again on the other side. Surely Lusang Laku must be on the other side. But it isn't. Four more hills and four more valleys. I'm at the end of my strength. But just as I am about to plead for another break, there's the unmistakable sound of a helicopter. Can't be. Either the heat is getting to me or they are shooting part two of *Apocalypse Now*. The setting would be right. But there's no 'Ride of the Valkyries' blaring from loudspeakers. Nor is there the fresh smell of napalm in the morning. Instead, just behind a palm grove I can see an enormous longhouse: Lusong Laku.

chapter seven

lusong laku

The throb of the rotor blades is getting closer until the chopper is immediately above us casting a dark shadow. It lands just in front of the longhouse, flattening the grass. The locals line the edge of the clearing. Silent. Motionless.

'Flying doctor,' says Patrick. 'Probably taking away the burned boy.'

We work our way closer to the scene, the concerned father running ahead of us. Everything happens rather quickly. By the time we get there, a medic has already examined the child and two crew members are now transferring the stretcher on board. A few quick father–son words of consolation and the helicopter starts its engine, sending spectators scrambling back to their original line-up. The machine's tail lifts itself up, and for a few moments the rescue helicopter hovers over the clearing before taking off in a sudden spurt over the treetops.

The day's excitement over, the longhouse inhabitants' attention is starting to shift towards us. They stand there, just staring, as Patrick approaches them. A rather lengthy monologue ensues as Patrick tries to explain our presence. There's no reaction whatsoever from anyone in the opposing force. Finally one man detaches himself from the group and motions us to follow him up the rickety steps to the veranda. So far, not a word has been spoken.

We take off our shoes and sit on the floor, surrounded by silent onlookers. The front row is made up of children, all of them smoking cigarettes or banana leaf cigars. I can't believe my eyes – some of them are mere toddlers, barely able to walk, but they handle their smokes like Hollywood film stars from the fifties.

Recovering from my shock, I decide to try the old icebreaker trick and hold out my packet of cigarettes towards the front stalls crowd to help themselves. Suddenly the motionless get into motion, scrambling for their share of the spoils. But there's still no interaction. Cigarettes are quickly snatched from the pack and the owners return to their respective positions.

In the middle of the mêlée there's a sudden, rather loud outburst from the end of the veranda, followed by a rapid-fire barrage of words aimed, apparently, at the children. Fast and heavy footsteps produce a tall young man advancing towards us with a *parang* in his hand. He looks fierce and for a moment I can even detect a hint of panic on Patrick's face.

The man moves about the crowd, chiding some of the kids. Then his stare lands on us and amidst his verbal waterfall I can only make out the words *'orang putih'* – white man. He looks at some of the elders questioningly. A quick discussion follows and fierce-man turns around to face us once more. His expression is stony. Not a muscle moves in his face. Then he turns towards me, bending down to a face-to-face close encounter and, like a flash, extends his hand to shake mine. He repeats the same performance, eyeball to eyeball, with Patrick and walks away.

'Does that mean he likes us now?' I ask Patrick.

'Yes. We're OK. Sit down, relax.'

This calls for a calm-down cigarette. Hesitantly, I proffer the pack to the crowd. The kids, in unison, retreat. But some of the older guys take up our offer. Still no one is talking. Patrick leans over to me and quietly starts explaining.

'I think that was the chief's son. He seems to be running things around here.'

No kidding.

'These people, believe it or not, are really rather shy and tend to feel somewhat uncomfortable with strangers – and that includes some of the neighbouring longhouse tribes, whom they don't trust as a rule.'

'Shy? My foot. That guy looked as if he were about to take us apart!'

'It's all show,' replies Patrick. 'He has to maintain his reputation as a leader.'

That puzzles me, because unlike other tribes, the Penan are not usually structured to have leaders in the traditional sense. They are free-spirited and much of the decision making is done by consensus of the whole group, including the women.

Apparently this longhouse is not a real reflection of Penan life. Lusong Laku has been set up by the government in one of its many attempts to 'settle' the nomadic people by enticing them with what they call a 'better life'. (Which often includes large sums of cash and in some cases a healthy share of logging concessions in return.)

Now these people can bask in the glory of Western development, with Coca-Cola, denim jeans, chewing gum, toothpaste, power tools and a host of other spoils from the 'civilised' world. There are, of course, some benefits – the short-wave radio, which enabled them to call the emergency helicopter, for instance. Another, a little more dubious, is a school complete with its own (Malay) headmaster.

My reveries are interrupted by a finger pointing at my camera. The finger's owner is a toothless old man.

'He wants you to take his photo,' explains Patrick.

Grateful for the opportunity to get some interaction going, I press the 'on' button and the zoom moves out, complete with its own sound effects. This takes the old man aback and several necks are stretching over his shoulders to see what's going on.

Laughter. At last. The flash goes off and the crowd explodes into wild excitement. Snap. Snap. Snap.

Now they're starting to line up for their personal mug-shots. The kids are at their best, posing with cigarettes hanging out of the corner of their mouths and grimacing for added effect. Before we know it, we've all become friends and a little lady even emerges with a tray of fruit, a tobacco box, betel nuts and several mugs of coffee.

A lot more relaxed now, we finally settle down. Patrick chats with the old folk. I keep demonstrating the 'magic zoom' to the kids, each of whom wants to have his own turn at pushing the button. Zoom in. Zoom out. Zoom in. Halfway through the programme, a young girl appears and asks us to follow her.

'We've been summoned to the headmaster,' translates Patrick.

'Aha. What for?'

'We'll be his guests for the night. There's a taboo on the longhouse because someone has died. Which means we can't stay there, unless we spend the entire mourning period with them.'

'So how long is the mourning period?'

'Seven days.'

'Let's go and see the headmaster.'

The school is located at the far end of the clearing, some five minutes' walk away. The modern prefabricated building looks much like any school one might expect to find in the tropics, with glassed louvre windows, plastic chairs and smudged blackboards.

Our arrival interrupts the headmaster's lesson, but he welcomes us warmly. He tells his four pupils to take a short break and wait for his return.

'That's a nice small class,' I comment.

'Oh, in the morning we have maybe twenty or thirty students. But they get impatient and many of them leave after the morning break. You see, school is not compulsory here, but we try our best, *lah*.'

Spoken like a true scholar.

The headmaster's cottage is just a short stroll along the riverbank. It's another prefabricated building, but with a few added features such as a wide veranda with several deckchairs, giving it the appearance of a typical colonial bungalow. Inside, a washing-line is drawn across the main room, with drip-dry khaki regulation schoolmaster uniform shirts suspended on hangers. Puddles of water are forming on the wooden floor.

We are shown to our room. Another washing-line, this one with sarong, Mickey Mouse T-shirt and bra. Two rolled-up sleeping mats are on the floor, next to a third one which is covered in all manner of parcels and plastic carrier bags.

'Hello John, hello Pati!'

It's none other than the illustrious Lily, ready to set up shop. How did she get here ahead of us? I ponder the question but prefer not to ask. It's nice to see even a vaguely familiar face in this place.

'I go and do some business now, and then I come back and we'll have a picnic by the river, yes?' she says enthusiastically.

We nod in agreement. Sounds like a nice idea. We have the whole afternoon ahead of us to relax and recover from the trek. A swim in the river, lazing about in the grass, slowly exploring the new surroundings – it all sounds very tempting. I walk out to the veranda and accept the deckchair's invitation to unwind. Soon I am sound asleep.

'Want to come over to the house, John?'

Half an eye open, I just manage to make out Patrick's smiling face, backlit against the bright sun like a cover shot for a ClubMed brochure.

'What time is it?'

'About one.'

I must have slept for well over an hour, and feel rested. But when I get up, my whole body aches, from my ankles right up to my neck. Slowly I put myself into gear and follow my fearless leader along the path to the longhouse.

There's no one around, but we can see two pairs of children's eyes watching us through wooden slats on the veranda. Under the stairs, an old lady talks, in turn to herself and to a scrawny rooster. When she spots us she hastily retreats.

The building itself is unlike any of the other longhouses I had seen so far: twice the usual length, and housing perhaps as many as sixty families. Its overall appearance is rather shabby, a rickety wooden construction topped with a rusty tin roof. What it lacks in comfort and style, however, is abundantly made up by its spectacular location on the Linau river, with the lush forest vegetation on the opposite bank as a backdrop.

Behind the house are several small gardens where a few vegetables are grown. At the end of the clearing some wild bananas grow, and scattered by the edge of the forest are a few *sago* palms. We sit down on a tree-trunk in front of the house, waiting for somebody – anybody – to emerge so that we can buy provisions for our planned picnic lunch.

A boat arrives. The boys have been out fishing and have returned with a sizeable catch.

Patrick picks out a rather large catfish with a wide-mouthed grin on its stunned face. The bargaining and haggling over an acceptable price is intensive, but in the end the visitors' team prevails and we walk away with our lunch.

'What are we having with it?'

Patrick points ahead of us. 'Whatever we can find in the forest.'

Evidently, there's a whole self-service jungle out there with supplies topped-up daily by mother nature: chillies growing wild on small bushes, miniature bright red pineapples, wild bananas, ferns, and a sufficient diversity of leaves to make up the most imaginative of impromptu meals.

To keep the fish fresh while we get changed and fetch our cooking accessories, Patrick builds a small dam around a few rocks in the river and drops Mr Catfish into his own private pool. I change into my swimmers, throw on a lightweight shirt and grab the camera on the way out. The water is beautiful and both Patrick and I have found ourselves a shallow pool each, away from the strong currents that gurgle all the way down over the mighty waterfall, just metres away from us. It's total bliss. Cool. Refreshing. And miles away from urban life. I wonder (with a great deal of satisfaction) what my colleagues back at work are doing right now.

The picture-postcard scenery is awesome. Huge vines hanging down, their tips barely touching the water, occasional screeching of birds somewhere amidst the trees, and greenery in every hue imaginable forming a secretive blanket over the forest. Amongst it all, the roar of the river as it thunders with tremendous force over the precipice that breaks its path. There are no crocodiles here in the fast-moving, clear water. Apparently they prefer to lurk in the muddy shallows further along. As I lie there, idle in my little rock pool, the music from *The Mission* slowly emerges in my mind and engulfs me totally. This place really is like the Amazon, and I can't imagine any spot in the world more beautiful than this.

'Hello!'

I know that voice. And I did enjoy the tranquillity while it lasted. Lily comes bearing a message from the chief: it's

OK to swim in the river, but we must not take any pictures of the waterfall as it is sacred.

Interesting. But further prompting on the subject yields little additional information. She just shrugs her shoulders.

'Something about a man and his wife hiding in a cave just under the waterfall. Their lives were saved by the river. There are powerful spirits in the area, *lah.*' That's all I can get out of her.

While Lily babbles on, I recline my head just enough to submerge my ears below the water surface. Peace. The only sounds come from the river, whose gurgling is now amplified. I like this.

Patrick gets out of the water. From my cool vantage point I observe him as he builds a little fire on the pebbly beach. Then both he and Lily are off towards the bush to help themselves to produce the ingredients that will accompany our main course. Curious, and dripping wet, I join them. We don't have to walk far; Patrick finds a chilli bush and picks several plump, red-hot, ripe ones. Not to be outdone, Lily points at some juicy shoots at the top of a clump of bamboo. A few swishes from Patrick's *parang*, and there are our vegetables.

On the way back, we pick a few young ferns (my favourite) and finalise the menu with tiny 'ladyfinger' bananas which taste delicious barbecued, if somewhat floury and stringy. As we return to the beachside campfire, we find that a whole bunch of cigarettes (with kids attached) has gathered, waiting for something exciting to happen. This is obviously far better than school.

Lily volunteers to administer the last rights to Mr Catfish while Patrick heats up some oil in a pan, adding a few chillies, various leaves and a sprinkle of spices from a tiny wooden box. In goes the fish with a loud sizzle and suddenly, as the herbs and spices are starting to release their aroma, I realise that I am quite hungry.

The children around us, in the meantime, have diverted their attention to something else. I go over to have a look. They point a some large blades of grass on top of which is a very small snake. One of the boys picks it up and offers it to me (in a gesture of friendship, I presume).

'Is it venomous?' I ask Patrick.

'Yes. But it's only very small, so it's OK to handle it carefully.'

It's a beautiful little snake, with a bright green belly and an intricate dark pattern on its back. But like so many small snakes in Borneo, its bite can pack a punch – often final.

In a way we're lucky in Australia, I guess. Although our snakes are among the most deadly in the world, they also tend to be very large and therefore much easier to spot.

'Would you like me to cook him?'

'He's too young,' I lie, 'I think we should let him go back to play with his brothers and sisters.'

Patrick agrees and the boys release the snake, which slithers away amidst the blades of grass.

Lunch is served, and oh boy does it taste delicious. Stomachs full, we lie back and listen to the noises of the forest. Coffee would be nice. Coffee. I haven't used my little camping espresso maker yet! With a jolt I jump up and run towards the bungalow.

'What's the matter, John?' I hear Patrick calling out behind me.

'A surprise! I'll be right back!'

Digging through my pack, it doesn't take me long to retrieve the necessities of life and return to the riverside restaurant. The packet of Italian Mauro coffee lets out a hiss as I break the vacuum seal and the aroma of fresh roast is released into the air. I hand the pack around and everyone takes a long, appreciative sniff.

'You brought this with you, all the way from home?'

'Yep.'

Lily is not quite sure about it all. 'You make coffee in this small pot?'

The lady doesn't know her espresso. But Patrick seems delighted. He is well-travelled and has had encounters with Italy's contribution to civilisation before.

I pack in the grinds carefully, screw the top and bottom of the espresso-maker together and place it on the fire, straddling two solid branches. Our mugs won't fit under the twin spout, but we improvise with a small saucer, transferring the black liquid back when the machine finishes its gargle.

Patrick sips appreciatively. Lily complains that there's not much coffee in her cup. I close my eyes and take in the aroma.

The serenity of the moment is short-lived as a party from the longhouse marches towards us. News travels fast. They're all here to see the strange little contraption and partake in what they perceive to be a free coffee tasting session. I make some more and hand it out as it emerges from the little machine, which is now working overtime.

One man has a sip and laughs. A second one spits it out. Others are non-committal. They leave without saying a word, having wasted my precious coffee grinds. Maybe this was not such a good idea after all. Nonetheless, I make another round of espresso. But Lily decides to pass, opting to go back to her quarters for a brief siesta instead.

So it's Patrick and myself. The coffee is good. And the waterfall spirits smile upon us as we sit there without a care in the world.

After a while of quietly contemplating the thick jungle on the other side of the river, Patrick breaks the silence.

'Tomorrow, we'll enter a different world, you know, none of these luxuries.'

'No, I guess not. Tell me, do you think we'll encounter some nomadic Penan in there?'

'Hard to say, John. They move about a lot and cover very large areas. But we should find some signs of one group or another, and with a bit of luck we'll be able to make contact.'

'And what about you, Patrick, do you call this home?'

He ponders my question and answers slowly.

'Yes, it is. These are my people and I lived in the forest when I was a young child. But that's a long time ago. My mother married into a Kelabit family up in the highlands; they were Christians and one of the missionaries arranged for me to go to school.

'I am very grateful for this, but whenever I come back here I feel that this is my home. The forest with all its beauty and mysteries is like my mother, and all the animals in it are my brothers and sisters. It's our own little world within the bigger world outside. But, you see, we never lay claim to it. It doesn't belong to us – we belong to it.'

I find this outlook on life, which many tribal peoples have in common, fascinating. In fact, Aboriginal people in Australia claim that they belong to the land, which has been their mother since 'Dreamtime' when the Earth was born. The people themselves are mere custodians of the land, passing through.

A few drops of rain send us warnings of an imminent downpour. We hurriedly gather our belongings and before we reach the headmaster's bungalow, the sky has turned black and massive sheets of rain move towards us.

We just make it on to the veranda when nature unleashes its full fury, sending torrents of water down on the idyllic landscape. The noise of the falling rain is deafening and not particularly conducive to conversation, so we each recline in a deckchair and stare into the gloomy landscape, left to our own thoughts. My mind wanders to what's ahead of us. The next few days will be different indeed; whether we make contact or not, it won't change the way we'll live in the forest. It will be back to basics. Real basics. And strange as it may sound, I am starting to look forward to it.

The rain is easing. Patrick is snoring on the deckchair next to me. I feel fidgety. Perhaps this is the time to rearrange my belongings and shed some of the items I won't need in the jungle. As we're coming back through here, I'm sure the headmaster won't mind if I leave a few things in his care.

I empty my backpack on the floor and put the non-essentials to one side: they are gifts destined for longhouses along the way and include a variety of souvenir T-shirts (featuring kangaroos, the Opera House, the Sydney Olympics logo and an assortment of Koala Bears in diverse sleeping positions), Swiss Army knives (made in China), as well as colourful stickers, holograms and removable tattoos for the children.

Next to go are my towel (the versatile, multi-purpose sarong is a much better alternative), the mosquito net (mosquitoes are abundant in secondary jungle, but there are hardly any in primary forests), my velcro-fastened trekking sandals (tend to get stuck in the mud), and toilet paper (which is hardly used in these parts of the world – it also spoils the scenery).

I hesitate at the espresso-maker, but common sense prevails and I leave it behind.

Now for the essentials: first aid kit (malaria pills, aspirin, antiseptic cream, tablets for gastric disorders, antibiotics, bandages, sterile dressings and snakebite kit), passport, money, police permits, film and camera (all in waterproof pouches).

Clothes are at a minimum: two pairs of trousers with zip-off legs, two shirts with lots of pockets, two T-shirts, underwear, woollen socks and floppy hat. That's it. (The reason for doubling up on most items is simply that clothes on the body are perpetually wet from the humidity. Keeping a spare pair of dry clothes to change into before going to sleep is not only more comfortable, but also gives the wet clothes a chance to, at least partially, dry out by the morning.)

The 'utilities' department includes my poncho, torch, Swiss Army knife (the genuine article this time, made in Switzerland), some rope, a tiny nylon hammock, toiletries kit, two water bottles, water purifying tablets, eating utensils and emergency dehydrated food rations. Oh, and cigarettes for the desperate (myself) and the grateful (everyone else). Re-packing the bag only takes a few minutes and the difference in weight is remarkable. I should be able to manage this.

School's out (officially) and the headmaster returns after a hard day's work of shuffling papers in his empty classroom.

'Gin and tonic?'

'That sounds nice, thank you.'

Amazing what legacies the British have left behind in some of the remotest parts of the world.

Patrick stirs. 'Me too.'

The headmaster acknowledges his request.

The rain has stopped, leaving light wisps of fog hanging over the river as darkness descends upon our valley. Our host arrives with drinks, some crackers and two kerosene lamps which he hooks up on the veranda's rafters. The jungle, relatively quiet during the day, comes to life, slowly warming up like an orchestra awaiting the arrival of the maestro. Cicadas, frogs and a multitude of other nocturnal performers gradually join in a cacophony of sounds that builds into a crescendo, before mellowing down again into a gentle background score.

'So you're off tomorrow to the land of the Penan, uh?'

'Yes, John is particularly keen to meet some.'

'Ah, the Penan! They are lovely people, but so poor.'

'Poor?' I anticipate what's coming.

'Oh yes, you will see for yourself. These people lead a wretched existence. They are very poor. It's so sad because they are also very stubborn and resist all our efforts to make them part of modern society.'

Here goes the official government line.

'But are they happy with their way of life?'

'How can they be happy? No education. No healthcare. No future. Most of them don't even know how to speak the national language of their country. They are missing out on the modern way of life that the rest of Malaysia enjoys. We are constantly trying to bring them out of the stone-age into a better life, and we are already making progress. For example, before we built logging tracks through the forest, which made contact easier, they did not even know that aspirin could cure a headache and that antiseptic cream would heal their injuries. The only thing they knew were the traditional herbs and roots they used to cure illnesses with. Yes, fortunately things are slowly changing. Just look around you – right here in this settlement – we have managed to teach them how to brush their teeth, bathe with soap and shampoo their hair.'

'And go to school.'

'Yes, yes. They go to school now!'

Not wanting to offend our host, I do not pursue the argument further but propose a toast instead, to him and his students.

'Thank you. I go and make dinner now.'

'Can I help?'

'No need. Very easy.'

As the clutter of pots and pans begins in the kitchen I look at Patrick. He has remained silent throughout the conversation.

'What do you think, Patrick?'

He answers in typical Penan fashion. 'He's OK. He genuinely believes in what he says. He means well for our people.'

The insects are buzzing around the kerosene lamp. Hundreds of them in colours and shapes that would send the average entomologist into a frenzy.

Dinner is served on the veranda. Rice, chicken (not the old lady's sparring partner, I hope), some vegetables and lots of sliced chillies sprinkled over the top. During coffee I start to yawn relentlessly. And so do the others. Time to unroll our sleeping mats.

An almighty clap of thunder. Before me a tree splits in half. I am soaked to the bone, and try to climb the steep slippery slopes of the mountain. But each time I take a step forward, I slip back two steps.

The water is pelting down. Again I manage one step up, but instantly slip back two steps. I am utterly exhausted. One step forward, two steps back. I'll never make it to the top. But there's no other way out of here. Would the helicopter rescue team be prepared to lift me out if I paid for it? Another step forward. Two steps back. A loud clap of thunder. The rain hammers down on the tin roof.

I wake up, bathed in sweat.

chapter eight

linau

Breakfast is pretty basic. A few rice cakes, vegetable curry, crackers and coffee.

'How did you sleep?' asks Patrick from behind a huge yawn.

'Not bad, until I started having these nightmares about climbing back up the mountain. It's a funny thing, how things seem to be so much worse when you're in a state of half-sleep. Everything seems amplified and exaggerated. But now, with the sun out, I feel fine again.'

'Should be a great day.'

Outside, our new travelling companions are already waiting. Jok and Ajang are joining us for a couple of days in the jungle. For them, it's a change of pace from the settled way of life in the longhouse and an opportunity to do a little hunting or gathering. It's also their way of staying in touch with their original habitat. As I shoulder my backpack, Jok gestures towards it, offering to carry it. I decline politely, determined to carry my own share of the load, especially since Patrick is also looking after our provisions. But our new friends won't hear of it: they quickly divide our loads up evenly between the four of us, adding some of our belongings to their cane shoulder baskets.

Parangs strapped to the waist and blowpipes in hand, they motion us towards the river, which is already a hive of activity. Numerous longboats have gathered, ready to take locals to various destinations up-river. One of them contains no less than the illustrious Lily and her chattels, ready to go and terrorise some other nearby community, it seems. She waves a big goodbye to us and shouts 'See you soon!' over the roar of the outboard engine as the boat swerves around and points its bow straight against the current. They briefly battle diagonally across the rapids until they reach the calm of the opposite shore and slowly disappear in the distance.

'We – here,' says Ajang, pointing downstream and leading the way towards the waterfall.

The track takes us past our little picnic spot and soon disappears downhill into thick vegetation. Here the riverbank is quite steep and seems to incline even more as we proceed. The thunder of the waterfall becomes more pronounced, and finally we emerge on a small beach immediately in front of an enormous wall of cascading water. 'Wow!' is the best I can come up with as I stand awe-struck in front of this spectacular production of nature. The fall must be well over 200 feet high and presents and ever-changing spectrum of moods and colours. At the very top, a sparkling rainbow spans its way across the width of the river, partially obscured in places by the thin mist of spray that hovers above the precipice. I reach for my camera but Ajang quickly intercepts my intention.

'*Maaf*, I'm sorry, I forgot.'

The camera goes back in its pouch, with a great deal of regret on my part. We all sit down and silently watch the awesome panorama in front of us. The deafening noise prevents conversation, but none of us seem to mind. A tap on my shoulder. Patrick flicks his head sideways towards a small bay downstream, where a boat is just tying up against a semi-submerged log. Must be our lift. Our boatman looks frail and ancient. But looks can be deceptive, I realise, as he grabs me by the arm and almost single-handedly lifts me and my backpack into the centre of the hull. Reverse throttle, the bow swings around, points into the current, and we're off.

The going is nice – for about a hundred metres until a series of ripples indicates the first set of rapids. Oldman-boatman takes them all in his stride, veering to the left, veering to the right, engine screaming in reverse, and back again into the centre of the action where we slide, as if guided by unseen hands, straight into a narrow passage between two huge rocks. Emerging on the other side, the water is calm and deep. Unlike the upper part of the river, the landscape here is dramatic; gigantic cliffs surround us on both sides, some with sheer faces as high as a hundred feet. In between, and sprouting from even the slightest crevices, is an abundance of lush greenery, accented by small waterfalls that cascade their way down into the river. Around any bend now, I expect Adam or Eve (complete with apple and snake) to pop up from behind some bushes.

'Hold on, John!'

The impact is violent as the boat hits the rapids. We are thrown from left to right and back again, and soaked through to the skin. My cigarette is wet and soggy and probably a write-off. The old man, however, looks statuesque as he assesses what's ahead of us with a calm but tense expression on his face. Jok laughs. Patrick smiles. Ajang looks stern. And the boatman is ever so cool.

I must admit, racing through these rapids is fun. The adrenalin pumps and you hold on for dear life – a sensation not unlike a child's first exposure to a wildwater ride in an amusement park. But as with all forms of repeat exposure, one tends to tire of it after a while, and getting a good soaking every few hundred metres may be refreshing but not overly conducive to taking photographs.

Jok, standing up near the bow, eagerly looks out for imminent action and signals the boatman accordingly. In some ways he looks the part of a traditional Penan, with long earlobes, a bone necklace, short, straight fringe and a stream of long hair hanging down over his neck. If it weren't for his shiny Reebok training shorts and the fake Rolex on his wrist, he could easily be featured in a Sarawak Tourism Commission brochure. Ajang, on the other hand, is a quiet sort of character. He doesn't smile much and doesn't say much. Almost brooding. But he is very polite, ever ready to lend a helping hand and contribute to the general well-being of the group.

The water flow seems to have settled down, and other than for a couple of stretches where we have to carry the boat around obstacles or waterfalls, we are progressing at a good pace, the engine gurgling away happily through the otherwise rather silent forest surroundings.

'Time for lunch, John. Are you hungry?'

'Yes, I could eat a monkey or two!'

'Ah! You like monkey? You like real Penan!' (Jok, of course.)

Everyone laughs in appreciation, even Ajang who doesn't understand a word of English.

The boat pulls up at a little sandy beach, covered in fresh wild boar tracks.

'*Babi!*' hoots Jok, and before we know it he, Ajang and the old man are off into the bushes, blowpipe and spear in hand, in hot pursuit of what may turn out to be lunch (in the form of wild pig).

Patrick and I follow some distance behind, but as we enter the tangle of greenery we are faced with the reality that we have no idea where they all went. We return to the beach and start building a little fire. Patrick rummages through our provisions in search of lunch (just in case the *babi* run faster than the Penan), while I finish off the last of my drinking water and refill the canteen, popping a couple of purifying tablets into its neck.

Chores completed, we relax by the edge of the water. The Linau River is at its scenically-best along this stretch, as it winds its way down towards the Indonesian border. But casting my mind back to the number of rapids and waterfalls we had to tackle over the last few hours, I suddenly understand why Josephine was so adamant about opting for the land route instead. It looked so easy on the map – catch a boat and zoom all the way down the river. But the maps (most of which could win awards for outstanding efforts in inaccuracy) didn't show all these obstacles along the way.

The peace and quiet is interrupted by a troupe of monkeys that noisily makes its way down from the treetops towards a little beach right opposite us. First to reach the ground seems to be some sort of scout, who looks around, makes a few authoritative noises and proceeds to the edge of the river where he scoops up water in his hands and throws it over his head. The others follow and the monkey party is underway. There's a lot of splashing, underscored by an assortment of yelps and screeches. But the revellers quickly tire of this and break up into individual little groups, some settling on the rocks, picking fleas (or whatever), while others chase each other across the muddy shores.

Patrick and I sit perfectly still in order not to alarm the merry tribe. The unsuccessful Penan hunters, however, emerge out of the bushes, sending scout and followers scurrying back up into the trees.

'No good. *Babi* gone.'

Thought so. Resigned to their fate, the hunters retrieve little parcels of banana leaf-wrapped rice and place them on the fire. Patrick follows suit, adding leftover bits of catfish to the menu.

There's time for a swim before lunch and we all jump into the cool, clear water, splashing around like a bunch of boy scouts on their annual outing. Refreshed and dripping-wet, we settle down around the campfire. Lunch tastes great in these natural surroundings. Jok takes a swig from his canteen and passes it around. There's a lot of appreciative noises and lip-smacking before the bottle reaches me. I should have known – *tuak*.

Ajang breaks the silence by addressing Patrick with a succession of guttural sounds. Translation: the hunters have come across a signal message of carefully placed leaves and notched branches, left behind by a group of nomadic Penan. According to this message, the group has split in two – one heading up into the mountain, the other making its way back to their base camp near a large rock outcrop, about a day's walk down-river. Signals of this kind are routinely used by the forest dwellers to inform other groups of their whereabouts, intended movements, potential hunting areas and other bits of jungle news worth covering in this unique bush version of CNN.

'So we're in luck?' I ask.

'Yes, maybe. We know that they're here. But things change quickly. I think our best bet would be to go to their base camp and see. We could also leave some messages, but they may not necessarily respond. We'll just try our luck. No promises, OK?'

Agreed. Spurred on by the news, I collect my belongings and make it obvious that I'm ready to move on. But the others won't hear of it. Their stomachs are full, the sun is warm, the *tuak* still flows. It's too nice a day to go bashing around the bush. Cigarettes come out. Patrick is making coffee. Maybe I can be talked into staying just a little while longer.

The afternoon journey has a dreamlike quality about it, as we glide along gentle currents and frequent long stretches of water so calm that not a single ripple can be detected on its surface. The serenity of nature is perfect and the hours go drowsily by, gliding through this awesome tropical landscape where foliage grows in such abundance that trees touch each other across the river and dangling creepers form massive walls on its sides.

The air here is somewhat lighter and less stifling, but what I notice most amidst this vast expanse of untouched beauty is an almost inexplicable sense of freedom and well-being.

For the first time in years, I no longer feel the back pain that had been riding along my spine for so long. And all the cares (and stress) associated with urban life seem to have vanished. Without the hectic pace imposed on us by our material world, I feel that I am 'connecting back' to nature and for the first time in my life, perhaps, I understand the true meaning of this concept.

Patrick is asleep, sprawled out in the bow section of the boat, one leg dangling over the side. Ajang scans the treetops for any signs of life. And Jok sits cross-legged in a puddle of water with a gentle smile on his face, taking in the scenery. Even the boatman seems to have found his inner peace in the magic of the moment. My mind wanders back to the city: sirens wailing as ambulances take the latest heart attack victims to the operating table, police cars responding to petrol station hold-ups, shouting matches in board rooms, drivers abusing each other in traffic.

On the other side of the river a mouse-deer and its young are drinking from the cool river, interrupting their activity only briefly to watch us go by. Patrick stirs. The sun has disappeared behind the cliffs and he suggests that we start looking for a suitable site to pitch camp for the night. We don't have to travel far; within half an hour Ajang spots a jungle shelter, high above the water. We pull in near a large rock that protrudes out of the river and Jok climbs up a tree to fasten a line some thirty feet up. My raised eyebrow brings an answer from Patrick, 'In case the river rises overnight.'

Our gear is unloaded and we start our trek up yet another steep embankment. I huff and I puff as usual. At the top, we find that the shelter occupies prime real estate, with sweeping views over the valley and the river bubbling away some two hundred feet below us.

'OK, this is it. Choose your sleeping place and make yourself comfortable, John.'

There aren't too many options and the principle of choice does not really apply: our abode for the night is no more than a raised bamboo platform with a few palm fronds to keep out the worst of the rain. But it's a room with a view and I pick the most scenic aspect. Jungle camps such as this are common throughout Sarawak, and can be found anywhere along the gigantic network of age-old tracks used by indigenous people for hunting or for travelling from one longhouse to another. Mostly these shelters are spaced out to coincide with the end of a day's march. They can be used by anyone, as long as some basic 'jungle hospitality' rules are observed, which includes repairing any damaged sections of the structure and replacing any dry firewood used. Sometimes there are even urns of fresh drinking water and small amounts of rice left behind for the next visitors to use. Again, common etiquette requires visitors to replenish such supplies.

While I unpack my belongings before darkness sets in, Ajang is busy building a fire, rice-pot filled and ready to go on. The old man and Jok are rearranging the roof and Patrick and I are left with nothing to do. It must be six o'clock – the jungle chorus is starting to rehearse.

'I love this time of day,' says Patrick, 'it's so peaceful and relaxing.'

'Yes. Out here, all the cares of the world seem to go away.'

I relate my thoughts of urban life that popped into my head while we were on the river this afternoon. Patrick smiles, 'I know what you mean. It's so fast and frantic. Everyone wants to achieve things, to get a better life, I think.'

'You're right. We are pushed to excel the moment we start school. Then, when we grow up and start working, we become ambitious and competitive, because that's the example which is constantly being held up before us. But does what we achieve really bring us a better life?'

'I don't know. When I went to the city I was told to work hard so that I could go to University and carve out a better life for myself. Now I know a lot more about the world, but I'm not sure that I am more satisfied with my new life than these people are with theirs.' He points at our friends who are reclining around the fireplace, enjoying the warmth and the peace of the moment.

'They lead a simple life and material pursuits don't seem to come into the equation, mainly because they're not aware of them,' Patrick continues, 'they probably find their 'riches' in other things.'

An interesting point of view, which reminds me of an incident during a course of Aboriginal studies I once attended at Sydney University. The lecturer answered a student's question on perceived 'laziness' among Australia's Aborigines and I found his reply fascinating:

Tribal Aborigines have different sets of values. Their life is based on living in harmony with nature, first and foremost. They get up in the morning and attend to their daily chores: the women gather roots and plants, the men go hunting.

This only takes two or three hours. Having fulfilled their immediate needs, they have time left to engage in leisure pursuits for the rest of the day and devote themselves to art, story-telling or spiritual matters.

In Western society we call that 'quality time'. The difference is that we keep working harder and harder striving to achieve it – which mostly happens when we retire. Then we die.

Something smells good. Ajang dishes out the steaming hot rice, topped with a few spiced-up vegetables. A simple meal, but I don't think I ever appreciated a humble bowl of rice as much as I do right now, sitting in a gentle breeze above the river, serenaded by a thousand different voices from the enchanted forest around us.

When the fire goes out, I slide into my sleeping bag and see a million stars through the gaps of the roof. Stars I never see in the city.

chapter nine

penan

The way down is always harder than the climb up. This is due to a thing called gravity – something that pulls you down much faster than you really want, in the direction you want to go, usually through alternating layers of mud and tangled roots. I reach the bottom with a thump. At least Patrick is used to me and doesn't laugh. The others just look at me in amazement.

The boat is still there, but its bow has been lifted into mid-air as the river level lowered during the night. Better than having to board from a tree branch, I guess. It's a bright sunny day, great for an early morning dip. There are no formalities here: strip and splash. Wash and shave. And move downstream for any other business on the agenda. The river is rather shallow here and I manage to find a nice solitary rock to sit on and enjoy a leisurely shave, while Patrick prepares breakfast of coffee and tinned mackerel on crackers. I take mine back to the rock where I can enjoy uninterrupted views of the river.

The old boatman is peeling layers of jungle weed from the outboard's propeller.

'More coffee?'

I nod. Somehow time seems to stand still in the jungle. There's no hurry to do anything or go anywhere. But eventually our little party sets itself into motion and we push our longboat towards the centre of the river, where a slightly deeper channel enables us to re-board and slowly begin our journey towards the next set of rapids. It doesn't take long to get used to the routine of unloading and reloading the boat every time a waterfall blocks the way – or to hang on to hat, backpack and provisions whenever the tell-tale ripples of a new set of rapids appear.

But this time, the waterfall ahead is bigger than previous ones; complicating matters further, it is flanked by sheer cliffs and the way around them appears too impenetrable to carry the boat. We are pretty close to where we think the Penan may be camping and so decide to secure the boat under some trees and walk the rest of the way. As we clamber up mountainsides, follow tracks that don't look like tracks, take detours around obstacles and frequently change directions, I am starting to lose my sense of orientation. Everything is just a blur of greenery and tangles designed purposely to confuse the hell out of me.

'How do these guys know where we're going?' I ask Patrick.

He laughs and calls out to Jok, translating my question.

'*Mal cunuk*,' he replies. 'They follow their feelings.'

Just like that. But their built-in bionic PGPS (Penan Global Positioning System) seems to work: after two hours of dripping my way through nature's sauna, the forest opens up and there, right ahead of us, are plumes of smoke wending their way up through the trees.

As we approach I can just make out a hut in the background. And another one. An old lady sits on the ground in front of it, weaving some rattan with nimble fingers. She has already spotted us, but keeps on weaving until we're right next to her. She smiles at us and doesn't display the slightest bit of curiosity. It's as if we were the milkman dropping by on his daily rounds. We sit down next to her and my Penan friends strike up a slow conversation. I don't have the faintest idea of what they are talking about, but periodically the old lady looks at me and says, '*Bah.*'

Not to be outdone, I say '*Bah*' to her and return her smile. I think we're on our way to becoming friends.

While the locals chat, I get an opportunity to cast my eyes over the setting that surrounds us. Eight huts constructed similarly to our previous night's shelter, but built more solidly, are dotted among the trees around a rather small clearing. These *lamin*, which tend to accommodate one small family group of three to four people each, are built on wooden poles about two metres above the ground and are accessed by the usual notched log. Although devoid of embellishments or furniture of any kind, they are rather cosy, each with its own earthen hearth, slightly raised platforms for the dogs and sometimes even some simple shelving to store everyday belongings under the roof. There is no one around, other than Lady *Bah*.

Taking advantage of a lull in the conversation, I ask Patrick where everyone is.

'The men are out hunting and the children went with their mothers to make *sago*. They'll be back later and then we can meet them all.'

Jok produces a few guttural sounds and Ajang nods, picking up his *parang*.

'Come on, John, we'll build a house for the night.'

'A house? Just like these?'

'Yes, the *lamin* are all occupied, so we have to make our own. It's very quick, you'll see.'

Ajang hands me a *parang* and leads the way into the bush. Just a few minutes into the scrub, a brief conference takes place. Ajang points at a few trees and allocates them to individual members of the work detail. I get a small one. Aim. Big swing. Blade bounces right back, hardly leaving a dent in the wood, but jarring my wrist.

Patrick is right behind me, watching. He takes my hand (which miraculously is still holding the machete) and slowly moves it back in an arc, aiming the blade down at an angle. And there it is: an ever-so-slight cut! Much encouraged, I start chopping away in earnest, working my way around the thin trunk. A crash. And another. My friends are felling their trees merrily around me, while I still try to get the hang of this. Suddenly a creak – from my tree! I've chopped my way down to a pencil-thin pylon in the centre and the sapling is about to move in my direction. This requires quick thinking: left, right or behind? I opt for the latter, which turns out to be a good move as the tree starts to bear down on my companions who quickly scatter into the four corners of the forest.

'Is it safe?' A snide little remark from Patrick who emerges from behind one of the bushes.

But I think I did all right, as my fellow workers are starting to produce some of their strange gurgling sounds, simultaneously patting me on the shoulder. Rather pleased with myself, I eagerly proceed to stage two: chopping off all the branches, a task that turns out to be much harder than it looks. All around me it's chop, chop, chop, with the occasional *clunk* (me) in between. I'm up to the third branch on my tree. The others have finished. We each collect our own trees and weave them like knitting needles through the thick undergrowth.

Back at the camp the old boatman has already collected a whole heap of *nipah*, palm fronds, now neatly stacked and readily for use. Ajang marks out four spots between a few trees, a respectful distance away from the other buildings. Jok starts banging the saplings into the ground with a rock, creating a square so that the horizontal poles (which are tied to the base structure with rattan) can be laid down accordingly, and *pronto!* we have a floor for our little abode.

Another square made from smaller saplings is tied to the top where our boatman is already starting to lay down the palm frond roofing. Not wanting to appear useless, I help him and for the first time I can actually detect a hint of a smile on his face. This is exciting. I've never built a house before, and here it is, nearly completed. The whole operation took less than an hour.

The old lady hasn't moved, sitting in the same spot, splitting rattan with a small knife and talking to herself. Suddenly the quiet is pierced by a faint *'ooohaaahooo'* sound from somewhere in the distance across the river. Ajang cups his hands and replies with a similar noise.

'The troops are back from the hunt,' explains Patrick, 'they'll be here soon.'

More 'oohs' and 'ahs' from both sides. The pace is picking up and the sounds are closer now, somewhere on the mountain-top opposite us. If it weren't for the tropical surroundings, I'd expect Julie Andrews and the Lonely

Goatherd to pop out of the bushes any minute. Instead, an advance party of three hunters appears on the riverbank, waving from afar. In as much as I can make out from the distance they are *au naturel*, sporting only a tiny loincloth to protect their assets.

'Let's make some coffee. It will be a while until they get here.'

After all the hard work in the building and construction business, I couldn't agree more.

The hunters trickle into camp one by one. They look weary and tired, the strain of the past few days showing on their faces. When the last of them finally arrives, it becomes clear that the hunt had not been very successful. All they have to show for three days of hard labour is one rather small monkey, and their disappointment is evident as they collapse, exhausted, around the small campfire.

Our presence seems to go by almost unnoticed, until one of the younger men gets up to shake our hands. A couple more follow suit and the remainder simply acknowledge us with nods and smiles. It's as if we were neighbours from up the road, dropping by to borrow a cup of sugar.

A few voices from behind the bushes signal the arrival of the women and children, who are returning from their *sago* gathering. One little boy, on seeing his father, lets out a cry of delight and rushes towards him. Dad manages a smile and a hug, but his body displays the signs of the long walk home, with deep, red marks on his shoulders where the rattan straps of his carry basket has cut into the flesh. Patrick asks them about the hunt and translates the answers for me.

'They say that they walked for three days, looking for wild pigs. Although they came across some tracks, there was no sign of the pigs. They killed a couple of birds along the way, which they shared among themselves. There just didn't seem to be any wildlife.'

'Is it always that hard for them?'

'No. Sometimes they're lucky and do rather well. But the old man says that things have changed over recent years. They used to go out for a day or two and come back with enough provisions to see them through for two or three weeks. But now it's becoming harder. There is less wildlife about as the logging activities in surrounding areas drives the animals away.'

'And what about fish? Surely there must be plenty in the river.'

'Same thing. The loose soil from denuded areas washes into the river, making it muddy. As a result, the fish move on.'

The sound of snoring near the campfire interrupts my thoughts; one of the men apparently decided not to wait for nightfall. The others are sitting around, talking quietly.

Unlike our Penan guides who are partially decked out in vestiges of Western civilisation (including one pair of shiny Homer Simpson boxer shorts), these people sport their original tribal look, from head to toe.

Panhandle hairstyles are de rigueur, although some grow their hair to shoulder length at the back. What strikes me most is their physical appearance. They seem to be taller than most people I have encountered in Borneo, and above all they are rather fair-skinned as a result of living in the perpetual shade of the forest.

Adornments are few: some men wear a couple of rattan bracelets below the knees, others have necklaces with beads or boar's tusks and, unlike other tribes in Borneo, they seldom wear tattoos. The one adornment that has me fascinated, however, is a pair of boar's tusks protruding from the pierced earlobes of an old man. (Patrick tells me that originally these hottest of fashion accessories were invariably teeth from the cloudy leopard, but as these are hard to come by due to the depleted population of the legendary cat, wild boar's tusks are often substituted.) To confirm his suspicion, Patrick asks the old men about the tusks. Animation at last. The old guy bursts into life as his bruised ego sets out to put the record straight: No, they are not 'fakes'. Yes, they are the genuine article, obtained from a rather large clouded leopard he personally stalked for a whole night.

At this the old man gets up, drops down on his hands and knees, and re-enacts both the cat's evasive manoeuvres from tree to tree and his own leaps and bounds during the entire chase sequence, all the while trying to keep his blowpipe steady in readiness for the moment of truth.

The rest of the men are now coming alive, following the old man's antics with whoops and yelps. They've obviously heard the story before. As a *grand finale*, the ancient performer takes out the leopard's teeth, inserts them under his upper lip and looks around for general acclaim which, other than for a few half-hearted giggles, is not forthcoming.

But I appreciate the man's performance and start applauding. The other Members of the Academy obviously don't think his act deserves a nomination; nevertheless, one by one they join me and give the man his due. He sits down, looking rather pleased with himself.

While all this has been going on, the women have prepared some food and are now emerging from their individual *lamin* carrying bowls of *sago* and platters of vegetables, looking much like a procession of stewards making a grand entrance into the dining room of a Caribbean cruise ship.

'Help yourself, John.'

The food looks good, but the portions seem sparse. In the centre is a large bowl of rice – our contribution to the meal and a somewhat unusual offering, as the Penan don't cultivate it. Their staple diet is *sago*, which grows wild in the forest, and meat. Lots of it when the hunting is good. Following local custom, I take a small amount of rice out of the bowl, work it into a small ball in my hand and dip it in the soupy vegetable dish. The hunters seem quite hungry, judging by the way they are shovelling the food into their mouths. Yet time and time again, they motion us to partake of their simple meal.

'Don't be shy, help yourself,' says Patrick, trying to encourage me.

But I feel ill at ease encroaching on these people's meagre rations. Patrick disagrees.

'If you don't eat, they will think that their food is not good enough for you. Here everything is shared equally. It's the Penan way. They are proud people and that's why they are not shy or coy. When you come here, you live with them on their own terms and you will be treated as one of them, without apology for poverty or lack of comfort. If you are hungry, they will share their food with you as a matter of course. And equally important to them is the act of 'taking' without hesitation.'

Looking at the circle of people around the fire I can't help noticing a feeling of total harmony within this small community. Simple conversation between young and old alike, exchanges of pleasantries, enjoyment of a moment of togetherness as night descends upon the jungle. I share my observations with Patrick.

'Yes, you are right. They are a gentle people, slow to anger and prepared to listen to one another's opinions. They call it 'listening to the heart'. In fact, feelings such as anger, jealousy or envy are quickly pushed aside, to be replaced by warmth, love and consideration for one another. They need that to survive in such a close-knit community.'

This intrigues me, because simply looking at them gives an impression of fierce and wild jungle dwellers, ready to send a poisoned blowpipe dart in the direction of the nearest intruder from the outside world. Thinking of the shudder that went through Josephine at the mere mention of the word 'Penan', I decide to broach the touchy subject.

'Tell me, Patrick, am I right in saying that the Kayan and Kenyah don't seem to like these guys all that much?'

Patrick ponders the question. 'It's probably not so much a matter of dislike, more a sort of fear of the unknown. Most longhouse people feel uncomfortable in the forest, which to them is the abode of countless spirits and demons. As a consequence, anyone who lives here is regarded with a high degree of suspicion. It's a fear that is quite irrational, because among all the tribes of Borneo, the Penan are the only ones who never practised headhunting. They are just happy to be left alone in their own world where they live in total harmony with nature.'

I help myself to more rice, and the old man with the tusks nods at me in approval. The stars have come out above us, adding to the magic of the moment. A few of the men, weary from their non-productive hunt, are retiring towards their *lamin*. One of them comes up to me, says a few words and hands me a small, beautifully woven rattan bracelet.

'It's a *jong* – a dream bracelet. He wants you to have it so that you can keep the memories of tonight in your heart.'

I am speechless, literally, and take his hand, thanking him merely with sincerity in my eyes. He nods, picks up his small son and disappears into the family shelter. A few remaining stalwarts stay on with us as we share a nightcap of coffee. But we don't linger. It's been a long day and my yawns are becoming increasingly pronounced. Someone is extinguishing the fire behind us as we clamber up the tiny ladder to our sleeping platform.

It's too hot to use my sleeping bag, so I spread it out on the bamboo floor to make myself a soft bed. As my eyes are closing and I am about to slip off into dreamland, I hear a song drifting through the trees from one of the shelters. It's a gentle tune with a soft, lilting melody. Suddenly, several people from another *lamin* join in and soon, it seems, the entire camp is partaking in this impromptu forest recital.

I sleep well, holding on to my dream bracelet.

There are about 10,000 Penan living in Sarawak. (Government source).

There are about 7,000 Penan living in Sarawak. (A different Government source).

There are 'approximately' 6,545 Penan in Sarawak. (Yet another Government source).

It all depends on who quotes the figures. The reality is that, unless some enterprising souls are actually prepared to wet their feet and spend months in the jungle trying to track down every last one of the elusive Penan, the real number will never be known.

To confuse the would-be statistician even further, there is a sizeable overlap between 'true' nomads and 'part-timers' who are officially settled (according to government records) in permanent longhouses, but periodically revert to living in the forest.

Although the government has managed to convince many Penan groups to move into permanent settlements, the realities of settled life have often been disappointing. Adopting rudimentary forms of agriculture, such as the (often unsuccessful) planting of tapioca or rice, only provides enough food to replace their traditional diet of *sago* for a couple of months in the year. So here's an instant dilemma: why put up with the harsh sunshine (to which they are unaccustomed) in the paddy fields and lead a boring life in an alien environment the rest of the time, when their original home in the jungle provides such an abundance of food and activities? Jok and Ajang have found their own compromise by 'commuting' between the two, living in the twilight of the colliding worlds.

Others have never succumbed to the temptation of government promises. But their numbers are dwindling rapidly: of the total Penan population in Sarawak, it is estimated that only between 5 and 10 per cent still lead a nomadic life. In other words, somewhere between 500 and 1,000. And fourteen of them are now splashing about in front of me in the river. My arrival does not interrupt their frolics. In fact, it almost seems to go unnoticed.

Stepping carefully amidst a veritable underwater Legoland of precariously stacked pebbles, I make my way towards a waterhole not far from the group. But they call out for me to join them.

A little distance from us, several small fish are jumping. Suddenly, one of the girls calls out something and everyone goes quiet. She cups one of her hands and brings it down hard on the water, producing a sound that resonates like an organ pipe as she sweeps her arm along, just below the surface. Another girl takes a turn at this, but instead of letting the sound fade out of its own accord she plunges her other hand into the water in a cutting motion, which alters the initial sound completely.

I stand there, dumbfounded by this unique experience. By now, the rest have joined in, each one producing their own notes, which end up in a symphony of haunting sounds that carry across the water and gently fade away among the ripples of the river. Ajang explains in sign language how it all works. He starts the sound with his cupped hand and then cuts across it with the open palm of his other hand. This changes the pitch, which can be altered depending on the depth of the cutting motion. I try my hand at this, but all I can produce is a splash as my hand enters the water. By now the group has seemingly lost interest and is heading back to the shore. I decide to postpone my attempts at a solo until I can practise some more, perhaps in the bathtub back home.

When we return to the camp, Patrick already has the kettle on, and some parcels of compressed rice in banana leaves topped with a few morsels of fish are waiting for us.

'Today is a rest day, John. The guys are pretty tired from their hunt, so maybe that's an opportunity for you to observe life around the camp and take it easy yourself. Would you like to do that?'

My head nods repeatedly and very fast. A small huddle of men is having what appears to be a little meeting some distance from us. They talk quietly among themselves, drawing little symbols in the dirt with some sticks. Most likely they are planning their next moves. In front of one of the huts, several women have gathered, weaving colourful baskets and hats. The children have disappeared in the scrub, followed by the ever-attendant pack of dogs.

Life seems too simple and uncomplicated here. And in many ways it is. Camps such as this are usually set up as semi-permanent settlements, in areas determined by the availability of *sago* and fruit as well as the proximity of wildlife. These base camps tend to be used for anywhere between three to six months, depending on how quickly the available food supplies are depleted. When that happens, the entire group will simply abandon the camp and move on to a new location, giving the old surroundings time to regenerate.

As a rule, the base camp tends to be inhabited by women, the elderly and the very young, while the men split up into small hunting parties that forage in the jungle for food. As this can sometimes take them over considerable distances, individual groups tend to establish temporary settlements on the way where they may stay for several days, until they once more move on in pursuit of fleeing wildlife. This simple pattern, which is based on necessity, enables the Penan to live in harmony with their environment without inflicting any permanent damage upon it.

'Want to try some *sago* pancakes?' Patrick has just whipped up a batch, using some of the starch flour the women have extracted from palm trees. 'They're quite tasty.'

I bite into one. Not bad at all. In fact, they remind me of the famous *latkes* sold in your average New York Jewish deli. All they need is a little apple sauce. Patrick is already on to his second batch and I'm intrigued by the way he prepares them. He pours *sago* flour into an old soft drink can with holes punched in the bottom, adds a little water, and presses small dollops of the squishy mass straight into a pan filled with hot fat. As the pancakes brown to a golden colour, they rise to the top and Patrick scoops them out with a small branch. Simple. I can do that. And to make sure I don't forget the 'recipe', I write it down in my little notebook.

'Do you know how *sago* is made?' asks Patrick.

'No, I don't have the slightest idea. All I know is that it comes from palm trees.'

'OK. I think the women are about to go and make some. Why don't you go along and watch them?'

'If that's all right, I'd love to!'

'Sure. I'll tell them. They'll probably be glad to have an appreciative audience.'

He walks away. Giggles from the women's hut. They emerge with broad smiles and motion me to join them. I grab my water bottle and follow them barefoot into the jungle, feeling like one of them. 'Ouches!' here and there, but by and large I seem to manage. In fact, I feel a lot lighter and more sure-footed than with my bulky boots on.

The stand of *sago* palms is only a few minutes' walk away, and as soon as we reach the area, the women get down to business. Each one seems to have their own pre-assigned task and I am left standing around, feeling like a spare wheel waiting for a puncture to happen. I sit down on a fallen tree-trunk and watch, fascinated, as stems of palm trees are being transformed via this unlikely assembly line into the fine flour that produced such unusual pancakes earlier on.

The procedure is rather complicated and looks very labour-intensive. First, after agreeing on the number required, the girls select some suitable palms. A few well-placed blows of their *parangs* quickly produce a pile of stems, ready to be split. Once the pith inside the trunk is exposed, it is scraped out with a sharpened piece of wood and the loosened fibres are placed on a woven mat, which is stretched over a raised wooden frame.

This frame, in turn, is placed over a second mat that catches the *sago* after it has been tread-pounded with water on the upper mat. (Something like a topless grape treading competition – minus the black scarves – at a remote village in the Italian Alps.) The resulting white substance is then left for a while until a sediment forms, when the remaining water is drained and discarded. To finish the process, the *sago* is dried in small chunks over a fire before being stored as pure starch in finely woven rattan bags, to be used later.

The most common way of cooking *sago* is to boil it in water to a pasty consistency (not unlike the glue we used to make in our woodwork shops at school) and then eat it like a fondue from a common pan. In its paste form, *sago* can also be baked or fried, topped perhaps with small pieces of meat or fish.

As I watch the slender girls, I am amazed at how easily they perform their arduous task – which so far has taken them several hours. My reveries are interrupted by a familiar voice behind me.

'Beautiful, aren't they?' Patrick has managed to sneak up and sits down beside me.

'Uh, yes,' I say, slightly embarrassed – not knowing whether he is referring to the topless bits or the girls in their sarong-clad entirety. Change of topic.

'It seems a lot of work for just a little *sago* flour. How often do they have to go through this pounding exercise to keep up their provisions?'

'The average yield lasts them about a week. Then they start all over.'

'And what happens when they run out of *sago* palms?'

'Usually they move on to another area. But they rarely run short of food because everything is shared. If one group has been successful in a hunt or has surplus food, some of their members will walk for hours to bring a nearby family their share of the spoils. It's a system that works very well and one that ensures the community's survival.'

'Yes, I've noticed how things are shared. The monkey they brought back yesterday was carved up into equal portions and handed out to all the families.'

'That's right. They gave us a piece too. It's something they learn from an early age. When children find some berries, for example, they immediately distribute them among themselves. And although they respect individual space and property, they have no hesitation in borrowing something without asking. It's all quite natural to them; so natural, in fact, that there is no word for 'thank you' in the Penan language.'

The girls are starting to pack up their belongings and we make our way back to camp, which seems to have transformed itself into a market square with mats spread out everywhere, loaded with exotic plants, sticks and stones.

'Wow! What's all this?'

'The pharmacy,' says Patrick, laughing.

'The pharmacy? What do you mean?'

'They've been out gathering and most of the things you see here are used in everyday life for food, handicrafts or as medicines.'

He picks up some gnarled roots, '*Laku kubaba* – these are boiled in water and used for toothaches. And these flowers called *apujaka* are applied to open wounds.'

Patrick weaves his way through the tangle of plants the men are sorting out, pointing at different natural remedies.

'For headache. Skin rash. Broken bones. Stomach ache. Too much drink. Fever. This one I don't know.'

My naturopath would have a ball here. And, one would presume, so would many of the world's largest scientific companies – if they would only listen to the voices of the forest.

According to some of today's foremost botanists and biologists, some 25 per cent of modern drugs were first used in traditional folk medicine. Yet of an estimated 80,000 species of plants found in the Amazon alone, less than 500 have been studied and analysed. Considering that nearly 70 per cent of plants in tropical forests are known to have anti-tumour properties and any one of them could lead to a breakthrough in cancer research, the lack of interest – or unwillingness to investigate – by modern science is astonishing, to say the least.

But medicine is just one area that seems to ignore the immense storehouse of nature. According to Dr Wade Davis, an eminent Harvard University ethnobotanist, the tropical rainforest offers some 75,000 edible plants, of which a mere 150 are used commercially in a world where the number of nations experiencing famines is increasing daily[3].

And there's more: a type of palm seed oil that is indistinguishable from olive oil; a tree that produces resin that will, unprocessed, run a diesel engine; shrubs whose fruit contain natural compounds 300 times sweeter than sucrose; lianas impregnated with biodegradable insecticides. The list goes on.

Perhaps David Suzuki had his finger right on the pulse, when he referred to modern science as focusing on 'areas of specialisation' rather than using a more holistic approach[4]. During one of his visits to the Amazon, he met several PhDs and students of herpetology who could spot and name the most unusual, tiny frogs in the middle of the night. Yet when asked to identify a flower or insect, they replied, 'Don't ask us, we're herpetologists.' In contrast, the Kaiapo Indians, deep in another part of the same Amazon rainforest, had a name and a story for every single organism Suzuki pointed out.

Like the Penan here, who are now busy sorting through their bounty from the jungle, there are countless indigenous peoples throughout the world whose combined knowledge is far more profound and extensive than anything science currently provides. Yet these very people are disappearing as rapidly as other species in the forest. The potential loss of their knowledge is beyond imagination.

Patrick continues, '*Gatimang*, antidote to poisoned darts. These leaves over here repel mosquitoes and bees. This is for snakebite. This one for luck in hunting.'

'Any for luck with women?'

'No. But this one will stop you from having babies, in case you do get lucky.'

My diary entry for that day reads: 'Not much happening around camp in the afternoon. Used the time to relax and explore the surroundings. Washed clothes (four items) in the river and reorganised film in various waterproof pouches. Early dinner (*sago* and small fish full of tiny bones that get stuck between my teeth). Haven't seen Jok, Ajang or the old man all day. Patrick says they went to visit some "cousins" whose group is camped on a hill a couple of bends further up-river (some prompting establishes that there are some very pretty girls in that group) to "pound some *sago*".

The meaning of this eludes me, until Patrick's face breaks into a wide grin. Interesting turn of phrase.

The sun is already up and the smell of coffee wafts through the trees as I tentatively crane my neck out of our shelter.

'Good morning, did you sleep well?' Patrick looks full of beans and ready to party.

'Fantastic. What about you?'

'Oh yes, I always sleep well out here.'

The conversation dies as I try to get used to the bright daylight and Patrick stirs up the fire. I join him, warming my hands by the fire. Nights can be quite chilly up in the mountains.

The others are returning from the river in little groups, chatting among themselves. It appears that everyone else has already eaten, so I heat up some left-over rice and bake some plantains in leaves. While I sit there, cup of coffee in hand and trying to wake up, some of the men are emerging from their huts, bearing blowpipes and all sorts of accessories.

'Are we going hunting?'

Patrick, sipping his coffee, nods. 'Uhum. Just around the area. They've seen a few tracks down by the river.'

Next to me, one of the Penan is taking small wooden darts from a quiver. He checks their points and then dips them in a sticky white substance wrapped in a leaf.

'*Tajem*, a very potent poison,' explains Patrick, 'they collect it from the latex of the *ipoh* tree. But there are many others. Some are so powerful that even the tiniest little prick from a dart can kill an animal in just a few minutes.'

'And what if he accidentally pricks himself?'

'Then it's a quick goodbye to friends and family. But there are antidotes of many kinds. They know which ones to use.'

I ask the man next to me if I could have a look at his blowpipe. He picks it up and starts explaining its intricate workings in great detail, all of which is lost on me. His lesson finishes with a quick demonstration: he inserts the dart, lifts the blowpipe to his mouth and holds it there, quite still with both hands, for several seconds. Then a sharp blow. I look vaguely in the direction he fired, but can't see the dart.

My blowpipe coach takes me by the hand and guides me towards a hut, and past it to a tree-trunk, and past that to a very thin sapling where the dart sits happily implanted at the fork of a thin branch some fifty feet away from where he fired it.

My turn. He hands the *sumpitan* to me. It's not as heavy as it looks but quite long, as I find out when I rest it on the ground and its top reaches way past my head. I insert a plain dart (mainly for the safety of the others), hold up the pipe with both hands as shown, take a deep breath and – flop. The dart lands a few feet from me.

Encouragement. I need encouragement. But looking around full of hope, I see that the best they can manage is a couple of non-committal nods. I try again and this time the dart actually flies a few metres. The nods turn into slightly animated mumblings and a couple of guys even shout a few words in my direction. (I could swear they meant 'fantastic', 'good try', 'keep it up'. But then again, I am not so fluent in Penan.) The cheers get louder and louder. I get ready to take a bow. However, in the nick of time I discover that the acclaim is not aimed at me, but rather at our three returning local heroes emerging from the bushes behind me, wearing ear-to-ear grins. The *sago* pounding must have been good.

While they recount their nocturnal adventures to a rapt audience, I inspect the hunting equipment. Right next to me is a pile of long spears with tips fashioned from old soft drink cans (which have replaced the bone arrowheads once used). These spears are used for large (and thick-skinned) game such as wild pigs, tapirs and perhaps the occasional crocodile.

But what really attracts my attention are the blowpipes; fashioned from the toughest of hardwoods, they are a marvel of engineering. For the darts to gain the correct velocity and actually fly (let alone travel considerable distances with a mere puff of breath) the bore has to be drilled precisely and very straight. Power tools would help, of course, but the folks out here do it all by hand. The procedure is not complicated; however, it requires a great deal of skill and, above all, patience. A good start, I am told, is to find a suitable (and presumably reasonably straight) piece of wood, cut it into a two metre length and roughly smooth it down to eliminate any lumps, humps and bumps. The wood of the *nyagang* tree is ideally suited for this, but others can apparently work equally well.

Stage two consists of building a high platform so that the blowpipe maker can start the slow task of drilling a vertical bore with the help of a long metal drill. This can take a few weeks, though still less time than in the old days when they used sharpened stone implements. Once the drilling is completed (and the craftsman presumably indulged in a little rest) the exterior of the weapon is smoothed down to a fine finish with the help of *bekela* leaves, a sort of plant substitute for sandpaper. As a nice last touch a metal blade is fastened to the top, much like a bayonet on a rifle, so that the blowpipe can also double as a spear.

There's movement in the camp. The stories of nocturnal exploits have apparently been exhausted and the crew is getting ready for the hunt.

'What shall I take with me, Patrick?'

'As little as possible. Take your water bottle and camera. But make sure you don't wear any belts, clips or pouches that can make a noise. And leave your insect repellent behind – the animals can smell that from a distance.'

This is exciting – going hunting in the jungle. The group has assembled near the path and an old one-eyed man seems to be the leader of the pack. Curiously, despite his affliction, he is the only one carrying a rifle (which any self-respecting antique dealer would pay good money for). I ask Patrick how the old man can shoot with one eye (and wonder if he still shuts the other one to aim, but refrain from mentioning it).

'I think the rifle is just for show. He may use it in an emergency, but shooting is not a good idea as the noise will send any wildlife fleeing from the area. Blowpipes are much more efficient. They are silent and just as deadly.'

Food for thought. The group starts moving in a single file, myself at the end like a United Nations observer. We walk for about half an hour until the old man motions us to sit. Two large trunks, facing each other, provide us with a congenial setting. All that's missing is a coffee table and a

Landing stage at Kapit – the last government outpost on the mighty Rajang river and a meeting place for tribal people from remote longhouses.

Tuak time: author enjoying Kayan hospitality while being honoured with a traditional welcome song.

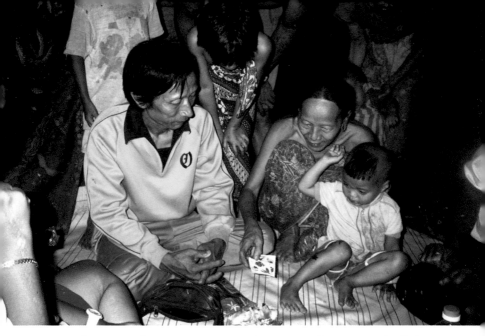

The novelty of removable tattoos has these semi-settled Penan enthralled.

*Rice storage hut at Rumah Apan,
beautifully decorated with intricate Kayan designs.*

War canoe in the making: boatbuilding largely remains a manual skill along the Balui river.

After hours of trekking through leech-infested jungles, the longhouse at Lusong Laku suddenly appears on a clearing.

Slippery when wet! Stairs leading up to longhouse verandas take a lot of getting used to.

Travel in Borneo is mainly by longboat,
but settlements are few and far between.

Beaded battle shield and baby carriers
featuring traditional Kayan dragon-dog design.

Iban longhouse: the rickety elevated platform is made from split bamboo that bounces and creaks with every step.

One of the most beautiful places on earth, Sarawak offers a never-ending spectrum of awe-inspiring scenery.

*Express boats, essentially old aircraft with their wings chopped off,
can be a frightening experience as they scream with a
deafening roar up-river into the heart of Borneo.*

Unlucky warrior: captured head on war canoe

Fired up by copious amounts of tuak, a young warrior performs the hornbill dance to the sound of gongs and the sape, a single-string instrument with hauntingly beautiful sounds.

Their hiding place discovered, curious longhouse children assess the visitors from another world with mixed reactions.

deck of cards. The troops are all puffing away on their local tobacco cigarettes, talking quietly. The old guy is chewing on some betel nuts, the bright-coloured juice trickling down the sides of his mouth. It's only a short break and after just a few minutes cigarettes are dropped, almost in unison, on the jungle floor and we move on. I can't get used to the local custom of simply dropping lit cigarettes on the ground. But then again, unlike back home in Australia where even the slightest spark will set off a potentially devastating bushfire, here everything is perpetually wet and the soggy, butts will rot and distintegrate within a few days. (A process that washing powder manufacturers would in all likelihood describe as 'bio-degradable'.)

Suddenly it dawns on me that Ajang, Jok and the boatman aren't with us, and I ask Patrick about it.

'I think they really came along for the girls. Hunting was just a nice way of putting it. By now, they are probably fast asleep.'

Our conversation is interrupted by one of the men up front, who suddenly squats down and makes a peculiar sucking noise with his mouth. Everyone else immediately crouches low and we remain totally silent. The lead-man points toward the sun, where a troop of monkeys has settled in the treetops. One of the men to my left silently disappears into the bushes and I lose track of him. Several others take off in different directions and vanish, seemingly into thin air. Our forward scout, still from a crouched position, lifts the blowpipe to his mouth and fires a dart.

I think he missed. The monkeys keep going about their business. We remain quiet and motionless. Then, out of the blue, a furry body plummets through the branches. The poison has started to take effect. Screeches from the treetops as the group flees. The mortally wounded animal lands with a thump some distance from us. But no one moves.

'They're giving him time' whispers Patrick, 'otherwise the monkey will try to run further, making it harder to retrieve him.'

I get myself into a more comfortable position by sitting down. We wait. It seems like an eternity, but at last the men get up and start making their way to their quarry. When we reach the spot, we find the monkey wedged between two large buttress roots, looking peaceful as if he were having a brief siesta. The group stops and the hunter who killed the animal steps forward, bends his head and starts talking.

'What's he doing?'

'He is apologising to the monkey for killing him and talking to the spirits of the forest, asking them to take good care of him in his after-life.'

I feel somewhat unsettled. Seeing an animal being killed is a chilling experience. Yet I do enjoy steak. The contradiction weighs down on me heavily as the hunter straps the monkey to his back with several lengths of rattan, and we set out to continue our journey through the now quiet forest.

The Penan are once more talking among themselves, knowing that most of the wildlife would have fled by now. We walk for half an hour or so, before our leader suggests another break. I can't take my eyes off the monkey which lies, face towards the sky, on the wet jungle floor. The group seems to notice my unease. One of the men sidles up next to me and puts an arm around my shoulder. Two more move closer and the old one-eyed man squats down in front of me, talking quietly with slow, measured words which gradually turn into humming. The others join in and begin to sing, almost in a whisper. Patrick, not wanting to disturb the moment, gives me a telegraphic summary of their actions.

'They are trying to explain to you that this is the way their mother – the Earth – has taught them to live and survive. The song is part of *Oia Aheng*, an age-old epic that is passed on from generation to generation and recounts the creation of their world.'

I don't ask questions. What is happening before me does not require translation and the comfort these simple people bring to my troubled thoughts defies description. At the end of the song, I thank them the only way I know they will understand: by placing my fingers on my chest and pointing the palm of my hand towards them. It's a traditional greeting that means, 'I will always keep you in my heart.' I smile, and they respond in unison. To seal the occasion, the man who had performed for us when we first arrived at the camp pulls a cheroot from one of his earlobes and offers it to me. Everyone lights up and conversation resumes. Patrick looks at me.

'You all right?'

'Yes. I'm sorry, I didn't mean to become the centre of attention. I'm OK, really. It's just a new experience for me. Somehow it's different when you buy your dinner ready and shrink-wrapped at the supermarket.'

He laughs at the comparison. As we get ready to move on, images of television news coverage flash through my mind: truckloads of tomatoes being dumped by protesting farmers in Spain. Followed by footage of children foraging for dried-out roots in hunger-stricken areas of Africa.

There are, of course, practical explanations for these contradictions. But out here, they somehow don't make sense. The Penan will only take from the forest what they need. This not only applies to hunting, but to all forms of life including plants, which will never be up-rooted or damaged unless they plan to use them.

My thoughts are interrupted by yet another alert from one of the men. He points at the ground and the group gathers around some fresh wild pig tracks. Like a well-practised army platoon that has stumbled into a suspected ambush, the men split up and silently disappear in different directions. Patrick motions me to keep low as we follow the leader. No one is making a sound – except for me. No matter how much I try, my feet produce snaps, crackles and pops wherever they land. Yet there's no sign of reproach from anyone in the hunting party.

Sounds echo through the forest. The bush telephone in action, message: 'Tracks washed away. Game gone.' Cigarette break.

Team members are emerging from the bushes without the slightest hint of their imminent approach. Suddenly they're just there. Materialised out of nowhere.

'How do they do this? Why don't they break twigs or splash mud when they walk?'

'For a start, they don't wear boots.' Patrick is delighted at taking a swipe at my cumbersome jungle gear. I cringe at that, mainly because I know that I would be equally as noisy with my boots off.

He continues, 'Of course, there's something called lifelong experience. Stalking is a skill they acquire from the moment they take their first steps around the campfire.'

'Are there any tricks to it?'

'No tricks. But I can show you something that will help.'

He exchanges a few words with the others and one volunteer steps forward.

'Watch as he walks along the track.'

The man sways past bushes, walks through ankle-deep water, picks his way past thorny vines and brushes aside branches that obstruct his path. All without the slightest bit of noise.

'He almost slithers through it all like a snake,' I say in amazement.

'That's right. And you know why? Because he doesn't use his feet.'

'His feet? What do you mean?'

'Exactly that. When we walk, we tend to concentrate on our feet. And that's how we end up making noise. But if you shift your centre of gravity to your pelvis, and concentrate on that part of your body, you will find that your feet follow. It's a lot easier and also far less tiring. Why don't you try it?'

I'll try anything once. So I move towards the track.

'Remember, John, concentrate on your pelvis. Move it forward slowly. That's right – now bring up the legs.'

I do as I am told. Snap, crackle, but no pop. Perhaps there is some hope for me yet.

'Keep going. Follow the man!'

I try it a few times and gradually the system kicks in. It's quite amazing and feels like a well-oiled machine that pushes forward and slowly puts down its various attachments as it progresses along the way.

'Good, you're getting the hang of it!'

'OK, let me try a stretch on my own.'

I pick a section of entwined vegetation and head straight into it. Hips go up and twist sideways past some bushes. My arms stretch out to brush aside some hanging stuff. The feet sink down gently on a batch of leaves. I twist the hips again and can actually feel energy and propulsion coming out of them. This is fun! *Crash*. Had to come.

'Keep on going, John. I think you are getting the idea.'

I am indeed. The whole thing reminds me of some of the martial arts that use the flow of *chi* – the inner strength in all of us – to achieve seemingly impossible feats.

'Why don't you practise this on the way home? You'll see. You will be able to walk a lot easier and you won't get so tired. And if we are all lucky, you'll also make less noise!'

I'm on cloud nine. This is fantastic. But the best is yet to come: while I learned to sway my hips like a novice hooker along a busy stretch of highway, the guys back at the treetrunks have brewed some coffee.

Pepped up by my newly-found energy and a sizeable caffeine hit, I actually manage to keep up with the locals as we make our way back to camp. Ajang, Jok and the boatman are waiting for us, all packed-up and ready to go. A quick conversation with Patrick and they start shaking hands with me.

'Where are they going? What about our boat?'

'Don't worry. We won't need the boat. A few of the Penan from here will guide us over the mountains tomorrow into Ukit territory – you know, the 'invisible' people.'

'Really? But what about my gear I left behind in Lusong Laku?'

'Oh. I forgot about that.'

Another quick conversation with the Three Amigos. 'They say they will send it ahead to one of the longhouses we will be visiting along the Balui river. Is there any gear you will need before then?'

I make a quick mental inventory, but there's nothing I desperately need. In fact, most of the things I left behind could be regarded as disposable, except for my treasured espresso maker, perhaps, and a few gifts I brought along. I convey that to Patrick.

'Then it's settled. You'll have your belongings in a few days.'

'Are you sure?'

'No, but let's give it a shot.'

Strangely, I don't feel uncomfortable with the idea. Maybe I am starting to get used to the way of the jungle where plans are meaningless and arrangements are changed at the drop of a loincloth. Smiles all round, followed by enthusiastic handshakes.

'*Selamat jalan*,' I say, wishing them a safe journey back.

They reply with the traditional, '*Jumpa lagi*' pointing at their hearts in unison, and disappear in the thicket. On the far side of the camp I can see the hunters dissecting the monkey, handing out pieces to all the families.

'So tell me about tomorrow, are we really going visit the 'invisible' people?'

'Well, we will be going into their territory, but first you can witness an interesting event – a Penan trading day where they meet people from other tribes to exchange goods. We'll probably have to spend a night in the jungle before we move on into the land of the Ukit.'

'Will we be going on our own, just the two of us?'

'No, I don't think that would be wise. I have already asked a couple of guys who know the area to accompany us and they agreed.'

While dinner is bubbling away in its big black pot, Patrick fills me in on *tamu*, the trading day. According to one story, it had its origins a long time ago when a group of Kayan travelled through a patch of Penan territory to visit relatives in longhouses scattered through the area. To avoid carrying all the gifts with them, they decided to stash some of them away on top of a large rock, to be retrieved on their return journey. But things didn't quite work out as expected, because the Penan found the stash and, believing it to be gifts from the spirits, took them back to their families. Most were items they were unfamiliar with: *parangs* made of iron, fabrics woven from cotton, rice, glazed Chinese jars.

To comply with tradition and thank the spirits for their generosity, the Penan returned the next day and left some of their own offerings behind: beautifully woven baskets, handicrafts, blowpipes, mats and jungle produce. Needless to say, the look of surprise on the Kayans' faces upon their return would have made for a priceless picture occasion. But they were delighted, believing the gifts to have come from the spirits, in the same way the Penan did. The story made the rounds, other tribes decided to test the system, and so began a regular pattern of lucrative trading.

Whether there is any truth in this story or not, is hard to tell. But the ancient tradition of the *tamu* so impressed the British when they arrived in Borneo that they formalised it by promptly setting fair prices and introducing a regular timetable.

'But the Penan don't have a written language, how can they read a timetable?'

'With a piece of rattan. I'll show you.' He calls out to no one in particular. A young woman acknowledges his request and returns with the 'timetable' – a long string with knots tied into it.

'They are given one of these and each knot represents one day. The Penan simply untie one knot per day and when they get to the end, they know its *tamu* time. A simple system, but it works.'

Dinner is ready. (Oh no, mum, not monkey again!) The sky opens up and sends down buckets of water. We hurriedly pick up our food and retreat to the relative dry of our individual shelters. I chew on the tough, stringy meat and daydream of a strong cup of espresso with just a touch of froth floating on the top.

It's still pitch-black when Patrick wakes me up.

'Come on, John, time to get up. We've got a long day ahead of us.'

Outside, the rain is coming down relentlessly. I decide to take a shower instead of a bath and climb down the ladder, splashing through puddles in my underwear. Patrick joins me and we both stand there, face to the sky, soaking up nature's waterworks.

A couple of women walk past us, bending slightly and bowing their heads in a customary sign of respect. In the background, I can barely make out a family inside a hut, their faces partially lit up by the fire in their hearth. They look wild and fierce. Yet in the past few days I have learned that these are a gentle and peaceful people. When there is potential for an argument they tend to avoid confrontation, preferring to settle matters through talk. They respect each other's feelings and views and act accordingly. And once they have overcome their initial shyness, they will welcome strangers into their midst, forging friendships that will often last a lifetime.

Their habit of never looking anyone straight in the eyes – a characteristic Josephine described as 'shifty' – is no more than politeness, as the Penan perceive direct eye contact as a form of aggressive challenge. Patrick's coaching in the ways of the Penan has been invaluable, enabling me to show some respect for their customs. I never step over a meal on the floor. I bow before a plate of food that is handed to me. I avoid direct eye contact, and never call anyone by their name (a bad omen).

In turn, the group has started calling me *pade* – brother. As strange as it may sound, I feel very much part of their little community and regret having to leave their uncomplicated world where material possessions are meaningless and nature supplies a spiritual wealth most Western people spend a lifetime trying to achieve.

'I'm singing in the rain . . .'

I can't believe my eyes when I turn around and find Patrick dancing through the puddles, sending splashes of mud towards me in his own interpretation of Gene Kelly's famous routine.

'Where do you know that song from?'

'I saw a video once – come, join me!'

I'm already wet and full of mud, so what the hell. We dance and cavort and sing at the top of our voices, which are partially drowned out by the thunderous downpour. The Penan are starting to line up on their platforms, amazed at the spectacle before them. But not sufficiently shocked to resist the temptation of a little fun, it seems, because one of them comes racing down with a small bamboo instrument that resembles a Jews' harp, which he starts playing, mimicking our song. Before long a woman joins in with a nose flute, followed by two kids banging away at some old kerosene drums. Mud is flying in all directions. Laughter resounds through the jungle. The rain eases and daylight starts to break, revealing patches of fog that creep silently through the woods.

'Let's eat!'

I couldn't agree more. We return to our shelter and unpack some of the rations we have brought with us: dehydrated curry and rice, followed by a couple of Powerbars each.

'So how far are we walking today?'

'I don't know, but probably around three or four hours. There's a logging road over the mountains and that's where we'll meet the others – mostly people from neighbouring tribes. Kayans. Kelabit. Kenyah, and whoever else shows up. The road is as far as the Penan will go, because they don't like leaving the forest. So trading takes places on the edge of their turf.'

Outside, the camp has turned into a hive of activity. People are loading their carry baskets with barter goods and as we stroll through the jumble Patrick points at some of the wares about to be packed.

'These baskets are highly prized by outsiders. It is said that the Penan women produce the most beautiful woven handicraft. You can see how fine the workmanship is; beautiful dark dyes, thinly-split rattan to give them density, and intricate patterns that make for striking designs.'

He'd make a good advertising copywriter.

'The longhouse people usually sell them to the Chinese traders who, in turn, will sell them on to tourists with a huge mark-up.'

Spread out on the ground are hats, mats, pouches, baskets, arm bracelets and a selection of bamboo containers, all beautifully shaped and crafted.

'These *parangs* are interesting.' Patrick picks up one of the machetes and hands it to me.

'The blades were not made here – the guys probably bought them at the last *tamu*. But since then they have carved and decorated the sheaths and attached adornments. Now they will sell them on to the outsiders.'

The much sought-after hardwood blowpipes are lined up in a row next to the *parangs*, together with a couple of sets of paddles and some animal skins. Patrick spots an elderly man who is carefully placing some stones into a small pouch.

'Guess what these are!'

'Semi-precious stones? Diamonds?'

'No. They are gallblader stones from a monkey. They are said to have strong healing properties and the Chinese merchants will pay a good price for them. They are very rare and hard to find. As you can see, the man is also selling deer horn and a number of healing plants.'

The medicine chest in front of me reminds me to take my malaria tablets. As I search for my first-aid kit, Patrick calls out that the trading caravan is about to set out on its journey. I hurriedly stuff my belongings into my backpack and do a last check around the shelter (a habit I've picked up when leaving hotel rooms) to ensure that I haven't left anything behind – camera, film, hat, backpack – and I'm off to join the others.

It's already been a long walk and the worst is yet to come: ahead of us loom the mountains we're about to traverse. Puffed as usual, but using my newly acquired 'slithering' skills, I plod on, one bush at a time. We've crossed countless rivers (I'm getting better at these, too) and encountered seven separate species of snake. Borneo has the richest snake fauna in South-East Asia. There are racers, cobras, kraits, rice snakes, rat snakes, coral snakes. Some 160 species in all, and we seem to have met most of them this morning. Some were just beautiful to look at (from a distance). Others frightened the living daylights out of me – especially the bad-tempered ones that rear up, hiss and spit and generally behave in a very anti-social manner. Not all of them are poisonous, of course. Like the keeled rat snake that came to check out my backpack during a rest stop. At ten foot plus, it's not the sort of thing you immediately want to share your biscuits with.

But one species I found fascinating was the famous flying snakes. We saw one just as we were approaching yet another river. There it was, performing bungee jumps from one tree to another. Strictly speaking they are gliders rather than flyers, because they draw in the belly so that their underside becomes concave, like a sort of wind tunnel that enables them to glide downwards, sometimes over considerable distances. To witness this type of performance is spectacular. To stand under a tree where one is about to launch itself can be unsettling.

The mountains are getting closer. As we clamber up the first steep hill we hear voices from the top, another group of Penan on their way to the market. The reunion calls for a break and out come some local delicacies: wild bananas, *sago* wrapped in leaves, a few berries I can't identify, and a tin of Spam.

'These people are from the same group as ours and have been in the area for a few weeks. Apparently there will be others joining us, so you'll soon meet the whole tribe.'

Sure enough, as we are starting to pack up a fresh group emerges, made up almost entirely of rather young people, three of them carrying babies on their backs.

As we progress up and down hills, our little procession is steadily growing in numbers and the whole thing is beginning to take on a carnival atmosphere, with lots of banter and joking along the way. The road must be on top of the next hill. Bathed in sweat, I work systematically, grasping for young trees and bushes to pull myself up along the vertical path. Next to me, a couple of old-timers are chatting casually, walking up the incline as if it were a Sunday stroll along the beach. Their bodies are taught and trim, their short-toed splayed feet well adapted to the jungle floor.

More hills, but there's light on the horizon as Patrick points towards a swathe of denuded forest just ahead of us.

'Not far now, John. That's where we're going.'

It looks quite some distance away, but to my surprise we get there in less than quarter of an hour. It seems that we're the first to arrive and I am a little disappointed as I expected hordes of people waiting to greet us. Everything is quiet and the early morning sun is already burning down on the exposed logging track. My Penan friends retreat to a relatively level spot on the edge of the forest and make themselves comfortable among their diverse wares. News is exchanged and there's a lot of subdued chatter. But no action. I feel like an early arrival at the party and bide my time taking in the landscape.

The road is right on top of the ridge, but unlike 'our' part of the forest the other side shows ugly scars of heavy logging. Large tracts have been carved out of some of the hillsides, leaving sizeable open areas to find their own way back to their former selves.

Then I notice something unusual: several trees on our side of the road bear faded markings painted in red and showing the letters 'X' and 'P'. I question Patrick on their significance, and he explains that they are the remains of the controversial Penan anti-logging campaigns of the early eighties.

'The 'X' means 'don't cut', the 'P' identifies the trees as Penan property. It was a last-ditch effort to try and save some of the traditional lands, by appealing directly to the timber cutters' conscience.'

'Did it work?'

'No, of course not. But it was not for lack of trying.'

And try they did. At first there were only relatively small incursions by the timber companies, sweetened by gifts and smooth talk which the accommodating Penan took in their stride. But things gradually deteriorated when the state government announced that over one million acres of Sarawak's rainforests where to be converted into cocoa and rubber plantations. The plan was to resettle both the nomadic and the longhouse people in the area, into new townships where they could find 'gainful employment and join modern society with all its benefits'.

The Penan, in particular, did not understand this, let alone want it. Theirs was a life that was lived in their ancestral homelands, the forest giving them everything they needed in abundance. But as the timber companies forayed increasingly into their lands, the Penan realised that the noise of chainsaws caused wildlife to flee in droves, and not return to the now barren land. To make matters worse, the rivers were becoming polluted by the loose topsoil washed down the hills with the frequent rains. Where once sparkling streams bubbled through the rapids, murky brown waters now forced the oxygen-deprived fish to migrate further and further upstream.

The Penan were beginning to starve. Their patient, good-natured approach saw their representations to the state government repeatedly fall on deaf ears. They decided to get tougher and demanded that all logging in their homelands be halted and compensation be paid for areas already destroyed. Again to no avail. Enter Bruno Manser, one of the quirkiest characters ever to carve out a place of his own in Sarawak's history books.

The Swiss artist, while browsing through books at the university, stumbled across pictures of a nomadic people living deep in the forests of Borneo and made the decision there and then to seek them out in order to learn more about the deep essence of humanity. Given the timeframe, this whim could easily have earned him the label of being a left-over from the hippie generation. His plans were mostly dismissed by a shrug of the shoulder.

Armed with a sketchbook and a supply of pencils, Manser set out to make contact with the Penan and ended up living with them, even adopting their lifestyle (including their trademark bowl-cut hairstyle). He recorded daily life in the forest, made innumerable sketches of plants, animals, medicines, customs and traditions, and obviously enjoyed the bliss of his newly-found alternative lifestyle – until the day the military put a price on his head and the chase was on.

It all started when Manser began to get caught up in what is now known as the Penan Struggle. Inexperienced in worldly affairs (such as dealing with government officials), the Penan sought Manser's help, who apparently concluded that using the usual tactics of pressure, publicity and protests would attract attention to his friends' plight. A delegation (dressed in little more than loin cloths and a few feathers for effect) travelled to Kuala Lumpur to ask for the government's help in halting logging operations. The Malaysian government responded promptly, with the now famous Forest Ordinance that prohibits interference with logging operations, prescribing long jail sentences and stiff fines for offenders.

Around about the same time, the government's Men in Black were let loose, their mission to find Manser and deport him in the most expedient way possible. And thus began a farce of hide-and-seek that lasted some six years and that is still being recounted by the locals with glee whenever the occasion arises.

The official reason for the hunt was that Manser's visa had expired (which, by now, it had), a relatively minor offence by most standards. The government unleashed a seemingly endless succession of police patrols, and even called in the military, but failed to find the man. Sightings were often reported, but by the time the troops got there, Manser had vanished into thin air – hidden by his Penan friends or crossing over the border into Indonesia until the air was once again clear.

Spurred on by the excitement of the hunt, rather than counting his blessing and escaping back home, Manser's determination grew with every close shave. He taught the Penan to form human barricades, lay down in front of logging trucks, and enlist the help of the international community. The sort of thing any self-respecting 'greenie' would do.

The army and police responded in kind, arresting everyone in sight. Protesters were carted off by the truckload. Bail was set for offenders. (But money was an unknown commodity to the Penan.) Fines (which remained unpaid) and jail sentences were handed out with great enthusiasm. And the people of the jungle ultimately lost the war.

Manser, escaping over the Indonesian border (the exact circumstances remain undisclosed), returned to Switzerland and his book[5] became a bestseller of sorts, at least in some circles.

Wild tooting as a cloud of dust approaches: the traders have arrived. First one truck, then another, followed by a motorbike! The Landcruisers are loaded to the hilt, with passengers hanging off the sides like peanut vendors on an Indian train.

'Disco T-shirts!' One fellow can't wait to get off the truck. There's a mad scramble as baskets, plastic bags and all manner of goods are being unloaded and spread on the ground ready for inspection. The Penan stay put, motionless, a plateau frozen in time. A blast of music erupts from the motorbike and over the thump! thump! thump! of the super-bass speaker a young Chinese entrepreneur sets up shop: cassette tapes, glow-in-the-dark T-shirts, batteries, Bart Simpson torches, candy bars and the latest in wrap-around sunglasses complete with reflective purple lenses.

Intrigued, the Penan watch him from the corner of their eyes. The man is no novice. He walks around his bike and retrieves a large bottle and several plastic cups from a seat side pocket. Casually, he places the bottle on the ground, pours himself a drink and leans back against the rear wheel, tapping his feet to the beat of the music. A picture of nonchalance.

His performance has the desired effect: several of the younger Penan plus some of the longhouse people from the truck walk over to inspect his merchandise. Quick as a flash, he pours a drink and offers it to the first person showing the slightest bit of interest. A succession of toasts made with *tuak* (or *borak* as it is better known in these parts) sets the atmosphere and paves the way for some happy trading. The old trick of getting the tribespeople pissed before they buy. And it seems to work, because the first goods are starting to change hands and soon the place is abuzz with the sound of haggling, claims and counter-claims and noisy slapping of hands as deals are sealed.

Patrick and I retreat to a slightly elevated vantage point. We make coffee and sit back, enjoying the activities below us.

'How often do they throw these shindigs?'

Patrick thinks for a moment. 'Not all that frequently, actually. They used to run them three or four times a year. But now they're a little more irregular, because there's more contact between them and the outside world. More Penan are working as timber cutters and they tend to bring back goods from their camp. And with logging roads penetrating further into the interior, things are much more easily accessible.'

A young Penan child from our group comes running towards us, proudly pointing at the Teenage Mutant Ninja Turtle watch his father has just bartered for a boar's tooth necklace. We duly admire his choice and he returns to the others, skipping and dancing all along the way.

'What's he going to do with that?' I ask, 'surely he can't read the time?'

'None of them can. But it's a status symbol and the family will probably take turns in wearing it.'

The penetration (and acceptance) of goods from the outside world is very evident at this *tamu*. A bright pink, white and blue-striped plastic sheet, just bartered for by one of the old men in our group, will replace someone's palm frond roof. Panadol is in great demand as a sort of cure-all, because that's the way it was introduced to the locals. And the personal headphone stereo one of the young men exchanged for a superbly crafted blowpipe will probably end up replacing the beautiful sounds of the bamboo flute one day.

According to Malaysia's Prime Minister, this is not a bad thing because it is the duty of the government to rescue these people from their misery and let them join the mainstream of modern society with all its wealth and benefits: 'We do not want their nomadic lifestyle to remain permanent so that they can become a museum piece and a source of research for Western anthropologists.'

A noble perspective in its own way, but by the sounds of it, not exactly a panacea to the complex problem. But it also reflects the polarisation of the issue, which is frequently underscored by an astonishing lack of cross-cultural sensitivities or understanding. A prime example of this can be found in a book by Malaysian journalist Khaidir Ahmad entitled *Save the Penans*[6] (a misnomer if I ever saw one). Some extracts:

The Penan told me that wild animals had become scarce. Even if they came across any, it was difficult to use blowpipes because the animals could easily detect them as the forest had become thinner. Would I be able to help them purchase a shotgun? I explained that it was difficult for the Penans to own shotguns because they did not have identity cards.

Or, on the subject of logging:

He asked me why logging activities were being carried out in the settlement areas of the Penans when they were entirely dependent on forest resources for their living. I did not give a reply to the question because they would not have understood.

And then, this little gem:

The presence of nomadic Penans during meals can kill the appetite of people who are easily nauseated.

Good thing most Penan can't read.

'Let's move down and mingle,' suggests Patrick. (OK for him, he can speak the language.)

But communication is not a problem, as I'm about to find out.

'Hello, you come to buy?' A pretty young Kenyah girl throws an ice-melting smile at me.

'T-shirt? Sarong for your wife? Coca-Cola?'

I oblige by buying a can of warm Coke. The Penan are starting to pack up, except for Mak and Jamun who will accompany us to the land of the Ukit. Patrick has spotted some friends (or at least acquaintances) from Uma Belor, a longhouse on the Balui River. He introduces me. A skinny old man with wispy shoulder-length hair and wearing nothing but a sarong shakes my hand. Several others follow.

'They're inviting us to stay at their longhouse on the way back.'

'Are we going past there?'

'Yes, it's right on the way – and a good example of a traditional Kayan community. I know some of the people there. It should be fun.'

'Great!'

More handshakes and they're off, loading their chattels on to the back of the Landcruiser. Our Penan group is starting to line up to bid us farewell. It's a sad moment for me as I have begun to feel part of their little community. They all do their 'I'll keep you in my heart' bit and I return the wish with sincerity – because I know I will.

The young Chinese Salesman of the Year fires up his engine with an almighty roar and he and his mobile disco take off under a cloud of dust. The two Toyotas follow in his wake. Suddenly everything is quiet and the voices of the jungle gradually return, beckoning us.

chapter ten

ukit

From the top of the hill, where we spent the night suspended mid-air in our tiny nylon hammocks, the huge expanse of forest before us looks sleepy. Yet somewhere in there live some of the most remarkable tribes on Earth: the 'invisible people'.

Our two Penan guides are already up, cooking some *sago* for breakfast. But there's no Patrick. His hammock is empty. Jamun, catching my searching looks, is eager to provide an explanation and squats down, making an explosive blowing sound with his lips, while pointing into a gully. I get the drift of what he is trying to tell me. When Patrick comes out of the bushes, he flashes one of his big smiles.

'Ready to see some invisible people?'

The contradiction in this statement is not lost on me, as one of my colleagues back at work used to tease me regularly with exactly the same line.

'Sure. Ready when you are!'

Over breakfast we chat about what's ahead of us.

'There are three or four tribes that can be described as 'invisible'. The Punan are probably the largest one – and that's where we're going now, just across the river down there.' He points at a dreamy little stream, nestled in a lush valley.

My eyes wander across to the land of the Punan. I feel a little apprehensive, as these people have little contact, if any, with the outside world. They have a reputation for being fierce and hostile towards outsiders. Even neighbouring tribes – and especially longhouse people are scared shitless by them and avoid going anywhere near their turf.

'And what about the Ukit? Do they live down there too?' Patrick quizzes the locals.

'They say, "perhaps". There were several groups of Ukit in the mountains on the other side. But their numbers are getting smaller – a lot of them have been resettled.'

As soon as we finish breakfast, Mak and Jamun shoulder their carry baskets and unceremoniously start walking.

'I think they want to push on,' says Patrick.

Right. Jamun, short and stocky, leads the way, followed by Mak who is nearly twice his size. Together they look like a pair of comedians from a silent film.

'Hi, ho! Hi, ho! It's off to work we go.' I whistle the Seven Dwarf's tune and join the single file at the end, feeling a little bit like Dopey while I try to do up my backpack as I walk.

The landscape is relatively open, with freshly felled trees scattered here and there waiting to be picked up by the mighty logging trucks. Seeing the irreparable damage that is being done to nature here is heart-rending, and it is easy to direct deeply-felt anger at the Malaysian government, whose country is the world's largest exporter of tropical hardwood. Yet it is equally easy (and convenient, perhaps) to forget that we, the proud 'developed nations', have already denuded 95 per cent of our world's primary forests to harvest timber or make room for agriculture.

'Hi, ho! Hi, ho!' I fall back in step with the others as our little procession winds its way down the hillside. It's a beautiful day, the going is easy and adventure lies ahead. Funny how time flies when you're having fun.

It's already late morning and Big Mak suggests we break for lunch. A perfect shady spot, almost at the bottom of the hill where a small logging track follows the course of the river that marks the boundary of Punan territory. We unpack our provisions and debate at length what we should have, deciding finally on some (relatively fresh) chicken and rice that we have just bought from the Kayans. Jamun cooks the chicken with some wild papaya which tenderises the meat (just in case).

While we bask in the glory of the day, chewing on some blades of grass, we hear a voice in the distance. It is, in turns, animated and subdued and gets louder by the moment. Then, out of the blue, an apparition on the logging track: a tall, fair-haired guy labouring his way up the track on a pushbike, his monologue spiked by what seem to be a lot of swear words.

I can't believe my eyes and look at Patrick, who is equally taken aback. Jamun and Mak's expressions defy description – they've probably never seen a bicycle before. To set the situation in its correct context would take a lot of explaining. A man backpacking solo through the jungles of Borneo would be an achievement in its own right – but not an impossibility. But someone riding a bike on a steep, muddy track to nowhere must be a first.

As the apparition is getting closer we can make out some details: tall, sun-tanned, blue eyes, torn T-shirt that has seen better days, knee-length camouflage shorts. The whole thing sits on top of a rather hi-tech-looking mountain bike, complete with side pockets, a backpack strapped to the front and a small Dutch flag bringing up the rear atop an old radio aerial. Almost in unison, we run down the hill to the roadside. The intrepid traveller spots us, but does not appear to be in the least surprised by the encounter.

'Hello!' He calls out, with undue stress on the 'o'.

He pulls up and dismounts, shaking hands vigorously with us.

'Jost,' he says.

Mak shakes his hand and also says 'Jost!'

'No, no, that's my name. Jost.' He points at his chest and repeats, 'Jost.'

Mak understands. We invite him to join us for lunch. As we climb back up the hill, I ask him where he was from.

'From Holland.'

'Where abouts in Holland?'

'Scheveningen.' (The 'ch' pronounced as in 'Loch'.)

Patrick, fascinated by the sound of that town, tries to repeat it, a feat that is nearly impossible for any person not born with chronic lung disease.

'And where are you off to?'

'Oh, just travelling around. I like it here. And you?'

We tell him of our plans over lunch and he promptly invites himself to join us for a few days.

'Good. I come too.'

'With your bike?'

'No problem. I carry like this.' He demonstrates how he will lug it, slung over one shoulder – through thick and thin.

Patrick tries to point out the impracticality of this, but he won't have a bar of it.

'Is OK. I come!' Big smile.

That's that then. Jamun retrieves the coffee from his carry basket, but Jost stops him.

'I have coffee. One moment.'

He takes off down the hill to rummage among the belongings on his bike, and returns with a fresh vacuum-sealed pack of Douwe Egberts Instant Espresso.

'Here. Dutch coffee.' His contribution to the meal.

Still trying to mentally size up the man, I ask him where he came from.

'From Holland'

'No. I mean now, with your bike!'

'From Holland.'

'You travelled all the way from Holland with your bike?'

'Yes, Holland.'

Silence all round. Then Patrick and I burst out laughing. The Penan don't know what's going on, but they laugh too. This guy might be all right after all. We pack up our gear, extinguish the fire and start our journey towards the land of the invisible people.

Jost collects his bike from the roadside and reorganises a few of his satchels ready for the river crossing. The water is not deep, but the currents are swift. I pick my way carefully through the pebbles, steadying myself on the occasional protruding rocks. Jost, with the extra weight of his bike, does not fare as well and swears in unpronounceable Dutch words as he slips and stumbles his way across the water.

Dripping from the waist down, we regroup on the other side and proceed into the bushes.

Crash, crash, crash. Not me, this time. It's Jost's bike causing the sound effects. We get to a small break in the vegetation and Jamun calls for a halt.

'So soon?' I ask.

'Yes, he's setting up a message for the Punan.'

I'm intrigued as I watch the man break off some twigs and leaves, carve a few notches into a branch, and assemble the whole thing before planting it into the ground.

'What does it say?'

'Hard to translate precisely, but essentially it tells them that there are five of us, that we are just passing through and that we don't intend to hunt. It also gives them an idea of the direction in which we will be heading.'

'In other words, we come in peace?'

'Something like that.'

A comforting thought. Patrick bends down and explains some of the symbols before us.

'These shavings on the ground indicate where we are heading. The knots in the rattan tell them how many days we plan to stay here. The two sticks in the shape of a cross mean that we have food to share and that they are welcome to join us. The other configurations I am not quite sure about. Except for this one.'

He points at another two sticks that are pressed into a branch.

'These two symbolise that we are from the same heart, a way of saying that we want to be friends.'

While we walk along I learn more about this extraordinary dialogue that enables groups to communicate with one another. While signals can vary and particular tribes may adopt their own ways of saying things, it appears that the most commonly used messages can be understood or interpreted by most of the nomadic people in the area. Folded leaves, incisions on sticks or saplings, roots or even stones placed in a certain pattern, can warn of danger, pinpoint areas where food or wildlife can be found, instruct others to return to a predetermined meeting place, or simply point out a stand of *sago* palms ready for harvesting.

The sound of cursing. Jost is at it again, swearing madly as he tries to untangle his bicycle from a maze of vines and roots.

'With all that noise, the locals will soon know that we're here,' I remark.

'I think they already know. I'd be surprised if they didn't observe us from the moment we crossed the river.'

Eerie. I look around. No one to be seen anywhere. Yet I can't help feeling a presence, as if eyes were staring at us from somewhere. It's an unnerving experience. Jost is still at it. We go back to lend him a hand in his struggle against the bushes. While untangling our hero, I casually remark how I find it interesting that some patches of jungle are wildly overgrown, yet adjoining parts of the forest are wide-open. Patrick knows, as usual.

'You just said it. It's the difference between 'jungle' and 'forest'.'

'Aren't they the same thing?'

'In Hollywood films they are. But strictly speaking it should be all forest. These patches, where vegetation has gone berserk, are caused by falling trees which suddenly make room for the sun to come through. Before you know it, all sorts of vegetation starts growing and you end up with this sort of mess, which they call jungle.'

He looks at Jost, who is plucking the last bits of greenery from the spokes of his rear wheel.

'Logging has the same effect. Except where the growth covers larger areas, they tend to call it 'secondary' forest.'

Looking around me, I come to the conclusion that I prefer calling it all jungle; it has a more adventurous ring to it.

The lights are dimming and the stage is set for yet another tropical storm, which manifests itself with a few plops as the first drops start falling, then with an almighty clap of thunder that tears through the silence. It's bucketing down and there's nowhere for us to go, other than to keep on walking. The fireworks above us are spectacular, with flashes of lightning zipping wildly between gaps in the canopy. Somewhere in the distance, a crash as one of the forest giants meets its fiery finale.

It has turned dark, almost pitch-black, and visibility through the driving rain is down to zilch. Resigned to our lot, we decide to stop and make ourselves comfortable around a huge tree-trunk, using the gigantic buttress roots as if they were designer armchairs. (Not the best of places in a thunderstorm I'm told, but where else is there to go?)

The eyes. I can feel them through the darkness, creating an atmosphere that is highly conducive to my vivid imagination. Fortunately the show only lasts about ten minutes. The rain eases off, the thunder is becoming more distant and someone is slowly turning the dimming lights back to normal. We all look like drowned rats. Jost is lovingly wiping down his bike.

'Any idea where we'll be pitching camp for the night?'

Patrick seems to have a little surprise in store for us.

'You'll see,' is all I can get out of him.

'Is it far?'

My pleading look is working.

'In fact, no. Just over that hill,' (he points at a mountain) 'and down the other side. It's one of Mak's favourite places and if we get there in reasonable time we'll be able to enjoy the rest of the afternoon relaxing.'

Yes! My kind of man. I pick up my pace with renewed vigour and scan the bushes for any sets of eyes that may be watching us.

'Tell me, Patrick. These invisible guys, are they, well are they friendly?'

'You mean are they dangerous?'

'I guess that's what I mean.'

'Hard to tell. In many ways, they are not unlike the Penan. But when the loggers came along and started chopping down trees, several of them ended up with darts in their backs. The loggers fled in panic without seeing the blowpipes or the people who fired them. Next day, the timber companies returned with armed escorts, who promptly fled when a spear implanted itself on a tree they had just ear-marked for felling.'

'So the good guys won.'

'Perhaps. They certainly managed to strike fear into the hearts of the timber workers. But only time will tell. For the time being, the forest is quiet.'

I stop for a moment and drink nearly all the water in my canteen. The mountain is starting to take its toll. Jost, finally relenting to repeated offers, is handing his bike over to Jamun who carries it astride his shoulders to the mountain-top where we rest. The weather has cleared up and the valley below is bathed in bright afternoon sunshine.

As I admire the dreamy landscape, the distinct feeling that someone is watching us returns. I mention it to Patrick.

'Yes, I can feel it too. It's strange, isn't it? Quite unsettling. But don't worry. It could just be our imagination. Either way, I don't think they would have any bad intentions towards us.'

Right. *We* know that, but do *they* know it? Cigarettes to the ground, and we're off for the final leg towards our surprise destination. Can't wait to see what Mak has lined up. At the bottom of the hill I can hear the unmistakable sound of rushing water. Another river. But as we break out of the foliage the full impact of the scenery before us has us stopping dead in our tracks: a riot of orchids in every shape and colour imaginable, dangling down from branches that placidly overhang a picture-perfect lagoon. The water is crystal-clear, revealing every detail of its underwater world, its mirror-smooth surface interrupted only by the ripples of a small waterfall that gently carves its way down the hillside finally to plunge into a rock pool on the opposite bank.

Jamun suddenly freezes and signals us to stop. But his caution is superfluous as our eyes are simultaneously drawn towards a crashing noise in one of the trees where an orang utan has just retrieved some fruit, clutching it under his arm like a handbag full of valuables. Damned camera zoom! The ape searches for the source of the noise and spots us. He jumps to a lower branch and dangles there, holding on with just one arm, eyeing us suspiciously. We remain still. But he's not too sure and takes off with a series of leisurely swings, looking like the Hunchback of Notre Dame weaving his way through a maze of overgrown gargoyles and church spires. Then he's gone. For once I'm speechless.

Jost is first to break the silence, 'Let's go look for him.'

A resounding double 'No!' from Patrick and me. Mak is already building a fire by the sandy strip of beach. Jost goes to where Jamun had left the bike, and returns with his packet of Douwe Egberts Espresso clutched under his arm, imitating our hairy friend. The Penan explode with laughter. I sit down and enjoy the amazing scenery before me.

'This afternoon we'll do some fishing,' remarks Patrick as he watches me stare into the clear water.

'I'd love to. Have they brought lines or are they going to build traps?'

'Neither, I think.'

'Poison?'

The Penan are famous for their ability to make up a concoction of crushed leaves, roots or plants, resulting in a toxic substance that stuns the fish and drives them floating to the surface where they can be gathered up by hand. These poisons disperse very quickly in calm water and are fully biodegradable, causing no permanent damage to the water eco-system. Patrick asks the Penan how they plan to fish.

'They'll use pebbles. You see, many of the fish here are fruit eaters; throwing pebbles in the water simulates the effect of fruit falling from a tree and the fish gather in anticipation of a feed. You then scoop them out with a net or a floating basket.'

'Ah, like the old 'clock' method the fishermen use in Holland.'

We look at Jost, who's busting to deliver the punch line.

'Yes, They tie an alarm clock on a stick and dangle it over the water. When the fish come out to see what time it is, the fishermen hit them over the head with a stick!'

We fell for that one. The Penan want to know what the fun was all about and Patrick obliges with a translation. But the joke misses its mark. They just stare at Jost, puzzled, while he prepares some more coffee.

Mak and Jamun take off into the scrub to collect some rattan for the fishing baskets and we sit around the fire, enjoying this moment in paradise. Huge bright blue butterflies flit between the orchid blossoms. A lone hornbill bird preens himself on top of a branch, the colourful big hump on his beak glistening in the sun.

'Anyone for a swim?'

In a flash, Jost has all his clothes off, runs down to the lagoon and with one mighty splash shatters its calm surface. I hope the fish don't mistake his various appendages for some tasty morsels of tropical fruit. We follow. Total bliss. The water is warm near the surface, but sufficiently refreshing further down to offer instant relief from the oppressive heat of the jungle. After splashing around for a while, we explore various parts of the lagoon and end up under the waterfall, just sitting there enjoying a gentle shoulder-and-neck massage from its cascading cool water. Through my waterlogged eyes I can just make out Mak and Jamun on the little pebble beach, splitting some rattan for the fish baskets. I let the stream from the waterfall carry me back into the lagoon, where I float, face-up, looking towards the treetops and the bright blue sky beyond them. The peace and tranquillity, interrupted only by the occasional sound of birds in the foliage, has an incredible calming effect. I wonder if they are watching us.

The fish baskets are ready and we are being waved out of the water. Jamun hops silently from rock to rock and stops at the edge of the water. I can't see the slightest sign of any fish, but he seems adamant and persists. Holding a long stick to which he has attached the basket, holding it over the water, he drops in a pebble, and two, and three. Nothing. He waits, patient as any fisherman anywhere in the world. Mak has set himself up at another spot, with equal determination. It's fun watching them. But not for too long. Another dip would be nice.

While I contemplate my options, there's action around Mak. The water surface is starting to bubble ever so slightly. Mak carefully lowers the basket, and with one swift move scoops out our dinner: two fish, each the size of a matchbox. For some reason, this seems to remind Jost of his homeland and he shares with me his favourite recipe for marinated herring.

The afternoon drifts by hazily and our fishermen, having tried their luck around different spots, return with their catch: five more matchbox fish and one reasonably sized prehistoric-looking specimen, complete with long whiskers and bulging eyes. Some sort of catfish, I am told.

Dinner will be early and Patrick suggests we string up our hammocks while daylight is still with us. Knots drawn tight, my little jungle bed sways slowly between two trees, looking very inviting. To complete my quarters, I suspend my pack from a branch, roll out the poncho ready to be used as cover in the event of rain (always a distinct possibility), and wedge my torch within easy reach into a tree fork. My clothes are still wet so I hang them up to dry on a makeshift coat hanger made from two branches. To complete my nightly ritual, I slide my boots upside-down on top of two sticks, firmly planted in the ground (an old Australian bush custom – keeps out spiders, scorpions and other creepies and crawlies).

The fish taste awful and I am having a hard time extracting the bits of brown flesh from between the bones. The whole experience is like eating a tough pin-cushion. As I lay in my hammock, picking bits of bone from my teeth, I think of some of the wonderful harbourside restaurants in cosmopolitan Sydney. Next to me, Jost is snoring; probably dreaming of herring.

Although I can feel raindrops, I'm too tired to reach for my poncho. I just want to sleep.

But whispers nearby convince me partially to open one eye. It's almost daylight and I can see Patrick and the Penan crouched low over something on the ground, talking quietly.

'What's up?'

They look at me in a start.

'Not sure. We've received a message from the Punan.' He points at an arrangement of sticks and stones left near the fire. This wakes me up.

'The invisible? Were they here during the night?'

'Looks that way.'

'What does it say?'

'A warning of some sort for us not to proceed in that direction.' He points past the waterfall. 'The rest we're still trying to work out.'

Mak seems to have definite views about the signal.

'He thinks that someone possibly died and that's why they don't want us over there. When that sort of thing happens, the group usually breaks up camp and leaves the spot immediately in order not to anger the spirits. But Jamun seems to have doubts. There's another bit to the message, which they can't decipher.'

The rain is getting intense and I dive for my poncho. It's cold and miserable as I stand there, watching the three of them trying to make sense of the pile of stones and twigs.

The really scary part to me is that they were here, right in the middle of our camp, and no one saw them. The Penan searched the area for tracks or any signs of their visit, but they didn't leave any trace. Not a single bent leaf. No broken branches. No footprints. They came unseen and seemingly vanished into thin air.

Jost is stirring in his sleep, trying to wipe the rain off his face. Mak finds his poncho and covers him with it. I fetch some water and put the kettle on.

'What shall we have for breakfast?'

Patrick points at the empty cooking pot. I shrug my shoulders. Suddenly I feel like something warm. Something wholesome. Something that reminds me of home.

'I know. I'll make some damper!'

'Some what?'

'Damper. It's a sort of bread we make in Australia, when we sit around the campfire. Very traditional. Goes back to the days of *Waltzing Matilda*. You know the song?'

'Yes, I've heard it in KL once. At a football match. A bunch of Australians sang it then. They drank a lot of beer.'

'That's it.'

To make damper takes very little: some flour (which I don't have), a little baking powder (which I brought with me, anticipating such an occasion) and water (although some Australians prefer to use beer instead).

'Do we have any of the tapioca flour left?' I ask Patrick.

'Should have. Let me ask the guys.'

The answer is affirmative and Jamun produces a small bag full of flour. I spread out my poncho, pour the flour and baking powder on it, make a well in the middle and add some water from my canteen. Slowly the gooey mess transforms itself into dough, which I roll into a ball and place in the cooking pot. We don't have a lid for it, but a few banana leaves wrapped around the dough should do the trick. The Penan watch me, fascinated, as I bury the pot under the hot ashes and desperately hope that this will work.

An hour later we dig out the pot. The smell of freshly baked, warm bread fills the air as we unwrap the hot banana leaves. We let the damper cool down a little. Patrick, at my suggestion, is slicing some wild bananas, which will make a nice topping for the fresh bread. The moment of reckoning: I break open the bread. It's heavy and hard as a rock, but it tastes nice and the others are impressed. Jost dips his piece in coffee and smiles, 'Just like a croissant!' We leave a piece behind for the invisible folks. Just in case they turn up.

Two hours. Vertical walking all the way. But finally we reach the top of yet another mountain, and even the Penan are puffing just a little. Jost, on the other hand, looks as if he is about to collapse – which he does, right on top of his bike. Using my backpack as a pillow, I stretch out on a soft bed of rotting leaves. The obligatory cigarettes are lit, but I'm too tired to join in the ritual. Within just a few minutes I'm fast asleep.

Brightly-coloured birds, butterflies, waterfalls, cups of coffee around the campfire – and the eyes. My brief dreams are interrupted by wild laughter. As I try to find my bleary-eyed bearings, I can see several heads in fast-forward motion, just to the left of the ridge. Curious, I make my way to the edge and find my travelling companions cavorting along a narrow logging track, trying to teach Mak to ride the bike.

I sit down and watch them from the distance. The track is relatively dry, but full of the type of obstacles even the experienced rider would find hard to manage – huge potholes, broken tree branches, murky puddles, sharp-edged rocks and a rather large lizard trying to escape the amazing happening. But Mak persists and doesn't seem to mind the frequent spills and falls, all of which contribute enormously to everyone's amusement.

'Hey, John, come and join us!' Jost just spotted me.

'I'm right, thanks.'

He climbs up the embankment and settles on the grass next to me.

'Aren't you worried about your bike?'

'Oh, no, it's titanium. Very tough. Like me!' He flexes his biceps.

It's Jamun's turn on the bike, an almost identical performance to that of his partner, complete with all the spills, thrills and bleeding knees. A particularly nasty crash into a roadside log, however, causes Jost to reconsider the many qualities of titanium as he frantically breaks up the party, retrieving his bike from a tangle of dead branches. Bike under one arm, he makes his way back up the hill, leaving the Penan looking like a pair of dogs whose bone has just been confiscated.

'We better move on, I guess,' says Patrick, 'we should get down to the bottom of the mountain by late afternoon and then we can rest some more and set up camp for the night.'

'And how long until we reach the river?'

'The Balui? Tomorrow we'll probably only have half a day's trekking. From then on it's boats and longhouses all the way to Kayan country.'

Relief in sight at last. I'll enjoy being ferried up the legendary river where so many battles have been fought by the local headhunting navies.

The downhill trek is a lot easier, as the mountainsides aren't quite as steep as before. It's nice, undulating country. But still slippery, as I find out when I suddenly progress a great distance on my buttocks, until I'm stopped by a gigantic log that blocks my slide. For once, I'm actually ahead of the others. Vegetation on the ground is becoming more abundant as we progress to lower levels. In the far distance I can make out glimpses of a large river, its tortuous bends glistening with flashes of bright silver in the afternoon sun.

Coffee time again. We settle at a small clearing overlooking miles of endless greenery, thick and seemingly impenetrable. While the others unpack the necessary implements and Jost settles down to extract leaves, thorns and twisted twigs from the spokes of his bike, I answer the call of nature and head for the bushes. A spot just behind a small hillock (a decent distance from my friends) seems a perfect place. Not that it matters all that much, but the views are superb. Sitting there, contemplating my surroundings, I am reminded of the delightful little country log cabin that my friends Jef and Robyn frequently let us use as an escape from city life. One of its many rustic features includes a typical bush 'outhouse' – a sort of ramshackle toilet with an old kerosene tin as its focal point and an ample supply of (dual-purpose) magazines. After routinely checking its interior for snakes, venomous spiders and other forms of unwelcome wildlife that could inflict serious damage to some lower parts of the body, I would settle there with whatever reading matter was at hand and contemplate the tranquillity of rural life through the entrance that had lost its door a long time ago.

The eyes. Somehow my surroundings here are not quite as serene. I suddenly feel rather uneasy and start slowly to scan the bushes and trees in the vicinity. Nothing. But then, for quite unknown reasons, my eyes wander back to a spot

I had just passed, and see a muscular leg protruding from some shrubs. My heart stops, and sure enough, after focusing closely on the bush, there is a man, standing perfectly still and staring at me. My mind starts to race. I'm in a very vulnerable position here. But logic also tells me that if he were after my skin, he could have bowled me over a long time ago. I lift my hand hesitantly and wave to him: '*Selamat petang!*'

My greeting draws no reaction. He probably doesn't understand Malay. But there's movement next to him, as one of his colleagues emerges from behind a tree. While I zip up my shorts, two more men emerge. Where the hell have they all come from? The group sets itself in motion – towards me.

'Hello! How are you?' I say, reverting to English and stretching out my hand.

A very short man comes forward to take a closer look at me. The others follow, crowding around me. I seem to pass the inspection, which is followed by an embarrassed silence. What shall we do next, guys? In a flash of inspiration I motion them to follow me to our little picnic area and they fall in behind me, single file. Wait till the others see what I've found!

Predictably their jaws almost drop as we emerge. They jump up in unison as if touched by electric cattle prods. Jamun is first to regain his composure: he starts talking to the group, who look at each other and casually sit down next to the fire.

At last, one of them talks – and talk he can, rattling away in a quick succession of incomprehensible words which

somehow seem to make sense to the Penan, whose language
is distinctly different but has sufficient similarities to be, at
least partially, mutually intelligible. The conversation goes
on and on, giving me an opportunity to study these Punan
with discreet detachment. Physically, they don't seem all
that different to the Penan. Same panhandle haircuts, same
pale complexion, same splayed, calloused jungle feet. But
they are a lot smaller close-up, about five feet including
spears, something I hadn't noticed from my crouched
position in the bushes when their muscular bodies looked
like those of giants. They are only wearing loincloths,
fashioned from bark, and carry long blowpipes tipped with
spearheads made of sharpened bone.

The guttural sounds eventually subdue as our visitors are
starting to run out of steam. Mak offers them coffee, which
they regard with suspicion but slurp noisily, nevertheless,
their eyes averted to the ground.

'They wanted to know who you are,' says Patrick, who
has just received a debrief from Jamun.

'Yes? What did he tell them?'

'That you are a famous missionary.'

Great. My son Dani (Jewish, observant, lives in
Jerusalem) would be proud of me.

'And they accepted that?'

'They don't care. I don't think they've ever seen a
missionary.'

'Did Jamun ask them about the Ukit?'

'I don't know. I'll ask him.'

Another lengthy conversation ensues.

'They say there are some Ukit around – mainly up in the mountains. Most of them are apparently across the border in Indonesia, but there's a settlement down by the river, where several groups moved to a few years ago.'

So there goes that idea. We can meet some Ukit, but most likely they'll be wearing Reeboks and Pepsi T-shirts. Not exactly what I envisaged. While I ponder our options, Patrick tells me that the Punan have invited us to stay with them overnight.

'What happened to our plans to camp down in the valley?'

'Not a good idea. They say that we should avoid the area because they observed some hornbills flying in the wrong direction – a bad omen. According to them, there are some malevolent spirits down there, which must not be disturbed. We will be much safer with them.'

'Will we be safer?'

Patrick hesitates, 'I think so.'

The camp is nearby. So close, in fact, that we must have almost stumbled upon it on our way, oblivious to its presence. Although in essence the site is not unlike a Penan camp, there are some distinct differences: the huts are more like lean-tos, constructed on rudimentary sapling platforms just a few centimetres off the ground. And they are built not on a clearing, but are rather well concealed among the trees.

There is no one around, except for an old man who is sitting, perfectly still, on a small rock. As we approach, he lifts his head briefly, but immediately returns to combing the fur of a small monkey nestled between his feet. There's a brief exchange of words between him and our two Punan, and the old man gets up to shake our hands and touch his chest to seal our friendship. He is a tiny man, but despite his age has a full head of black hair, tied in a knot at the back and reminding me somehow of Mrs Travers, my primary school maths teacher. And, just like her, his eyebrows had been plucked – a daily ritual common among the nomads who regard facial or body hair as poor grooming.

The monkey looks up at us, but soon thinks twice of it and scampers back to the old man's feet where he seeks refuge from the strange white apparition (me) and the yellow-haired giant (Jost) in front of him. He's probably never seen a Dutchman before. The old man looks at his little friend lovingly, and pointing at him says, '*Nyapun.*'

'Is that the word for monkey? I ask.

'No, that's his name. He is only a baby. The Punan kept him when his mother was killed in a hunt. Forest people will often raise orphan animals. It's part of their relationship with the environment. They never kill indiscriminately and they have an astonishing knowledge of monkey populations, their numbers, habits and whereabouts. To keep some sort of control, they tend to kill young males in preference to females. It's a type of cropping programme any average modern-day wildlife manager would heartily approve of.'

The old one raises his head, gently sniffs the air and directs his look to the left, listening intently, just like an animal sensing nearby prey. I can't hear or see anything, but a few seconds later two Punan silently materialise from behind the trees. They seem pleased to see us and greet our group with affection, as if we were old friends. Before long the entire group has returned and we all settle down for our evening meal, supplied from our provisions.

The Punan group is only small: two elderly women, a couple of young men, three girls, the old man, a baby boy and the monkey. As darkness falls around us, their faces take on eerie proportions under their fringed hair, their bony features partially lit up by the flickering fire. These are the so-called 'wild people' of Borneo, the feared forest devils whose reputation for deadly accuracy with their blowpipes strikes terror into the hearts of anyone prepared to venture into their territory. Yet they seem caring and loving and, above all, unexpectedly hospitable. While they converse quietly with our Penan guides, Jost and I discuss some of the 'invisible' aspects of our hosts.

To watch these people weave fluidly through the jungle is an awesome sight. There is a sense of unity between them and nature. They are aware of every sound, every slight vibration, every leaf out of place. Outsiders often call them the 'leopards' of the forest because of their stealth. A fair comparison, except that leopards leave tracks. The Punan don't.

One of the young men hands me a battered enamel cup.

'Just drink it and pretend it's tea,' says Patrick, 'and don't bring out your coffee (pointing at Jost) or they might consider using you for target practice!'

'What is it?'

'It's made from plants and roots. Good for your sex life!'

'Out here? You're kidding!' I say, averting my eyes from the two young girls. 'I don't want to end up with a poisoned dart in my buttocks.'

The concoction tastes awful, the sort of stuff Nishant, my Indian naturopath, would mix up. But I drink it, making appreciative noises along the way. For dessert, the old women bring out some *durian* – a large tropical fruit that emits a stench so bad that many airlines and hotels have slammed a ban on it. Definitely an acquired taste. Jost nearly chokes after the first bite, but perseveres heroically to live another day. Next to us the conversation goes on. I wish I could partake. There are so many questions I want to ask. But the Punan language is not one they taught us at high school.

'Why are they known as 'invisible' people, Patrick?'

'I think it's what you make of it. Many of the neighbouring people have deep beliefs in magical and spiritual powers. They also fear the forest. So when someone ends up with a dart in his neck with no apparent culprit visible, it's easy to believe that it came from an invisible source, some sort of supernatural act that can't be explained. Personally, I think the forest people are just very clever in the way they move about. It's their territory and they know it better than anyone else; through necessity, they have learned to stalk prey that way. They simply use the same techniques when strangers invade their space, which they tend to resent.'

The way Patrick explains it makes sense. Camouflage and stealth are some of the most basic skills required in jungle warfare. During basic training in the Australian Army we were taught some of its principles, and I vividly recall the demonstrations given by the army experts: someone lighting up a cigarette, visible for hundreds of metres in the dark of the night; a silhouette against open ground; colours that did not fit naturally in the surroundings; sounds that carried a long distance over water; movement; shapes out of context; even smells of aftershave or human sweat can be dead give-aways. They are the sort of things listed in conventional jungle combat manuals. But none could even begin to teach the skills that come so naturally to the people around us.

Patrick returns with a piece of *durian*. 'Anyone for seconds?'

We ignore him and he sits down next to us.

'The Punan have offered to show us the way to the Ukit settlement. They'll come as far as the river with us. From there, they say, it's an easy two-hour walk. Are you interested?'

Jost looks at me. 'You want to go?'

I, in turn, look at Patrick. 'What do you think?'

'I'm easy. It's not far, but I don't know these people. I guess it's worth a try – we can always pick up a boat and continue up-river if things don't work out.'

'OK, we go,' says Jost. He gets up and goes to bed without a further word. From inside his lean-to comes a string of Dutch expletives as he tries to fit his bike in the tiny shelter.

It's a beautiful day, full of the sort of 'zip-a-dee-doo-dah' feeling that makes you want to get up and go. Jost is already haranguing the natives with a detailed demonstration of his bike's features; but after some signs of initial curiosity, they can't see any possible useful purpose for the contraption and lose interest. Our two Punan guides are getting their equipment ready: blowpipes, bamboo tubes filled with water, *parangs* and, fastened to their backs below the waist, a folded-up sleeping mat that doubles as a comfortable cushion whenever they sit down.

A quick bite to eat and we're ready to go. Amun and Mak leave us in the trusted hands of their cousins, the Punan, and do their 'keep you in my heart' bit. Strange how, despite the language barrier and after such a short time, I've really come to like these two. To seal our friendship I offer them a brightly-coloured koala bear T-shirt each, which they accept gracefully. Mak points at the picture and asks what sort of animal it is. Patrick translates. I explain. Mak nods and asks another question.

'He wants to know if you can eat koalas.'

Now that's a tough one. Literally. But to save lengthy explanations, I nod and say, '*Bagus*' – very good. Hopefully he will never have to learn the meaning of 'protected species'. My reply seems to satisfy him as he takes Jamun by the hand, and they're off, back home where the wild pigs roam.

Having witnessed the gift-giving ceremony, our two Punan guides hover around my pack, looking expectant, but sufficiently polite not to ask for anything outright. I get the message. There are no more T-shirts, but at the bottom of my bag I find two of my fake Swiss Army knives. The Punan's eyes light up as I demonstrate the knives' many features. Bad move. Now the others line up. I scrounge around for anything that might look remotely like a gift and manage to hand out some Powerbars, an empty notebook and a pencil (duly demonstrating how to use it) and an old sarong for the lady of the house.

The goodbyes are brief and the local residents invite me to come back soon. I promise that I will, knowing well that the chances of that happening are remote, to say the least.

The way ahead seems easy and I slide into my newly acquired hip-swaying jungle mode, following the example of the Punan ahead of us. Behind me, Jost is crashing his way through the thickets. The vegetation here is dense but much more colourful than on the mountains where huge patches of moss and lichens dominate the landscape. A flying lizard – just like a flying snake but with legs – launches itself from a tree just ahead of me, scaring the living daylights out of me. In the treetops, a troop of monkeys is having a heated argument, squealing and screeching amidst daring leaps from branch to branch.

Our guides are way ahead of us and Patrick urges me to pick up the pace when I hear an almighty thump: one of the Punan has just managed to demolish a rather large snake that crossed his path. He now brings it back to us, dangling from his *parang*, and offers it to Jost.

'Provisions,' says Patrick, 'he wants us to have it for dinner.'

Jost looks around, clearly uncomfortable. But the Punan keeps poking the *parang* with the dangling, zebra-striped snake at him, urging him to put it in his pack.

'Take it. It's dead. We'll give it to the Ukit later on; they'll love it.' suggests Patrick.

Jost relents and picks up the snake between two fingers, holding it as far away from his body as possible. But the thought of putting it into his pack is where he draws the line. He looks around, picks some vines off a tree and ties the snake to the crossbar of his bike, where it remains for the rest of our journey. Satisfied, the Punan resume their trot and we follow, desperately trying to keep up the pace.

At least there are no more inclines to clamber up and down. The country is fairly flat and our slip-slides are mainly confined to the riverbanks, which are still numerous. It's peaceful but stifling. The heat just sits there, at the bottom of the valley, with nowhere to go. It's also getting a lot wetter as we find ourselves repeatedly crossing swamps and marshes, immersed in the squishy liquid which, at times, reaches up to our knees. A large python swims past us some distance to the left, heading for the safety of the wild growth. Our guides are too far ahead to see it, which is fortunate for Jost because his crossbar is already occupied and there's no more room left on his bike. I point it out to him, 'Do you want it?' to which he responded with curses.

Another river. On the opposite bank there is a sizeable cleared area and a small elevated shelter. Several small children are watching our approach, their legs dangling over the side of the platform. They seem to be non-smokers, except for one who sports a massive cheroot in the corner of his mouth.

A wild cry and our Punan friends establish contact. The kids jump off the platform and vanish into the scrub. Minutes later a couple of men appear.

'Here's your Ukit,' says Patrick.

They look pretty much like the Punan, with no visible differences that could identify them otherwise.

'How do you know they're Ukit?'

'One of the Punan just told me.'

Smart-arse. There's the usual small-talk (Where are you from? Where are you going? Who are the white guys?), none of which needs translation because the body language tells it all. They regard us with suspicion. We all sit down in a row on a long log and share cigarettes. Two women emerge from the scrub. Another group is crossing the river, followed by the bunch of children who took flight earlier on. Handshakes and more cigarettes all round.

While everyone puffs away merrily, Patrick asks some questions in Penan, which the Punan translate to the Ukit, who in turn send their reply back to the Punan, who approximate it in Penan before it reaches us in English via Patrick. The conversation goes on for quite a while and finally Patrick comes good with a brief synopsis.

'We've asked them about other Ukit who may be living in the mountains. They say that there are several groups out there, but they haven't seen them in a long time. The tall girl says that part of her family still lives there, but now that she's married and living in a longhouse she rarely sees them.'

'How far away are they?'

'I've asked them that. By the sounds of it, it would be about a week to ten days' walking. Up the mountains.' He says that with emphasis on the word 'up'.

'Aha. Maybe we'll just visit their settlement.'

'I thought you might say that. The Ukit are pretty much like the Punan – they're cousins of sorts, and I think you get the idea of what the invisible people are like.'

'I do. And I like them very much.'

'Still scared?'

'No! Not at all. I think they're great and I like their sense of humour.'

'Good. They are nice people and they can be very friendly. Once they get to know you and accept you as a friend, no harm will come to you. But sometimes I'm still a little uncomfortable with them,' he says, almost in a whisper.

'What do you mean?'

'Oh, nothing, really. Just a conversation I overheard last night, about a recent confrontation they had with some Kenyahs. I didn't understand every word, but from what I did understand it was not a pretty scene.'

I am keen to find out more, but Patrick seems reluctant to volunteer details and is saved by the bell when the Ukit motion us to get up and go. They tell us that their settlement is just a short distance away and they would like to 'show us' to the rest of the community. Nice twist. Now *we* are the subjects on show. Jost, keen to strike up a friendship, offers the snake to the prettiest of the women. He scores a big smile and some apparently encouraging words as the lady places the snake on top of some rice-planting utensils in her shoulder basket. Pleased as punch, he struts alongside her, bike on shoulder, trying to make conversation while throwing furtive glances at her bare, shapely breasts. The man has been in the jungle for a long time.

Signs of settlement increase as we pass rusty oil drums, discarded beer cans and an old outboard engine with a tangle of vegetation growing out of it. Some kids arrive to greet our group, but stop dead in their tracks when they see us. As we advance, they about-turn and run ahead, yelling out the news to the sleepy community. From a distance the longhouse looks shabby, a ramshackle collection of corrugated iron, blackened walls where the smoke of cooking fires escapes the interior, and all manner of debris strewn around the long veranda.

Things don't improve as we get closer. The house is in a bad state of disrepair. Broken steps. Planks missing or dangling half-attached from walls. Rubbish heaped high on the side of the building, emitting an unbearable stench under the midday sun. A row of children's eyes watches our every move from behind two long planks that, once upon a time, must have been railings for the veranda.

We weave our way through a collection of worn-out and torn sarongs drying in the sun like flags at a major sports event. The chief appears on the veranda and, after a brief exchange of words with his friends, he motions us to ascend a broken ladder leading up to the house. He seems friendly enough and invites us to stay for as long as we like, while his entourage looks on from a safe distance.

My eyes take a moment to adjust to the darkness as we enter the main part of the building. A loud muffled sound of continuous buzzing emanating from the interior turns out to be swarms of flies feasting on remnants of food and other rubbish littering the floor. In a corner a mother nurses a baby, whose face is covered in flies. I'm starting to have second thoughts about staying the night. Disillusionment on seeing these Ukit I had so looked forward to meeting must be written all over my face.

'Are you all right, John? You are very quiet.'

'Yes, just getting used to it all.'

Over afternoon tea (of sorts) on the chief's mat, I reflect on the deplorable state these once-proud jungle dwellers have sunk to. The contrast between this 'settled' community and the nomadic groups whose healthy, happy and uncomplicated life we have shared over the past few days is unbelievable. Patrick looks at me quizzically. I respond in the most diplomatic way I can think of.

'It's different.'

He acknowledges my feelings with a nod. Jost shifts around uncomfortably on his corner of the mat.

'I'd love to know how the chief feels about living here as opposed to the forest. Do you think we can broach the subject?' I ask Patrick, no longer able to contain my amazement.

'I'll try. Give me a few minutes. At the moment it's all the usual chit-chat and it would not be polite to throw in a delicate question like that.'

The women bring out more coffee. Nescafé, with lots of condensed milk. The stench, the flies and the stale air are oppressive. Through Patrick I ask the chief whether it would be OK for me to take a walk down to the river and look at the beautiful scenery. With a sweep of his hand and a big smile he indicates his approval and I take my leave, coffee cup in hand. Jost follows.

'So what do you think, Jost, should we stay the night?'

'Sure, we sleep here,' he says, pointing at the beach.

'Good idea. I hope they won't be offended.'

We wander along the river, enjoying the fresh air. A couple of kids are following us, whispering to each other and giggling a lot, hands in front of their mouths. Their eyes are covered in sores.

'So where will you be going from here?' I ask.

'Oh, over to Indonesia – down to Samarinda by boat and then I catch a ferry to Java to visit some relatives. They are still there from the Dutch colonial days.'

'How long will that take?'

'Oh I don't know. One month. Or three.'

The kids are right on our heels now, and I try to converse with them in Malay. But they just keep giggling, repeating my words again and again. A hornbill flies over our heads. I hope he's going in the right direction, providing us with better omens for the rest of the journey. So far it's been great and, despite all the mud, rain, snakes, river crossings and bad coffee, I'll be sad to leave the forest and its wonderful inhabitants.

When we return to the longhouse, Patrick tells us that he just popped my question to the chief, who is now in the process of delivering his deliberations, which promise to be interesting. More instant coffee arrives.

'He talks a lot and I don't understand everything because his Penan is as bad as my Ukit,' explains Patrick. 'But what is clear, is that he often longs for the life he enjoyed as a boy with his family in the forest. Then life was carefree and happy, he says. But they often went hungry. Now they lead an easier life. The government provides many things and they have learned how to plant rice. However, the young people are becoming lazy. They don't want to get up in the morning and they sleep a lot during the day. He is worried that in just one generation they will lose all that has been precious to them from a long time ago: the beliefs their ancestors passed on to them, their spirits, the skills, the songs, the love for Father Earth. Even the forest is starting to disappear.'

The chief watches Patrick's translation with interest. When our eyes meet, he nods in acknowledgement and adds one final point.

'They tell us we now enjoy an easier life. Maybe we do. But I don't think it's a better life.'

From a room at the end of the longhouse, disco music is thumping out of a battered cassette player. We spend the night on the beach as planned. The Ukit don't seem offended. They believe that we, just like our Punan friends, prefer the outdoors to the confines of a house.

Morning comes with the roar of an outboard motor. A young Ukit is fussing about with the engine of his longboat, ready to take us down to the Balui river. We skip breakfast, hoping to find a change of menu at the logging camp where our journey into the land of some of Borneo's reputedly fiercest headhunters begins. Nothing stirs in the longhouse, its occupants obviously still fast asleep, in spite of the engine's racket, the barking of dogs and the crowing of several self-asserting roosters. We thank our two Punan and wave goodbye as our skipper brings the boat about and steers towards the swift currents of the river. The Punan wave back and within seconds head towards the edge of the forest where once more they become invisible.

chapter eleven

balui

As suddenly as Jost had entered our lives, he is now taking his leave, leaning against his bike on the back of a Landcruiser, chatting up two ladies with shoulder-length earlobes in a mix of Dutch, English and sign language. The whole thing took only moments. While I was helping to unload the boat, Jost had spotted a departing truck, negotiated a fare and made friends with the natives.

'See you in Holland!' he calls out, as the Toyota throws a wild U-turn and disappears in a cloud of dust. The last thing I see is two hands waving wildly next to a fluttering Dutch pennant. We make our way up to a single hut on a slight elevation overlooking the river. The Chinese shopkeeper-cum-guardian of the camp is obviously pleased to see us.

'*Makan*? You want to eat? Scrambling eggs? *Kopi*? Beer?' he says, while pulling up two rickety chairs next to a small metal table. Patrick and I opt for *mee goreng* (fried noodles, usually supplemented with whatever leftovers of meat, vegetables and spices happen to be around), some hot Chinese custard buns and a couple of boiled eggs. A nice change from all the *sago* we ate over the last few days.

We have our coffee out on the veranda, taking in the superb views of the Balui river with its fast currents, rushing through spectacular canyons and past sheer cliff faces all the way up to Long Murun, where they become one with the Rajang.

espresso with the headhunters

'So do you think it will be easy enough to hitch a ride up-river from here?' I ask Patrick.

'Oh yes. Boats pull up here all the time to stock up on provisions, and if there's room we'll get a lift.'

The shopkeeper pokes his head through the door, checking our state of affairs.

'*Apa ada* cola?' I ask.

'Sure we have Coke. How many, two?'

I nod. The Coke is warm. I ask for ice.

'Sorry, generator no good, waiting for spare part, *lah*.'

Several Cokes and hearty burps later, there's movement on the river: three boats appear and drop their longhouse folk on the waterside mud. It's shopping time. The passengers make their way up to the hut. Our observation platform affords us a bird's-eye view of a colourful parade of large conical hats covered in intricate designs that passes below.

'These are Kenyah,' remarks Patrick, pointing out some of the motifs on the hats.

The shopkeeper, cash register ringing in his mind, holds open the door, smiling at the dollars that have just arrived. We wander down to the boats and Patrick manages to arrange a lift as far as Uma Lanahan, a fair distance from here. Conditions are rather cramped on board the longboat, which is overflowing with people, provisions and what appears to be an inordinate number of cases of beer and soft drinks.

'Looks like they're having a party,' I remark casually.

'Yes. It's *gawai* and this time of the year most longhouses celebrate the end of the harvest with festivities that often last several days. It's a time for visiting relatives and friends in other longhouses and big-time partying all-round!'

'In other words, a good time for us to visit. Do you think we'll be invited?'

'We're bound to be. I'm pretty sure that our timing will be right to see some cermonies in at least one of the houses. In fact, if we're lucky you might be in for a BIG treat: I heard that one of the communities is planning a traditional headhunting feast that usually lasts for several days. I don't know who's throwing the party, but I'll try and find out.'

On the boat, in front of me, is a row of hats as far as the bow, effectively blocking the view. A peanut bar is being passed down the line. Everyone takes a bite before it is sent back up front to its anonymous donor.

Just as I am settling back against a stack of beer cases, the boat veers sharply to the right and heads straight for a stretch of beach on which it lands with a sudden slurp, its bow firmly implanted in the mud. The hats disembark and more than half the provisions are being off-loaded. The whole operation only takes a couple of minutes before we're back mid-stream, continuing our journey with just four more passengers. Wonderful. I can stretch out and take in the scenery.

Ahead of us is an almighty gorge that looks dark and foreboding, with heavy black clouds hanging over the cliff faces, patches of fog suspended over the river. Near its entrance I notice a small structure high up on a hill, overlooking the river like a silent guardian from another world. It looks like a miniature temple and is decorated with fantastic carved swirls and stark tribal designs.

'The tomb of a chief,' explains Patrick. 'We're now entering the land of the Kayan, the most feared headhunters of them all.'

As if to underscore that statement, the sky turns pitch black as we enter the canyon. The wind is starting to howl, sending ghostly echoes along the steep cliffs on either side of us.

The river turns into a boiling cauldron as heavy drops of rain whip up its surface.

'And I shall fear no evil as I enter the valley of the shadow of death . . .' or words to that effect.

Shivering in the sudden downpour, I pull my poncho tight across my chest. In the distance my imagination sees a Kayan headhunting expedition furiously paddling large war canoes against nature's awesome forces. These raiding parties were commonplace not so long ago, and some have even gone down in local history. One in particular, known as the Great Kayan Expedition, saw the locals in full battle against some 11,000 Ibans in more than 300 war canoes. Under the auspices of Charles Brooke, the 'White Raja', peace was eventually restored and the combatants ended up feasting together for several days to mark the occasion.

The cliffs seem to be closing in on us as the chasm narrows and we enter a wild wash of turbulent rapids. The boat is thrown violently from left to right the moment we reach the first set, but our boatman seems to have anticipated this. He eases up on the throttle until we enter the next spin cycle, which somehow manages to almost lift the entire hull right out of the water, leaving the outboard engine screaming in mid-air.

The thump as we hit the water nearly throws me overboard, but I somehow manage to hang on to the sideboards. Several more tension-filled moments pass before we reach relatively calm waters and we resume our course in the middle of the river.

A large longhouse appears, decorated with intricate carvings and vibrant designs in black, yellow and bright red all along its walls.

'Kenyah!' shouts Patrick over the din of the engine.

My eyes stay glued on the building until we are well past it. These longhouses are entirely different from the functional, plain dwellings the Iban seem to favour. Set high amidst this awesome river scenery, they have an almost mystical quality about them. The sort of image one might expect to find in a fantasy novel.

We are nearing the end of the gorge and rays of sunshine tentatively emerge from between the heavy clouds. The river is a lot wider now, the harsh rocks replaced by gentle, green hills and palm-fringed shorelines. Uma Lanahan is straight ahead of us. We disembark with the others and the *tuai rumah* welcomes us to his small community, which is starting to unwind from the day's work on a series of mats spread out on the veranda. The usual chit-chat ensues over coffee and biscuits and the chief invites us to stay. But apparently we're expected at Uma Belor, a Kayan longhouse a short distance down-river.

So after a brief break and an opportunity to get ourselves dry, we set off once more, with a young man who has offered to take us there in his longboat. It's almost dark and the river is starting to take on freakish proportions. In my vivid imagination I can almost hear the sound of gongs in the distance, as a headhunting party sets out under the cloak of the night.

We can hear Uma Belor long before we can see it. Noise carries a long distance over water. When we arrive, we find that the party is already in full swing, and before even the first words are spoken we are handed glasses of *borak* and dragged along to meet the headman. Gongs are beating frantically. A group of women sing in a corner. Someone staggers around the floor, trying to remember the steps of his dance.

'Hello!' says a voice behind us. Our escorts were obviously pointing us in the wrong direction. The headman seems quite young. He introduces us to his family and calls for a top-up of *borak* before we get a chance to put our gear down. Having downed our drink and ceremoniously smacked our lips in due appreciation, the boss's wife and several other women show us our quarters. Tonight we'll sleep in style, as guests of the chief's family. Their apartment is very large, its walls decorated with an astounding collection of headhunting swords. As my eyes wander across the room, I spot my belongings, the few bits and pieces I had left behind at Lusong Laku, neatly stacked in the corner. On top of the pile, like a monument to civilisation, my little espresso machine. Next to it all, Josephine's Hello Kitty bag.

'Is Josephine here?' I ask the young daughter.

'Josephine? Ah, yes. She come one day ago.'

'Is she here now?'

'Yes.'

'Where is she?' A shrug of shoulders.

We return to the veranda and join the throng of people milling about. Food is brought out. Lots of it. The headman motions us to sit down us and we join him on the mat, where the women are starting to 'set the table' – plate upon plate of deliciously inviting bowls of vegetables, meats, fruit and spicy little side dishes. He passes round a small brass bowl of water to wash our hands in and gestures towards the food. The food is fantastic. While we all eat, an ancient-looking man points a bony finger at the laden platters and everyone goes quiet. Grandfather is about to tell a story.

'A long time ago, before we learned to plant rice, our food came from the forest. Fruit, plants, fish and the animals we hunted. But there was a time when food became scarce and the people of the *Ulu* went hungry. It all started with Burong Pong-Kapong, the tiny little bird that lives high up in the trees. His task in life was to call the flowers, so that they come out after the monsoon and start blossoming. You can hear his call from far away.'

The old man gets up and stretches his arms to mimic the bird's flight.

'"Koo koo koo, koo koo koo."'

A few children follow him around in a circle, repeating the call.

'Pong-Kapong got married to a beautiful blue-coloured female and together they had children. One day when they went to bathe their offspring in the river, a big Juak fish bit the baby in the leg. The mother was very upset and put some healing leaves on the bleeding leg. "I am worried," said the father, who was watching. "As long as we live here, our children will not be able to bathe or have a drink from the river. Maybe we should look for a new home."

'The problem was, he didn't know where to go, so he asked some of the animals in the jungle: the crocodile, the tapir, the leopard, the orang utan. But no one knew the answer. Then, from the top of a tree, Tok-Tarau, the nightjar called out, "Go to Sumatra! Go to Sumatra!" The family thought this was a good idea, so they said goodbye to their friends and left. Just like that.

'Everything was fine for a while, but when the rains stopped there was no one to call the fruit blossoms and the animals began to starve. They decided to ask the wise rhinoceros what to do. "Send a messenger to Sumatra and ask Pong-Kapong to come back." There was much arguing about who should go, but finally the fruit-fly and the butterfly volunteered.

'When they arrived in Sumatra they were surprised at how big the place was. "Where shall we start? How can we find Pong-Kapong?" they said.

'Antu Panas overheard their conversation and said, "I know where Pong-Kapong is. Come with me." They followed the cicada and soon they reached the top of Bukit Binjai, a very tall mountain, where they found their friends living happily in a large tree.

'The butterfly explained the problem and asked Pong-Kapong to come back. But the family liked where they were and did not want to leave.

'"I have an idea," said the mother, "I left three eggs in our tree. Take them to our cousin Tok-Tarau and she will hatch them for us."

'So the butterfly and the fruit-fly returned to Borneo with the good news. Cousin Tok-Tarau was happy to help, and soon three little blue birds hatched one beautiful morning in spring. "Koo koo koo!" they cried, and the flowers and fruit blossoms heard the call and came out.

'The animals were delighted. They laughed and danced and had a big party to celebrate. But the next day, when it was bathing time, the leopard remembered the problem with Ikan Juak, who was sure to bite the little birds when they splashed in the river. "I will talk to him," said the rhinoceros. By the river he called out, "Ikan Juak – Ikan Juak!"

'The fish appeared and asked, "What can I do for you?" The rhino explained that the little birds must not be harmed, otherwise they would also leave and all the animals would once more go hungry.

'"I understand," said Juak. "I will not bite them any more, if they follow the proper custom and ask me first before they enter my river." The animals agreed, and the Ikan Juak hasn't bitten any babies since that day. And if you listen carefully after the monsoon, you can still hear the Pong-Kapong call out the flowers every year. This is why it is important for us to follow proper customs in everything we do.'

The old man lifts up a plate and offers me some fruit. I find his story, even in its abbreviated translation, fascinating as it shows just how closely most indigenous people relate to nature, and especially to animals.

Here in Borneo the animals take on a human form in storytelling. Australian Aborigines give their camp dogs kinship names, which make them instant relatives. In the Amazon, animals are referred to as 'persons'.

Someone starts playing the *sape* sending its gentle, lilting melody fluttering down the longhouse veranda. Out come locally-grown tobacco and betel nuts. Fresh jars of *borak* arrive. The party gradually starts to rev up once more. But I don't know if I could last the distance. The past few days have been strenuous and I am dead tired.

'Do you think they would be offended if I had an early night?' I ask Patrick.

'I doubt it. The way they are going, they'll be beyond caring in about an hour or so. Just go and lie down whenever you like. I'm sure no one will mind.'

'Hello, Mr John.' A young man in Western clothes sits down next to me. 'You go see the land of Penan, yes?'

'Yes. We spent a few days with them. How did you know?'

'Chief say so.'

'Ah. And you? You live here?'

'Yes. But I work in Belaga, with commercial shipping firm.'

'That's interesting. You like your work?'

He shrugs his shoulders. 'Not much. But I have to work until I pay off my bride price.' Noticing my questioning look, he quickly adds, 'I am from a different longhouse. I am Kenyah but I marry a Kayan girl from here. The Kayan, they are very strict. Until I pay for my wife, I have to stay in her longhouse and work. Then I can go and she can come too.'

'Back to your own longhouse? Will she want to go?'

'I think so, it's not very far. Only one hour.'

He pours more *borak* and we seal our new friendship. Looking around, I can notice some subtle differences between the Kayan way of life and that of the other longhouses I have visited. Unlike the Iban, who live in a free-spirited and relatively egalitarian society, the people up here are highly stratified under a strict aristocratic system with four distinct tiers.

At the top are the *maren*, the true 'aristocrats' who comprise the ruling group. Theirs is a life of authority and countless perks, which include exemption from doing manual work and the opportunity to accept gifts (or 'contributions') from lesser members of the community. (A job description not unlike that of some contemporary politicians or government officials, perhaps.) The lifestyle these members of the ruling class lead affords them ample spare time to visit neighbouring communities and establish strong links with other leaders, thus perpetuating their authority from generation to generation.

Next in line are the *hipuy* and *panyin* groups, who are essentially 'commoners', with only subtle differences in prestige and obligations distinguishing them from one another. These groups are tied to the longhouse by a variety of rules and cannot leave to reside elsewhere without the express permission of the chief.

At the bottom of the pile are the *dipen*, or slaves, whose position is hereditary; most are descendants of prisoners taken during headhunting wars. Their status in everyday life is not obvious. They may belong to the household of the chief (in which case he directly controls their work and a share in any resulting wealth), or they may form an independent household that contributes periodically to his coffers, ensuring his continued well-being.

From what I can gather, the young bridegroom next to me belongs to the 'commoner' class.

'So how do you get on with the people in your new home?' I ask him.

He looks around, then leans closer to me and says quietly, 'It's very difficult. Here I can make no decisions, I have no say at all. The Kayan are very hard. Not like my people. I hope I can go back to my own longhouse soon, so I work very hard to make money quickly.'

The gongs are whipping up a storm and it becomes difficult to hold a conversation over the din. My eyes are drawn to a young lady who is approaching us. I met her earlier. Her name is Tami, and boy can she party!

'Have a drink!' she calls out to Patrick and me, and not waiting for a response tops up our glasses. She sits down on the mat and lights one of those huge joints, puffing away merrily to the beat of the music.

'You going to Rumah Apan for the big *gawai*?' she asks Patrick. Bingo! That's where the party must be.

'You mean the *gawai niau*?'

'No. Just a big *gawai* to celebrate the end of the harvest. But another longhouse, not far, they are having a *gawai niau*. You want to see it? I come with you!'

'Maybe. John would enjoy it. But we need an invitation.'

'No problem, *lah*. I talk to the *Phengulu* tomorrow. He lives not far from here.'

The *Phengulu* is the chief of all the longhouses in the area. An invitation from him is sure to bear some weight. Patrick tells me that the *gawai niau* is an important war-like event, celebrated in honour of a departed chief at the end of the official mourning period. It's a sort of celebration for the release of his soul, accompanied by a variety of headhunting rituals. Should be a novel experience.

So much for my plans to have an early night. After several attempts at my disappearing trick, I finally give up and go with the flow of the evening, talking to people who are keen to meet me, drinking, dancing and enjoying staggering amounts of food which just keep on coming.

Now I'm paying the price – with lots of little gongs beating away in my head. Most people are still asleep and I can only guess that they hit their mats not long ago. Patrick is down by the river, having his morning bath.

'Hi Patrick! Did you sleep well?'

'I haven't been to bed yet. Got talking to a lot of people.'

'I know what you mean.'

The water is warm, but there's a strong current. Must have rained last night. Refreshed, we both head back up the hill to the house, where the women are preparing breakfast in the kitchen: *taro* pancakes (made from the starchy root-crop), fern tips, tiny morsels of chicken and stale biscuits.

'Today we part company,' says Patrick casually. 'I'm going back to Miri in the afternoon.'

'Oh.' I say, mainly because I can't think of anything else. I knew that he had to return soon, but the suddenness of his announcement takes me by surprise.

'Yes, I want to see my family and then, the day after, I am meeting a group of Swedish backpackers who want to climb up to the pinnacles in Gunung Mulu National Park. I believe one of the visitors is a seventy-five-year-old lady.'

'So Josephine is taking over again? Where is she, by the way?'

'I don't know. She's around somewhere. But don't worry. She'll show up.'

I hope so.

'Let's have our coffee on the veranda,' suggests Patrick.

The view over the big river is superb and there is already quite a lot of activity: large tugboats pulling their loads through the currents; barges loaded to the hilt with sacks of rice; longboats returning from errands up and downstream; and the occasional fishermen waiting for Ikan Juak and his friends. Several people have started to form a circle around us. While we sip away at our cups of coffee, one of them slowly starts to sing.

'Your welcome song. This might take some time. But I'll try and translate as we go along.'

A diminutive man with thinning shoulder-length hair sits cross-legged on the mat, swaying slowly from side to side as he composes the first verse, his eyes half closed.

'You who have come from the other side of the world to honour us with your visit. You are welcome here and even though we are poor and cannot offer you much food, we will share what we have with you, because you are our friend.'

Borak is poured while the next person prepares his bit. Welcome songs such as these are an age-old tradition and are regarded as an art form. They are a pure 'stand-up poetry', with verses made up ad lib and sung to ancient tunes.

'Although we have little to offer you, we hope you will go back and tell your people about us, because our feelings come from our hearts.'

The song goes on. And on. Finally, after about an hour or so, the poetry seems to have exhausted itself and everyone joins in (yet another) toast to our friendship. The little gongs are starting really to hammer away in my head now, and I desperately need a rest. I go outside and take a stroll around the longhouse, through beautifully tended gardens, wild banana trees and huge flowers in the brightest of colours imaginable, planted all along the many paths.

A short distance away is a small elevated rice storage hut, decorated in wild Kayan swirls, its black, white and yellow colours entirely cover the walls providing a stark contrast to all the lush tropical greenery. The shade on one side looks like a perfect place for a little nap. I relent easily. But my bliss lasts barely a few minutes when I feel a hand gently shaking my shoulder.

'John? Wake up. We're going for a little excursion.'

'How long did I sleep?'

'Maybe an hour.'

'Oh. Where are we going?'

'Remember some of the chiefs' graves we saw along the way? A few women from here are going to visit their local ones. Want to come?'

I'm up like a flash. The headache is gone and I feel good. A short river trip takes us through a huge bend and there, on top of a hill, are three magnificent carved tombs, their wild carvings protruding from the trees against a bright blue sky.

While we struggle up the steep slopes, Patrick fills me in on some of the death rituals of the Kayan. The first and perhaps most important thing is to ensure a smooth transition for the departed to the land of the spirits. So at the slightest hint of a person about to throw in the towel, relatives gather their most important personal belongings and place the things next to the imminently departed so that they can accompany the final journey into the afterworld.

When the person dies, the body is wrapped in tribal blankets and placed on the outside veranda, while a coffin is carved out of a tree. This is usually done by producing two matching halves, which are hollowed-out to form a lid and a bottom. The body is then placed inside and the two halves tied together with rattan.

Depending on local customs, the coffin may remain on the veranda for up to two months (in which case a drainage spout is fitted – a thoughtful gesture in consideration of the surviving members of the community, who would otherwise have to suffer the consequences of the body decomposing under the tropical heat).

Once the initial period of mourning has been observed (which often includes the use of professional wailers), the coffin is taken by boat to its final destination, a *salong* high on top of a hill. John Ford, a member of the 1932 Oxford University Expedition[7], described a Kayan chief's burial procession:

The salong consisted of a stout, upright column, a tree-trunk about thirty feet high, carved with intricate patterns and painted in orange, black and white; resting upon this was a large structure, about five feet high, surmounted by a gabled roof. Along each of the four gables ran dragon-like carvings. The whole of this aerial house was beautifully and fantastically painted with perfectly balanced designs.

Nearby stood a painted and roughly-carved pillar. Strings of flags hung from it and from the four corners of the salong itself. A scaffold erected around the salong supported a platform about a yard in width, upon which some twenty persons, mainly wailing women, had gathered.

When the burial procession arrived, the men placed the coffin, by means of a small door, inside the 'house' and were now finally arranging the interior, laying spear, paddle, parang and war coat upon the coffin, and variously disposing of other goods that had been the property of the chief.

Once the official burial is over, the grave is rarely visited and the jungle slowly encroaches upon the tomb, which grows in beauty while the corpse is left to nature to decay.

As we reach the top of the hill with perspiration running down our backs, I am glad that nature has had plenty of time to do its job. The tomb is even more spectacular close up. The colours are bright and stark against the surrounding foliage. But what fascinates me most is all the minute detail in the carving. The main motif seems to be the traditional Kayan 'dragon' design, which is not really a dragon at all, but a dog that looks like a dragon. Called *Aso*, this recurring, highly stylised pattern is based on spirals and curves that sweep wildly towards one central point, thought to be the eye of the beast. No one seems to know where the Borneo 'dog pattern' came from, except that it has been around for a long time and that it can be seen just about anywhere – on paintings, tattoos, carvings and metal work which both the Kayan and Kenyah excel in.

The women are starting to sing – some sort of lament that celebrates the achievements of the departed and addresses his spirits, according to Patrick. But the solemnity of the moment does not last too long. Someone is unpacking a stack of party favours, promptly diverting everyone's attention to various snacks, drinks and tobacco.

Sitting there in their festive finery, the women are obviously enjoying their little outing.

Chatting among themselves and totally oblivious to us, they are a photographer's dream, the sort of subjects *National Geographic* would relentlessly pursue. One elderly lady in particular attracts my attention; her hands and forearms are covered in tattoos of such minute detail that, at first glance, one would get the impression that she had just immersed her arms up to the elbows in dark dye. It's almost as if she were wearing long gloves, ready to attend a formal ball at the White House. Her face is leathery and wrinkled, but her hair is still jet black and shiny, held in place by a colourful, beaded headband. Several heavy silver rings on each ear have stretched her lobes down past her shoulders. She must be well over eighty, but still sports a big cigar in the corner of her mouth.

Next to her, a younger woman with a small round hat (similar to those worn by fifties air hostesses, but topped by a single feather in colours that match her sarong) is chewing betel nuts, periodically spitting the red liquid in a well-aimed stream against a tree.

The engine noise of a boat pulling up way down at the river shifts our attention to the new arrivals.

'Hello John.'

Josephine, resplendent in traditional dress. I've never seen her like this before, wearing sarong, headband and silver jewellery. She's obviously getting into the swing of the *gawai* season. She looks up at the hill and thinks twice of it.

'You coming down, *lah*?'

We wave and start our descent. When she greets us like long-lost friends, I admit to myself that it's nice to see her again.

'We're going to the *gawai niau*!' she exclaims, 'I made the arrangements already!'

'When?'

'Now. We just go and get our things from the longhouse. I have a boat waiting.'

The intention might be there, but the reality of an immediate departure is not quite as easy, as it turns out. On our return to the longhouse we find that chief has lined up a dance for the night and insists that we stay. Josephine shrugs her shoulders.

'Never mind. We can go to Rumah Apan tomorrow.'

She goes to tell the waiting boatman who, sensing some action, immediately calls out, 'Party!' Looking at me he elaborates, as if he owed me an explanation.

'Many girls, drink, food, happy times, yes? I stay.'

He is round and stocky and his short legs look as if he were wearing thick football socks under his skin.

'My name is Kallang,' he says, smiling. 'What is your name?'

I tell him. 'Good, John. You are my friend. And we have fun tonight, OK?'

I hardly know this guy, but I like him already.

As the last rays of sun disappear over the hills, the river takes on another dimension. The valley is bathed in a soft pink light with purplish streaks running through the sky. The air is still and nothing stirs in the postcard serenity of the landscape. Dark shadows are cast where palm trees line the water's edge.

Inside the house the orchestra is warming up and people are shuffling around, forming little groups of spectators ready to take in the performance from their front-stall mats.

'I hope I won't be dragged out to dance again.' I remark casually to Josephine, who is pushing a couple of men aside to take up residence next to me.

'Probably not. From what I heard, tonight's dances will be quite different from the hornbill style we have seen. These are animal dances that are passed down from generation to generation and they require a high degree of skill. Not that your dancing was not good,' she adds hurriedly.

We don't have to wait long. Just a couple of shots of *borak* later, the gongs go into loud mode and a fierce-looking man leaps on to centre-stage. He is wearing a grotesque mask with huge tusks and his body is covered in a torn dark cloth.

'A wild pig dance,' explains Josephine.

Several oil lamps are being extinguished by the excited audience, adding a dramatic touch to the proceedings. The pig man gets down on all fours and heads for a group of small children, grunting and squealing in quite a realistic manner. The kids retreat as one.

Suddenly, out of nowhere, a hairy, slime-green mass advances towards the centre and slowly splits up to reveal a dozen or so dancers wearing fantastic masks topped with war headgear. For a while they sway in unison to the slow rhythm of the *sape*. Periodically, individual dancers step out and perform a brief but energetic war dance, before returning slowly to their place.

The pig sniffs the air and suddenly takes off towards the far wall of the veranda, squealing madly as the hunters follow him in wild pursuit. His lot does not improve when, halfway down the track, several doors of *biliks* suddenly open and young children, dressed as dogs, emerge and join in the fray. The music quickens. The audience is going berserk, cheering on the performers as the chase proceeds up and down the veranda and eventually disintegrates into a mad mêlée when things turn into a free-for-all. Exhausted, the performers collapse on top of each other in the middle of the arena until several longhouse belles come to their rescue with jugs of *borak*, amidst wild cheers from the audience. Food appears in front of us. I realise that I haven't eaten since breakfast and manage to put away three bowls full of rice and vegetables. Must be the exhaustion from watching all the high-energy dancing. The band strikes up another tune. This time soft and gentle. Perfect dinner music.

'What do you think, John? Did you enjoy this?' asks Josephine.

'Very much. I'm amazed at how well the dancers manage to mimic the animals.'

'The people of the *ulu* are very good at imitating animals. They are born naturalists and have intimate knowledge of animals' habits through observation. They know their way of life and are very good at copying it.'

'Wait till you see the next one,' remarks Patrick casually.

'Very funny.'

'And very naughty!' adds Josephine. 'But I think we have time for coffee before they start. You want some, John?'

What a question. While Josephine fusses around in the kitchen, I have time to observe the people in the room. Many are dressed in Western fashion, but by far the majority have maintained their traditional look: almost everybody is tattooed in one way or another. Most wear sarongs – brighter colours and patterns for the women, more sedate, 'earthy' colours for the men. Ear lobes are universally elongated, but slightly smaller and more discreet on the men. Topless is de rigueur for both sexes, although a few women have obviously succumbed to the missionaries' pleas and have started to wear T-shirts or simple bras. One very big lady next to me has donned a bright pink, shiny gothic bra for the occasion, probably in my honour. Thank you, ma'am, I appreciate your concerns.

Josephine emerges with her tray of coffee, in time for the next performance to start.

'Monkey dance,' she says. 'Very naughty.'

This is the second time she has emphasised that word. I wonder what she means, but no doubt I'm about to find out. To my surprise, the monkey turns out to be Kallang – our new boatman. According to Josephine, he is renowned throughout the Balui area for his somewhat unorthodox interpretation of the monkey dance.

Oil lamps are once more extinguished, except for a few that have been placed in a circle around the dance floor. The music starts slowly and Kallang sets the scene by spreading imaginary branches on the floor to simulate the treetops. He proceeds to walk precariously over a branch, looks around, and with several swinging leaps jumps over the heads of onlookers and lands smack-bang in the middle of a bowl of fruit, sending its contents rolling all over the floor. Instant hit with the audience.

He stops, looks around, and spots a banana. His facial expressions tell it all: the eyes move left, then right and back to the banana which he seizes with one single swoop before taking off in the direction of the door. A young man blocks his way and the monkey goes wild, screeching and flashing his teeth at the same time. Then he gets distracted and lunges for an old woman's head, searching frantically for fleas he appears to have spotted. He ruffles her hair, picks around in individual strands and finally finds what he has been looking for. Plucking his little snack from the hair, he examines it closely with crossed eyes, and proceeds to eat it with great gusto, smacking his lips while eyeing his audience.

His attention returns to the banana, which he now peels daintily with his thumb and forefinger. Banana held firmly in one hand, he walks sideways to the centre of the floor, pushing along with the knuckles of his other hand on the floor. He sits down and examines the fruit. This seems to be the moment the audience has been waiting for, and soon catcalls and words of encouragement egg him on into more daring territory.

He slowly holds the banana up in front of his lips and begins a series of highly suggestive licking actions. A toothless old lady calls out to him and everyone is whooping and yelling in support. He bites off the tip of the banana and the women cry out in unison. The monkey returns to his routine, lurching forward with knuckles dragging on the ground, looking around, spotting more imaginary branches to leap from and scampering about on the floor. The audience is urging him on to perform yet more outrageous acts of male bravado and he is obviously delighted to oblige. From a crouched position he jumps up and imitates an orang utan's mating call – which meets with similar responses from the lads in the audience.

His hips are now starting to gyrate and the movements leave little to the imagination.

One mating call from the audience keeps persisting. The monkey turns his head in the direction of the call, where a young man points at a pretty girl next to him. Without thinking twice, the monkey jumps on her, drags her to the floor and gets ready for the time of his life. But the girl keeps twisting and turning in a frantic attempt to escape, leaving our hero to finish his act in mid-air.

The audience goes wild over his antics while the girl returns to her group on the floor.

Monkey business finished, he sits down, breathing and panting heavily. He stares at the onlookers who have gone rather quiet, in anticipation of a big finale. Casually, he produces a cigar from behind one ear, lights it and lays back on the floor with a very content look on his face. The gongs pick up the beat and Kallang's performance is celebrated with obligatory toasts all round.

Time to mingle. I accept two more challenges to down some *borak* and chat with the locals. An hour goes by and I can see Josephine sitting in the corner, her mouth wide open in a big yawn. Now Patrick starts too. This is very contagious. Without a word, the three of us get up and retire to our sleeping mats. Under the rafters, some geckos watch over us, periodically making their presence felt with little *cik-cak* sounds. Outside, the party goes on.

chapter twelve

kayan

'John, get up, quick!'

Patrick gently shakes my shoulder.

'What's up?'

'The boys have just spotted a war party coming down-river. You might want to see it.'

A war party? At half past four in the morning? But curiosity has the better of me and I scramble out of my sleeping bag, quickly throwing on a T-shirt to keep out the morning chill. Patrick motions me to be silent as we balance our way down the notched log towards the river and position ourselves quietly behind an old canoe hull resting in the mud. The mist swirls quietly over the water as I scan its surface for any sign of life. Everything is perfectly still except for a slight rippling sound just near the river's bend, where patches of open foliage reveal glimpses of a large canoe progressing silently towards us. In the semi-darkness I can just make out the brown arms that swing the paddles in unison and drive the boat forward, hardly causing a ripple on the water's surface.

A faint flutter of feathers as a bird takes flight is the only indication of the war party's presence as it slinks its way towards us, hugging the banks secretively. There's a menacing, even scary feeling about the scene, which not so long ago would have meant some serious killing.

'They're carrying heads in the boat,' whispers Patrick, 'most likely on their way to a headhunting ceremony.'

The boat is now almost on top of us and I can see its elaborately carved bow clearly as it cuts its way through the water. Unlike ordinary longboats, this one is decked out to the hilt with war paraphernalia: colourful shields, blowpipes, spears and there, right in the centre and resting under a canopy of palm fronds, a large sand-filled box with skulls grinning as if they were enjoying their little morning excursion.

The warriors, some thirty of them, are dressed for battle with animal skins and plumed hats topped by large hornbill feathers that sway slowly to the rhythm of the paddles.

As the canoe glides past us I am surprised at its size – almost three times the length of an ordinary longboat. It is painted in vivid colours and is also built much sturdier than the usual hollow-hull models, with solid bamboo decking offering more sure-footed action (in the event of a hasty retreat, I presume).

As quickly (and quietly) as it had emerged, the boat is now disappearing into some rushes along the bank, and the river once more assumes its placid flow under the mist-shrouded scenery.

Still trying to clear the cobwebs out of my head after this extraordinary early morning wake-up call, I follow Patrick up the log, contemplating my options for breakfast. But he soon puts an end to my deliberations when he announces that we're about to leave, as he has to catch an Express Boat connection further up-river in order to get back home before nightfall.

'We can eat something at Rumah Apan, but there's time for a quick coffee, if you like.'

I nod under a big yawn. Daylight is breaking, revealing the full majesty of the river as it comes to life under the droning of outboard engines, boats zipping in and out of the currents, picking up passengers and dropping supplies at various longhouses along the way.

Comfortably settled in the boat among our own supplies, I take in the scenery. But I can't keep my mind from wandering back to the early morning war party. Although headhunting has been officially banned for some time now, vestiges of it obviously still remain. Most locals will vehemently deny that the practice is still alive, yet in a spiritual sense they seem to have reached a compromise by using the heads ceremonially.

At such events, headhunting stories are told and re-told by the elders, most of whom would have chalked up scores of their own on more than one occasion. Sometimes one can even detect in their eyes a degree of longing for days gone by. (Which can be mildly disconcerting – especially when their gaze falls directly upon friendly visitors like myself.)

The Dutch, on the other side of the border, were first to impose a ban on headhunting, meting out harsh punishment for offenders. But while the rules were strict, the practicality of catching someone in the act posed considerable difficulties; thus the age-old habit continued well into the twentieth century. Not to be outdone, the dynasty of 'White Rajas' in Sarawak imposed equally harsh measures, albeit with a generous degree of flexibility, allowing them to permit occasional headhunting forays against perceived enemies when it suited the political situation.

The ploy was based on the simple 'divide and conquer' principle: when the people of one tribe in the *ulu* became restless or caused more trouble than was reasonably warranted, the Raja would use another tribe to wage war against them, promising them that they could keep any heads taken. Thus many battles were fought with much gusto in the remote regions of Borneo while the Rajas sipped tea in the well-tended gardens of the *Astana* – the official government residence – hundreds of miles away in Kuching. Which doesn't necessarily mean that the high and mighty were cowards. On the contrary, the White Rajas were much-gifted entrepreneurs who managed to carve out an entire kingdom for themselves, which they ruled in a paternalistic fashion, preferring to consult with the headmen of local tribes, maintaining local tribal laws and traditions and preventing profiteers from exploiting 'their' people.

When the Japanese invaded Borneo in 1941 they met little resistance until they went inland where the Iban were waiting for them behind the bushes. Japanese heads became all the rage in up-river longhouse communities, where they can still be seen on occasion, hanging from the rafters as a special memento of the good old days. One of the heads, the proud possession of one Iban longhouse, is said to have belonged to the Director of Asian Endeavours in the Japanese Imperial Army. According to stories making the rounds, it still sports a pair of gold-rimmed spectacles on its partial nose, which the chief removes, polishes and reverently puts back every day.

Taking advantage of the temporary headhunting revival, a lone Australian SAS commando parachuted right into the middle of the jungle and organised the tribes into what must have been one of the world's most unusual resistance movements. It may have only been small, but it scared the hell out of the Japanese.

'You look deep in thought, John.'

'Yes, I was just thinking about the White Rajas. Didn't Charles Brooke spend some time up here?'

'That's right. Some of the older people around here still remember him fondly.'

'It sounds as if he was rather popular?'

'Oh yes, mainly because he kept his nose out of local affairs and the missionaries at bay.' Patrick giggles, 'Don't tell Josephine I said that!'

We both look towards the stern where Josephine is curled up in a puddle of water, fast asleep.

'So today you're off back home. It's goodbye then?' I say, settling back into the stack of crates and sacks.

'Afraid so. Your journey will finish soon, but I am starting all over again.'

'Do you enjoy your work as a guide?'

'Absolutely. I love every minute of it. It gives me a chance to meet people from all over the world and enjoy the outdoors at the same time. And the longhouse parties aren't bad either!'

The boat veers sharply to the right, sending the puddle of water sloshing with accelerated momentum against Josephine's cheek. She wakes with a start.

'What time is it?'

'Seven. And we're here.'

Our bow is pointed straight towards the mud and I hold on to the sideboards in anticipation of the inevitable sudden stop. Which I know has come the moment my glasses get splashed with thick grey slime. Kallang jumps out and, knee-deep in mud, helps us unload our belongings. I'm the last one out, and by the time I make it to the notched log that leads up the bank I am surrounded by giggling kids who have apparently targeted me as the day's entertainment. While I grapple with my laces in a supreme effort to take off my boots before entering the longhouse, Patrick comes to say goodbye. His Express Boat is roaring around the river bend, ready to land on our little beach. I want to go down with him, but I'm stuck midway in my boots.

'Enjoy the *gawai* – and send me a postcard from Sydney!'

And he's off before I can mutter another word. The Express Boat hits the mud with a thump, Patrick grabs a wrist tended by a deckhand, climbs over the rail, and the boat's engines scream away leaving behind a powerful wash of stirred-up mud.

'John, I want you to meet Uncle. He lives here.'

A short man with a round, smiling moon-face holds out his hand.

'Hello, Uncle.'

'Yes, yes! You can call me Uncle too!'

So here we are. New longhouse and instant family.

'I see you before. You with the Penan. Remember, on top of the mountain? We do trading!'

The man talks at a million miles an hour and suddenly it dawns on me – he's the one who talked to Patrick and invited us to the *gawai*.

'You stay with my family, OK?'

'Yes, thank you very much.'

Uncle chats away merrily to Josephine while we walk down a seemingly endless veranda.

This house is a solid affair. Big hardwood support beams. Massive, carved columns supporting the roof, and shiny wooden floorboards all the way. But what strikes me most are the painted walls featuring beautiful Kayan designs.

'Here – my apartment.' He opens the door and motions me to step in. 'Please.'

Inside are four women, standing in a row and waiting to greet us. In their sarongs they remind me of Singapore Airlines hostesses, ready to check our boarding passes.

Introductions over, we are shown our sleeping places. The apartment is huge. The room we are in could be used for a sizeable wedding or bar mitzvah. On the far end is a balustrade overlooking a light and airy courtyard that leads into an informal living-room and a large kitchen area on the other side where the women of the household reign supreme.

But what strikes me most are two large ponds in the middle of the courtyard; one is covered in a massive blanket of lotus and filled with carp, the other is for bathing. The setting is stunning and I compliment our host on it.

'Oh, it's not very much, I am sorry. We are only poor. But I hope you will be comfortable.'

After our recent accommodation in jungle shelters this is sheer luxury.

The women are busy preparing breakfast, but to keep us going coffee is being served.

Josephine, Uncle and I take our mugs outside and settle down in a little hut overlooking the river. It's a delightful spot, constructed to give shelter from sun or rain while local residents wait for a boat. A sort of bus-shelter with a palm-frond roof.

Rumah Apan is one of the nicer longhouses in the area and unlike typical Iban houses which are of a more temporary nature, and periodically shifted to follow new plantation areas. The Kayan and Kenyah residences in this part of the world tend to be more permanent. Although some concessions have been made towards the use of modern building materials, by and large construction still follows traditional methods, with solid hardwood and rich decorations dominating the architecture.

Social segregation, too, is more evident, with the Kayan class system separating the aristocrats from the more common folk in pre-determined living spaces arranged around various parts of the longhouse. Our apartment is near the centre, close to the chief's lodgings, indicating that Uncle holds a privileged position in the hierarchy. Furthest from the centre is a small connecting bridge that leads to a secondary longhouse, where some of the 'lesser' members of the community must be living.

A little girl walks towards us, very tentatively, a finger in her mouth. She stops in front of us and, eyes averted, says something to Uncle.

'Ah, breakfast is ready.'

I take my mug and follow Uncle. Josephine has spotted yet another relative and taps into the local news network.

The place is abuzz with activity. Along the veranda children are helping with decorations for the *gawai*.

'*Makai*! *Makai*!' The women are summoning us to breakfast, and Uncle gently nudges me along in the direction of the kitchen. As per custom, the men eat first while the women watch like silent waiters at a banquet. But Josephine, barging into the room, ignores tradition and, taking advantage of her guest status, joins us at the table.

The kitchen is unusual and, like the rest of the longhouse, full of cultural contradictions.

While we are eating at a table, the women are preparing food on the floor. Meals are cooked at a traditional hearth, yet modern crockery and cutlery are displayed on a large sideboard, the kind one might expect to be featured in *Country Life* magazine. The main living-room, too, displays signs of encroaching technology: a large-screen television, surrounded by a sizeable collection of headhunting *parangs*, provides entertainment via satellite for the aristocracy and selected invitees from the lesser classes whenever appropriate.

After breakfast, and at my request, Uncle gives me a guided tour of the numerous artefacts on the wall. Pride of place is naturally taken up by the *parangs* which, aside from their fundamental head-lopping function, are works of art in their own right. Their sheaths and handles are elaborately carved from bone in rich Kayan patterns. The metal blades are engraved with a variety of designs that are said to provide strong spiritual powers. And sprouting out from the top of the handles, bunches of human hair (or, more recently, monkey hair) make an unmistakable statement about their original intended use.

'Have you used any of these, Uncle?'

Embarrassed silence, followed by a diplomatic answer.

'These are mine,' he points at several swords, 'this one from my father. And this, my grandfather.'

I persist and re-phrase my question.

'How many have taken heads?'

He looks at me quizzically. 'Maybe all.' Subject dropped.

We proceed outside, where preparations for the big feast are starting to reach fever pitch. The atmosphere is not unlike Christmas Eve in the Western world, when everyone is lending a hand to get ready for the big occasion. Even the littlest kids are busy putting up decorations, getting ready to set the table, preparing sleeping quarters for visiting family members and helping with the preparation of food. The only thing that's missing is the mistletoe and lifts sliding up their cables to the tune of *Jingle Bells*.

'You want to take your bath now?' asks Uncle.

The idea of soaking in the lotus pond appeals to me. I change into my sarong and find Uncle, Josephine and her little niece already floating between the rocks. The water is warm and the setting serene. Just like a tropical beach resort – minus the swim-up bar.

Suddenly it strikes me that one can't answer nature's call in this pond, the way one simply does in the river. But there are real toilets – proper, dedicated, purpose-built rooms with squat-down pits, wooden ladles and barrels of water designed to use the 'splash' method in the absence of toilet paper.

After the bath and the rigours of breakfast, Uncle decides to take a nap and Josephine busies herself in the kitchen. I opt for a walk to explore the neighbourhood. The path outside the main house is lined with flowerbeds and exotic shrubs. Someone obviously loves gardening. At the end of the track are several elevated rice storage huts, decorated in stark black and vivid white dragon designs. A small snake is sunning itself on one of the notched steps. From the bottom of the hill comes the whining sound of a chainsaw. As I get nearer to it, I can see several men cutting timber planks for a boat that seems to be mid-way through construction. They stop on my approach and greet me with friendly waves, wiping sweat off their faces.

'Nice boat,' I say, trying to open the conversation.

'Only small, *lah!*' replies one of them.

I admire their workmanship – something I really appreciate as I am in the process of restoring an old wooden cruiser back home. There is not a single nail in sight. Nor is there evidence of any glue. The joints all fit perfectly and I have no doubt that the boat will be as watertight as any modern craft constructed with today's amazing technology.

Looking around, I see that the chainsaw is the only concession made to mechanical tools. The rest is shaped with *parangs* and a great deal of patient craftsmanship. Glad for the break my intrusion has offered them, the men light up their banana-leaf joints and we sit around for a while, trying to make conversation as far as the language barrier permits.

'After sun we *minum*, yes?' The chainsaw-wielding man throws down the gauntlet for a drinking session after sunset.

As I have no choice in the matter I nod, pretending to be enthusiastic about the challenge. Which encourages others to follow suit and one by one they vie for my attention, pointing at themselves and miming drinking motions.

At this point I make a firm resolve to avoid striking up further friendships with the locals, and head off towards the back of the settlement where the jungle encroaches upon the dwellings. The view from up here is terrific. But as I head towards a cleared patch of forest, I am stopped dead in my tracks by what lies before me: a construction site full of near-completed timber homes, neatly lined up in a row as far as the eye can see.

'You like our new houses?' It's Uncle.

'Your new houses?' I ask with obvious astonishment.

'Yes, yes. The government is building for us. Because Bakun will come soon.'

The dreaded Bakun Dam, whose planned construction will flood the entire valley. And these are the houses destined for the resettlement of this community. Although the building of the dam has been met with considerable resistance by the locals, economic projections paint a glowing picture of hydro-electric power being supplied to peninsular Malaysia, with residues, perhaps, even being sold to Indonesia and Singapore. Bakun is a gigantic project: a reservoir of 695 square kilometres flooding out some 80,000 hectares of primarily virgin rainforest – an area roughly the size of Singapore. In addition to the serious environmental impact the flooding of the valley will create, fifteen longhouses will disappear under water and with them a unique tribal way of life[8]. But for Malaysia there's a bright side to the story: before the dam can be built, the area can be logged – a bonanza in revenue which is expected to contribute more than half of the project's costs. Uncle walks with me. As we pass the beautiful rice storage huts, I wonder how their replicated successors will fit in with the new-look 'condo' up the hill.

Back at the main house, there's excitement; a group of people is crowding around a diminutive man who is engaged in friendly banter with a couple of women. At his feet are two large kerosene cans with hand-fashioned coathanger wires as handles, filled with a gooey mess that exudes an awful stench.

'What is it?' I ask Uncle.

'Fat. For cooking.'

I move closer. It's an oozing mass of entrails, gristle, floating fat and various other parts of animals that have seen better days. One of the longhouse chefs plunges her hand into the slop and examines a handful of its contents. A price is agreed upon and the man smiles, happy with the sale he has just clinched. The women invite him to stay on for a cup of coffee, but he declines; with the festivals at the doorstep, he is having a busy day with his deliveries.

As he leaves, there are shouts from the kids on the veranda and the bystanders' attention is diverted to the huge dragon-dog effigy which seems to have been completed and is now making its way towards us, carried by three splendidly attired warriors. It's an astounding piece of work, richly decorated and carved, its painted detail a blaze of colours. But no matter how hard I look, from every angle, I can't detect the slightest likeness to either dragon or dog. It looks fearsome, nevertheless. A warrior detaches himself from the group and approaches me, holding out a bowl.

'It's chicken blood,' says Josephine, 'take some and sprinkle it on the dragon's head.'

'With my hands?'

'Yes.'

All eyes are on me, so I do as I am told. The women begin to chant and the little procession slowly descends to the river where the dragon will be attached to the prow of a large war canoe, ready to 'bite' any enemy craft in sight. The warriors now place the carving on a small wooden platform erected next to the boat and the master craftsman walks towards it, holding an agitated chicken in his hand. With a swift move of his *parang* he ends the fowl's protests and drips yet more blood over the dragon's snout. In the old days, this ceremony would have used human blood and signalled the beginning of a major headhunting expedition. Uncle nudges me, two glasses of *borak* in his hands.

'Come, John, we relax.'

He heads towards the riverside bus-shelter and I follow, after taking a few snaps of the fantastic carving. The atmosphere around us is festive and jovial and, despite their reputation as fierce headhunters, the Kayans are a friendly, hospitable and progressive people, quite at ease with the compromise they seem to have struck between their bloodthirsty past and the realities of the modern world.

Traditions are maintained to a large degree through ceremonies, which form an important part of longhouse life. As headhunting has always played an integral role in most rituals since time immemorial, the idea is nowadays perpetuated as a spiritual link with the past, and tales of heroic deeds or other memorable headhunting occasions still make the rounds whenever opportunities arise.

One such story has been recorded by C.H. Hartley[9], an ornithologist and explorer who became a blood-brother to one of the Kayan communities in the upper Baram area:

On his way home from the farm, Unggang notices an old woman bent over a burnt tree-stump in a field. He is surprised to find her there, so late in the day when everyone else has returned home. There is something unsettling about this, and he stops for a moment to survey the scene.

The sun drops and the shadows creep over the jungle. The chirp of frogs and crickets is incessant, but no other sound is heard until a twig snaps on the edge of the forest and there emerges from the gloom the figure of a man. He crouches and advances, leaping lightly from stump to stump. The old woman looks up; a shrill scream and she hobbles as fast as she can to the other side of the clearing. But she's too late: the spear lands, the woman straightens and leaps forward as the steel flashes from its sheath.

The man raises his parang, but before he can complete his move there springs up in front of him Uggang. The surprise is complete, the aggressor makes for the bushes. A spear whizzes past him as he runs and the chase has begun.

But it is hopeless from the beginning. The panic-stricken warrior trips and recovers while he hears footsteps closing in on him; his breath comes in short pants, his eyes are straining towards the shelter of the trees. He feels the clutch at his flowing hair, and in desperation launches out with a backhanded slash. Too late. He falls heavily.

The victor bends over the writhing form. He straightens himself and waves his sword. His left hand now has its gruesome burden. His yell of triumph and defiance rings across the clearing and echoes from the jungle-clad hills.

As he makes for the homeward path, he suddenly sways slightly, and as he moves on, totters. He recovers himself and looks down. For the first time he realises that his enemy's despairing slash has taken effect. A look of surprise crosses his face; but he glances at the burden his left hand carries and again moves forward. Again he stumbles, collapses and crashes head foremost into the fringe of the undergrowth.

Something round and heavy bumps and jolts down the rough path until it meets a fallen tree. It strikes the log with a dull thud, rocks for a moment and is still.

There's excitement down at the fallen tree-trunk jetty: an Express Boat has just ploughed its way into the mud and is now spitting out hordes of visitors eager to join in the festivities. There are uncles and aunties, nephews and nieces, baskets of chickens, grandmothers, brothers-in-law, stepsons, secret admirers and a Chinese family. After countless embraces, handshakes and slaps on backs, the party is starting to make its way up the hill towards our little shelter.

'Ah, Loh!' exclaims Uncle.

The Chinese man breaks into a panoramic smile and comes towards us, both hands extended.

'This is John from Australia,' says Uncle, 'and this is my good friend Loh.'

'Hello, Loh.'

'Call me Erwin. This is my wife Lucy, and my girls Emma and Polly.'

Polite smiles and a few 'hellos' before they're off to settle into their quarters.

'Are you expecting many visitors for the *gawai*?'

'Yes. Many.'

'When will they all arrive?'

'Today. Tomorrow. Maybe after that. They stop at many longhouses,' he points up and down the river, 'many, many parties!'

I already gathered that. The festive season seems well and truly underway. By the time we finish our *borak* and reboard the rocking longhouse, Erwin has already settled cross-legged on the floor and surrounded himself with a selection of co-drinkers.

'Come, have a drink!' he calls out, waving a small round stone bottle.

'What is it?' I ask.

'*Mao Tai*! Chinese drink!'

He fills two small cups about halfway up. And that is fortunate, as I find out when, according to custom, I down it to hearty calls of, '*Kampei!*' and instantly lose my speech for a good minute. This stuff is terrible and packs a punch!

'Another one!' Erwin calls out enthusiastically, waving the bottle in the air.

I put him off by mumbling something about 'later, perhaps'. I notice that Uncle has remained quietly in the background, cleverly avoiding a ritual he must have experienced on previous occasions. I sit down next to him.

'You're not drinking?'

He pulls a face as if he had just bitten into a lemon.

'Like rocket fuel, *lah*.'

Paint-stripper would be a more apt description.

'So where do you know Loh from? He's obviously not a relation?'

'No, no. He comes from Singapore. He is an engineer and sells us spare parts for generators and outboard engines. He always visits. Maybe three or four times a year. Comes here for a long time!'

Erwin overhears our conversation. 'Yes, a long time, John. They're like my family. I love them. Do you like it here?' He moves closer, bottle in hand. 'You from Australia? I studied in Adelaide. Very nice city.'

'What did you study?'

'I have a degree in electrical engineering – and now I'm selling spare parts in the *ulu*. Funny, huh?'

'You obviously enjoy it.'

'Oh, yes. It's good money. A very large territory, all to myself. Maybe because no one else wants it!'

He roars with high-pitched laughter and then insists on us drinking a toast to Australia. Foolishly, I relent. He prattles on about Australia, the girls, the parties. But I can hardly make out what he is saying. My head is swimming. I can see his face as if I were looking through a kaleidoscope. Four ears. Now the eyes are under his mouth. His hair turns green and then blue. The rest I can't remember.

When I wake up, around seven in the evening, I find that my friends have transported me to a sleeping mat where I must have spent the afternoon in total oblivion. The room is full of people, watching an old episode of Seinfeld on the large-screen television. Few of them understand the dialogue, but whenever Kramer bumps into furniture or comes flying through the door, they just roll about on the mats with laughter.

Dinner is served in the kitchen, courtesy of Josephine and a few helpers who must have spent hours preparing the lavish feast of some twenty individual dishes. The headman joins us at the table as the women put down plate after plate of fresh river fish, exotically spiced chicken, mounds of delicious-looking vegetables and baskets of tropical fruit in the most incredible shapes and colours.

'Eat up, John. You will need your strength for the headhunting *gawai* tomorrow.'

'Why? Will my head end up in the rafters?'

Josephine laughs. 'Who knows what will happen if you don't behave yourself!'

The Chinese family appears, inspects every dish meticulously and then proceeds to demolish the neatly piled offerings with huge enthusiasm, praising the cooks at every new course sampled.

The chief looks on in amazement but seems glad that the guests are having a good time.

After dinner we retire, as usual, to the veranda where the decorations have been completed. The place looks festive with countless masks, wall-hangings, flowers and beadwork adorning the walls. Near the chief's apartment there is what appears to be a small altar with offerings of fruit and *padi* seeds placed on brass plates. Above it all is an empty basket. I can only guess at what goes in there. As my eyes wander down the veranda, I can see Erwin approaching, waving his bottle.

'No!' I scream. My entourage ignites into hoots of laughter.

As soon as everyone is absorbed in exchanging gossip and the dancing starts, I quietly make my exit. This time my disappearing trick works and I make it to Uncle's apartment without being stopped by tumbler-wielding tribesmen along the way. However, any notions I might have had of finding peace and tranquillity in my abode are instantly shattered when I enter the apartment and find that half of the neighbourhood has assembled, watching the ABC news courtesy of Australia's overseas broadcasting service. It's nice to catch a few glimpses of home. But before even the regional weather report appears (which is meaningless in these parts of the world where there is only one type of weather: sweltering) my eyelids are getting heavy, and I miss the forecast altogether.

The veranda is shaking with the tread of a war dance. Men fully dressed in goat-hair coats and wearing plumed helmets are wielding their *parangs* in a slow, steady rhythm produced by a gong orchestra deep in the bowels of the dark longhouse.

Although we managed to get up early this morning and reached the longhouse after only a short boat ride, the headhunting festival is already well underway. Our arrival is hardly noticed as we find an inconspicuous corner and settle down on the floor. While my eyes adjust to the dark interior I can just make out an altar under several lengths of colourful cloth fluttering lightly in the breeze. A warrior with extra-long feathers sits beside it, regally overlooking the proceedings. In his hands he holds a brass plate with a skull.

The gongs slow down to a muted whisper and a flute takes up a haunting melody. The dancers look fierce, their eyes flashing as they conjure up images of the enemy in their minds. So powerful is the sound of the flute of death that the Dutch banned it from being played altogether. For without the flute there cannot be a *kanjar dodo* – the war dance we are now witnessing, and which is central to achieving the trance-like state required to carry out a successful head hunt.

Although I know that the scenes before us are re-enactments of old traditions, I can't help feeling just a touch uneasy. Looking at the warriors, I find it somewhat astonishing that they encumber themselves with accessories and clothing as burdensome as bulky leopard skins, long protruding feathers and heavy shields, all of which must hinder their advance in the thick of the jungle. But who am I to argue? The blackened heads suspended from the rafters above me speak for themselves.

The flute-playing comes to an abrupt end. Dancers break formation and start mingling with the rest of the crowd, laughing and exchanging pleasantries. Food comes out and the gathering assumes the informality of an everyday party.

'What's happening?' I ask.

'Nothing,' replies Josephine, 'they skip the next part and wait for the heads to arrive.'

'What heads?'

'Well, they can't go out and hunt for fresh ones, so they normally borrow some from other longhouses and bring them back in pretend triumph, just as if they had returned from a real raid. It's a convenient way for them to maintain their traditions.'

The chief of this small community is a sturdy, elderly man who exudes leadership. He introduces himself and asks us to join him on his mat. He seems particularly pleased to see Loh, with whom he chats away as if he were a long-lost friend. Tea, sweetened with lots of sugar, is being served in big glasses. Much to my relief, not a single shot of *borak* in sight.

'Did you bring the presents for the kids?' asks Josephine.

'Yes, right here.'

'OK, now's a good time. I tell them.'

She proceeds to explain that I have brought gifts of friendship from far away, and would like, with the chief's permission, to present them now. Enthusiastic nods. The headman's children and several of their friends slide forward on their buttocks, in eager anticipation. From my shirt pocket I pull a small package of glittery stickers, several hologram pictures and a dozen or so removable tattoos. I spread them out on the mat and demonstrate the three-dimensional effect of the holograms. Lots of 'oohs' and 'ahs' from the appreciative audience. This, in turn, attracts the others, and before long the entire community has surrounded us, craning necks, trying to steal a glimpse of the magic I am unveiling.

The holograms are passed from hand to hand, and on several occasions I have to demonstrate the importance of viewing them at the correct angle in order to gain full effect from the light. The chief nods knowingly. Next come the tattoos. This needs demonstrating, so I ask Josephine to translate the steps involved. First I need to borrow a child. (Josephine translates.) No volunteers. Just shy looks. I smile, try to make fun of it all. A couple of children slide their buttocks back from the mat in response to my overtures.

Intervention by the boss: he points at his son, who reluctantly slides forward. Now I need some water. To speed up things, I use some left-over tea from my glass and apply it to the child's arm. He slides back. I follow. Before he can take off altogether, I manage to slap the image on the wet patch and hold it there firmly, watching the boy's terrified face. It's a long thirty seconds in total silence, but when I peel off the backing paper the butterfly tattoo shines brightly amidst the gasps of the audience. The boy's face turns into a huge smile and, excited, he jumps up and proudly shows off his new status symbol.

Now the rush is on – a flurry of little hands pushes towards me. I am about to start distributing decals of colourful birds, bright flowers and skulls with crossed bones (the most popular item), when Josephine takes hold of my wrist and stops me.

'Don't. Give them to the headman. It's his role to distribute them later, in a fair manner.'

I hand over the stash and he shakes my hand.

'John, do you have any more tattoos? For my kids?' Loh doesn't want to miss out on the freebies.

'Yes, plenty more in my backpack. Remind me tonight, when we get back to Rumah Apan.'

Just then, there's a long, drawn-out call from the river. We all rush to the side of the veranda where a man is climbing up the notched log, breathless and yelling something that sets the crowd off into wild whoops. He is a messenger, sent ahead to bring news of the victorious warriors' imminent return. The gongs resume their beat and a procession of women emerges from the headman's apartment, clad in their best sarongs and decked out like Christmas trees in their finest jewellery. They stop near the top of the ladder and watch the war party as it arrives in several canoes.

A tall warrior jumps ashore and, waving a *parang* over his head, shouts a few words that send everyone cheering and yelping once more. The heads, as far as I can make out from the distance, are kept in a large basket, which an old man cradles in his arms like a precious inheritance. In measured steps, he walks up the riverbank to a spot where several tall poles have been planted in the ground. He stops and puts down the basket.

Another pensioned-off warrior detaches himself from the onlookers. He is frail-looking but still cuts an imposing figure in his monkey-hair war coat and a solidly-carved headhunter's sword tied around his waist. Someone brings him a chicken – the first of many to be despatched into the eternal pecking grounds that day. One swift blow of the *parang* and its blood is drizzled over the new-arrival heads, to the chant of the old man.

For part two of the ceremony, the blackened skulls are placed in a spot of honour at the top of the poles, affording them a prime vista of the women below who have now begun to chant a welcome song.

'It's an age-old epic called *nimang*,' explains Josephine, 'chanted in honour of the heroes.'

'Which heroes – the ones with or without heads?'

'I'm not sure. But it's very moving.'

The returning warriors have seated themselves in a circle around the poles, looking very smug and lapping up the attention lavished upon them as part of their temporary hero status. Ear-piercing squeals behind me indicate that a sacrificial pig has just met its fate as a provider of omens. The chanting women are now breaking into a slow-shuffling dance, while the men retrieve the heads from their perches, placing them one-by-one into traditional blankets held by the dancers.

Led by the headman's wife, the women ascend the longhouse ladder where the heads are welcomed by the chicken-waving chief, who drips yet more blood over them as they pass by. The procession eventually comes to a halt in front of the elaborately constructed *pandong*, where the heads are placed on a beautiful mat on top of the altar, surrounded by various offerings of fruit, rice, *padi* seeds and a selection of everyday household implements.

More chicken-waving takes place before the warriors approach the altar and place their *parangs* in a circle around it. Once more the flute of death takes up its haunting spell and everyone returns outside, where the pig has been dissected ready for the omen-giving liver inspection. This, I am told, is an important ritual, for if the signs are favourable, harvests will be plentiful in the coming year. ('Harvests' is obviously a concession to modern times, replacing the word 'heads'.)

Another member of the old guard sprinkles rice over the involuntary organ donor and then extracts its liver, putting it on a plate where he examines its most minute details. The verdict is favourable and calls for celebration, which ensues without further prompting. Snacks are brought out and each child is handed a can of Coca-Cola. Everyone seems in a great mood, enjoying the frequent breaks in the proceedings as much as the ceremonies themselves.

I want to take a closer look at the skulls and start circling the altar in a nonchalant manner, smiling at people here and there and casually lighting a cigarette. There are seven heads on the small mat and I am surprised at how small they all look, until I discover that none of them have their jaws attached. Someone nudges me, interrupting my inspection. '*Makai.*' The headman's wife holds a bowl of rice in front of me and motions towards the heads. Josephine comes to the rescue.

'She wants you to feed the heads.'

'What?'

'It's a great honour, reserved for important people. Just take a few grains of rice and place them in the openings.'

'Like what, the eyes?'

'Any openings: eyes, nose, ears.' She looks at me sideways, obviously relishing my unease. I take a few grains and start dropping them in the various orifices in front of me, making sure that everyone gets his share.

The bowl is handed around among other people who have now joined us and the process is repeated with many variations: some people are adding their own little treats and titbits to the rice, others are supplying drinks (poured straight down the eyes). One fellow puts a lit cigarette up a particularly blackened skull's nose, giving it a grotesque appearance.

Back on the mat I try to reconcile some obvious contradictions in my mind: are these rituals designed to respect and honour the guest-skulls, or are they a form of mockery? Josephine seems a little unsure herself.

'I think it's a bit of both. On the one hand, they are scared to offend the spirits and so they treat the skulls with genuine respect. On the other hand, it's a show of superiority: the heads are now at the mercy of the victorious longhouse inhabitants, and they better remember it!'

I look at Loh for his opinion on the subject, but he couldn't care less: he is trying to work out how much these heads would fetch with the tourist trade back in Singapore.

Break over, the ceremonies resume to the beat of muffled drums. More flapping chickens are brought in. (Chicken soup tonight. Definitely.) As the first one meets its maker, one of the warriors holds it up high above the heads of the dancers and proceeds down the line of chorus girls to dab spots of blood on their foreheads and throats. The dancing gets more animated as the long line of women moves its way up and down the veranda, their mournful chant periodically accentuated by shrill cries and grimaces thrown at the heads.

Loh has nodded off in a corner, his head propped up against the wall. Near him, small groups have formed on the floor. The older men watch the passing parade with grave, solemn expressions on their faces. But some of the younger ones are chatting away, seemingly oblivious to the conga-line of village belles that weaves its way past them. To them, the rituals are probably no more than a form a Hallowe'en – a quaint tradition that is amusing rather than spiritually inspiring.

As the morning wears on, the same pattern of ritual, followed by refreshments, followed by yet more ceremonies is repeated over and over. Having apparently placated the spirits of the visiting heads, the focus is now shifting towards another important player: the Brahminy kite, which I am told is the Kayan's most sacred omen bird. To ensure that he gets his share of the spoils, the longhouse braves are now preparing sacrificial poles by shaving off the bark to the rhythm of a single bass gong. As the *parang* blades reach the bottom of the poles, the beat of the gong is joined by muted thumps of several drums, which momentarily stop when the last piece of bark has been removed. The wood shavings are collected and decoratively arranged around the poles. Some are tied together in attractive curls and placed near the bird-feeding platforms at the top.

All this, according to Josephine, is serious business, as the handling of offering poles is spiritually as dangerous as the removal of heads from their places of honour in the rafters.

Another break while the meat offerings are being cooked. But it seems that the humans, too, are about to be fed: when we return to the house, chickens, pigs and other local fare has been placed in front of each door, ready for cooking. While the women attend to the preparation of our midday meal, the first pieces of roasted meat are extracted from the fire and taken to the poles so that the ceremony can be completed.

A brief incantation conveying the longhouse's needs to the omen bird, and the pieces of meat are spiked on small skewers that protrude from the poles. As a grand finale, the piece of bamboo on which the meat was roasted is split in half lengthways and both parts are thrown in the air. To ensure a favourable omen, one piece has to land on its side, the other with the curved side facing down.

The first throw is unsuccessful, but no one seems perturbed. Apparently the dice are loaded in favour of the players: three tosses are allowed. Throw number two produced the desired result and there's instant jubilation. In the midst of the excitement, a young boy calls out, pointing at the sky. A kite soars in circles, high above the valley. It's going to be a great year. The troops pile back into the building and out comes the longhouse aperitif while we wait for lunch. Jugs of *borak* appear as if by magic, and it does not take long before merry-making takes over from the strains and rigours of prescribed ritual observance.

Loh is having fun. 'This is my favourite part, *lah!*'

Lunch is finally ready around three o'clock. By now, the braves and their families are well and truly ready for it, systematically working their way through everything that is set before them.

The skulls look down from the rafters, silently observing the feast in their honour. I need to go for a walk. These Sunday brunches are starting to get to me. But there's no relief from food outside the house either, where the locals are hanging out around the barbecue, looking for any bonus handouts that could come their way. Pieces of meat, skewered on to length of green bamboo, are roasting in the open fire. Someone is arranging small squares of cooked meat neatly on platters, and cups of *borak* are lined up in a row on the ground.

'*Makai! Makai!*' the chef calls out as he spots me. But I decline, patting my full stomach in a universal sign that says politely, 'I'm full!'

A sleepy Josephine emerges from the house.

'Did you have a good nap?'

'Yes, but I think we should get going soon, before it gets too dark.'

We eventually find Loh and our boatman, but only promises of more partying back at Rumah Apan lets us tear the protesting pair away from their drinking cronies. As we silently glide down the river, the fire ashore blazes up briefly, revealing a sea of shiny dark faces. In the background the sound of the gongs gradually submerges. For a moment I close my eyes and see a row of smoke-blackened human heads, their fleshless faces returning my gaze. One of them has a cigarette dangling from an ear.

There's a hush over the longhouse. Nothing stirs, not a sound. It's as if Rumah Apan has entered an enchanted state.

'Where is everyone?' I ask.

Josephine shrugs her shoulders. Quietly, as if to avoid disturbing the peace, we enter the longhouse. A loud burp greets us from somewhere in the interior. Josephine nudges me.

'Did you bring your torch?'

'Yes.' These trekking shirts have a pocket for everything. The beam of the torch reveals a veritable battlefield. Sleeping bodies sprawled out everywhere. Empty bottles and upturned cups strewn across the floor. Flies feasting on scraps of food. A few people wandering around in a daze.

'Party's over, *lah*.' Loh seems disappointed and goes to look for his family. Entering our apartment we find the large-screen television snowing and hissing. Josephine, stepping over several bodies, finds the controls in someone's hand and turns it off.

'What now?' I ask.

'Let's go to the kitchen. You hungry?'

'Nope. But coffee would be OK.'

We find Uncle, Auntie and two of their daughters sitting around the table.

'Hello, did you have a good time?'

We recount the day's events.

'And what about you?' Josephine asks, 'Looks like everyone is pretty exhausted!'

'Oh, just a break. Too much dancing and celebrating. Except for Jodi (he points at one of the daughters). She is never too tired to dance. Too much energy, *lah*!'

Jodi smiles. She's a pretty little thing and I've noticed her before, when her gracious dance movements spread a hush over the otherwise noisy audience. One day she's going to be a longhouse star.

'*Selamat malam!*' Loh has found his family.

'*Selamat malam*, Erwin, come in! You want coffee?'

'Any tea?'

Auntie gets up and puts the kettle on. It's a pleasant little gathering, and a nice way to relax after our day with the smiling heads.

'So tomorrow you are leaving us,' comments Uncle. 'So soon! You can't stay a little longer? For the rest of the *gawai*?'

Josephine explains that my trip is coming to an end and that I have to catch a flight from Kuching at the weekend.

'Until then, we'll stay in Belaga and drop in on a few nearby longhouses to see my relatives. I think John will enjoy that. Nice and easy.'

'Uh, uh,' volunteers Loh, 'a longhouse pub crawl.'

'A what?' asks Uncle.

'Australian tradition, *lah*. Go from place to place to drink. Like a progressive drinking party!'

I brace myself against that thought. Surely they're not serious!

'No, no,' interjects Josephine, 'some of our longhouses are Christian. Dry. No drinking.'

Phew.

'You had your bath yet?' Uncle gets up to fetch his sarong. I do likewise.

Jodi is talking to the fish in the lotus pond. A lone *sape* resumes its strumming on the veranda. Revellers are starting to emerge. I think I'll stay here and soak in the pond for a while.

A farewell committee has gathered down by the river. Uncle and his tribe. A sleepy Loh (minus family). The chief himself. And a dozen or so other people, many of whom I don't recall having ever seen before. They're all sitting in a line on a big tree-trunk that is half-submerged in the mud.

Uncle stirs, nudging the person on his right to move up. The line moves along a couple of spaces and I take up the vacancy, with Josephine squeezing in between us. The chief, without looking at me, starts to talk half in Kayan, half in English. From what I can piece together, he is thanking us for visiting his longhouse and, in particular, he wishes me a safe journey back to my far-away home. The others nod and mumble in agreement.

I get the feeling I should be replying and get off the log to face them, forgetting about the mud. But I keep my cool, steadying myself as my boots keep sinking lower and lower while I say my words of thanks. There's laughter as I extract my feet with a squelch each. Back on my perch I find a small parcel of food tied up in a banana leaf.

'It's from the lady over there,' says Josephine, pointing at an amazingly tattooed old woman. I thank her in Malay and she replies, 'OK, *lah*!' pleased as punch with the opportunity to show off her English.

Suddenly it strikes me that in a couple of hours I'll be in Belaga, where the local time will be eleven o'clock and my watch will have to be set forward a thousand years. I'll miss my longhouse friends, their extraordinary way of life and the awesome beauty of the jungles that surround them. But I don't have time to wallow in nostalgia, because the roar of an engine signals the approach of our Express Boat.

A hurried final goodbye, the chief passes my backpack to a deckhand and three people give my buttocks a shove as I attempt to clamber up the bow towards the under-foot safety of a steady deck. A long toot, the mud churns up under the water as the engines are thrown into reverse, and we're off, heading full-speed up the river. In the distance I can see the farewell committee slowly sauntering up the narrow path towards the house. ready to resume their seasonal frivolities in due course.

A sudden swerve and I nearly lose my backpack. The boat is jam-packed with holiday crowds, and holding on to the half-open window of the cockpit I look around for a place to safely stow my pack. There's standing room only. I ask the man next to me whether he could pass it to someone below deck, but he doesn't understand. The captain, noticing my dilemma, asks me to pass it through the window. He gives it to his co-pilot who is busy scoffing a bowl of noodles and seems to resent the interruption. With one hand he passes my pack back to a deckhand who manages to hang it on a hook behind the cockpit door.

Josephine has made herself a little nest on a coil of anchor ropes and is fast asleep. Standing up on the narrow side-ledge of the boat affords me a prime vista of the river's ever-changing scenery. In spite of the cramped conditions with the wind blowing through my hair, I can't imagine a better place to be right now. Fragments of song, accompanied by a lone drum, periodically drift towards me whenever the wind changes direction. Someone's getting into party mode up on the roof.

We stop several times along the way. But instead of people getting off, more passengers are taken on at each stop, dashing my hopes of finding a seat. By the time we approach the Belaga pier, people are hanging from the rafters.

chapter thirteen

belaga

A real jetty awaits us. No mud. No slippery logs. Instead, a long set of concrete steps leading up to the town. It feels strange being back in 'civilisation', a fact I am reminded of when I get my first glimpse of the lively bazaar on the other side of the village square. Shops! I can buy anything I want. Drinks. Cigarettes. Laundry detergent. Toothpaste.

My pace quickens, and in an unexpected role reversal Josephine calls out for me to slow down.

'Take it easy, John, we've got two days here!'

But her plea comes too late: my searching eyes have spotted a coffee shop and I head straight for it, before she gets a chance to object. By the time she catches up with me I've ordered coffee, bought a copy of the *Borneo Post* and stocked up on cigarettes.

'Didn't you want to check in at our hotel first?' she asks.

'Never mind, we've got two days here!'

She laughs at my little jibe and resigns herself to my outlook on life (which, by the way, she shares whole-heartedly). Coffee turns into brunch as we both find it too hard to resist the smells of fried *mee goreng* and steaming hot buns. This is the life. Covered in mud, we sit here, enjoying the passing parade. Josephine, in particular, relishes the attention she is getting from the constant flow of people who stop to chat with her. The lady seems to know everyone in town.

Belaga is truly a microcosm of the *ulu*, as is evident from the faces of people in the street. The diversity of the up-river tribes is obvious; there are Kayan women with colourful beaded baby-carriers on their backs; Kenyahs with their intricately woven conical hats; Lahanans with *parangs* strapped to their jeans – even a sprinkling of Iban who, for one reason or another, seem to have erred this far up-river. Most of them are here to trade, stock up on supplies for the *gawai*, or attend official business at one of the government offices. But once chores have been completed, the coffee houses become the focus of activities, with time whiled-away meeting up with old friends, exchanging gossip and catching up on local news.

'So where's our hotel?' I ask Josephine, who is lolling back in her chair.

'Upstairs.'

'What, here? Above the coffee shop?'

'Yes.'

I pay the bill, sling my pack over one shoulder and follow Jo up the stairs. Traditionally, 'shophouses' such as this have an upstairs residence where the owners live. But in this case, the family home has been converted into a half-star hotel. There's a desk in the narrow hallway, with a television blaring away in the corner. We remove our shoes and wait. My bare feet feel cold on the worn old linoleum. Josephine rings the bell on the desk. A rotund man appears, stops in his tracks and then surges forward in a flying tackle, embracing Josephine enthusiastically.

'This is my cousin,' she says, planting a loud kiss on his bald patch. The commotion brings out the rest of the clan –

a couple of small children and two middle-aged women (one with and one without the fashionable earlobes) – who promptly set out to make our 'welcome' coffee. I am treated as guest of honour.

'You get room number one, Mr John – just over there,' says cousin, pointing at the door. (A superfluous gesture, given that there are only three rooms.)

I open the creaky door and am instantly confronted by a blast of icy, gale-force wind from the air-conditioning unit someone has jammed into the window frame. I switch it off, drop my pack on the floor and let myself fall back on the bed, bouncing up and down a couple of times. A real bed, with mattress, pillows and a wool blanket. The room is very clean, but I don't much go for the green-on-green colour scheme, which has been delicately accented with pastel-blue door frames. The plastic flowers on the bedside table add a quaint touch of pink to the otherwise bare room.

First order of the day – a shower. Wash off the mud. Shave. I step behind the plastic curtain to find an amazing contraption with handles, knobs and several handwritten instructions: 'TURN HERE. PUSH BUTTON AFTER. DON'T TOUCH. PULL – HOT WATER.' It looks like Willy Wonka's Chocolate Factory. I stand there for a moment, trying to work out the technicalities and finally start pulling, pushing and turning, until a stream of cold water gushes out in several short bursts and then stops. I wait. Nothing. So I repeat the intricate procedures and eventually establish an equilibrium that maintains the flow of water, which periodically changes colour from dark brown to light green. (But I give up on the hot water, which doesn't seem to be forthcoming no matter which knobs or handles I turn.)

This is great. I feel like launching into my shower Pavarotti number, but this could cause alarm among the locals so I just stand there, soaking up all the wet I can get from the small hose fitting that dangles above me and doubles up as a shower rosette. When I finally emerge from my waterworks I find that a sizeable puddle has gathered outside the shower, flooding a good part of the floor. But there's a mop leaning against the little 'FOR DRYING FLOOR' sign on the wall. Thoughtful hosts, Josephine's folks.

A knock on the door. 'John? Are you all right?'

I must have stayed in the shower longer than I thought.

'Yes, yes. I'm coming!'

More coffee.

'So what do you want to do this afternoon?'

'Oh look, I'm just happy to hang around town. Go for a walk. Sit and have a cold beer.'

'Good. Then I can go and visit my family. But don't forget to go and register with the police!'

The red tape. I had forgotten all about that. We finish our coffee and Josephine takes off.

'See you tonight – we have dinner at a Chinese restaurant. My auntie's,' she says proudly.

I change into my comfortable trekking sandals, hang my boots out to dry on the shower contraption, and throw myself into the throng of people in the street. All the action is right outside my hotel, concentrated in a single concrete block that boasts about a dozen shops and a handful of restaurants. Beyond that, there's not much to this little frontier town. To one side of the square lie several sleepy government buildings. On the other side, an ancient longhouse that once was the original bazaar, established by Chinese traders at the beginning of the century.

All cashed-up with my original stash of money I never had a chance to spend in the bush, I'm ready to hit the shops. But I find little use for plastic brooms, shiny satin bras, jumbo-sized bags of sweets, chewing tobacco, shotgun cartridges or canisters of kerosene. One shop looks interesting, though – handicrafts and antiques. A little bell tinkles as I push the bead curtains aside. None of the Chinese staff seem particularly interested in me, offering only cursory sideways glances over the chopsticks that mechanically work their way back and forth between bowl and mouth. I say hello and receive half-hearted nods from a couple of dripping chins. The place looks amazing and I start browsing. On the walls, exquisitely-carved *parangs* and fierce-looking masks. Shelves full of carved boxes, tobacco containers and small statues. A whole crate with blowpipes, neatly standing in a row. Woven mats. Monkey skulls. Boar's tusks. Necklaces. Earrings. The place is fantastic, and a quick glimpse at price tags tells me that bargains are to be had. Must come back and have a proper look around.

Outside, the population has just doubled with the arrival of an Express Boat. I'd love a cold drink, but am reluctant to start fighting the crowds that are congesting the open shop fronts. Maybe this is a good time to get my passport stamped. The administrative centre consists of a small school, the *polis* station and a *klinik*. I head straight for the cop shop where a lone, bored-looking officer slowly taps a pencil between his straightened-out blank notepad and the neatly-placed cap near the edge of the desk. A rotating fan in the corner of the room partially lifts the top page of his pad every time it blows towards the desk, gently replacing it on its way back. The policeman gets up.

'Hello, how can I help you?' Big smile.

'Hi, I'm here for a permit.'

'Ah, please sit down.' He pulls up a folding metal chair. I hand him my passport.

'Mr John. Yes. You been to Lusong Laku, yes? With the Penan?' He smiles.

How the hell did he know that? He slowly goes through the pages of my passport, stopping at every stamp that looks halfway interesting. He stops at the Thai stamp, turning it upside-down to try and decipher it. When he reaches the last page, he rifles through the passport once more for good measure. Without a word he gets up, extracts a Permit Application Form from a filing cabinet and hands it to me.

'Please fill this in.'

First question: Where do you plan to travel beyond Belaga? This throws me: I have already done the travelling beyond Belaga. My initial permit entitled me to travel beyond Kapit. But somewhere along the line, I had crossed the district border and entered Belaga through the backdoor. I explain this to the man. He contemplates the situation for a minute, then says, 'Nevermind, *lah*. Just complete the form.'

So I put down: 'Linau and Balui Rivers.' This seems to satisfy him. He makes several photocopies of the permit, stamps the original and hands it to me.

'No problem. Enjoy your trip.'

'Thank you. Er, my passport?'

'It's OK, we keep it here. When you come back from your trip, we return it to you.'

This is getting complicated.

'But I'm not going anywhere. I am staying in Belaga and leaving for Kuching on Sunday.

'It's all right. Only for your own safety. Come back on Sunday to collect it.'

'I am leaving on the early Express Boat, at six o'clock.'

'Come back tomorrow morning.'

There's no point in arguing. I fold the permit that entitles me to stay in Belaga and beyond, for half a day, put it in my shirt pocket and say goodbye with a smile. He smiles back and returns to his pencil-tapping.

Outside, a couple of kids are laying in wait for me. They had been watching us through the window.

'Hello Johnny! You speak English? We learn English in school!'

I start to chat, but this proves too much for them and they take off. As I walk past the *klinik* I notice that the waiting room is nearly empty. A good time to stock up on some Vitamin C, which may help ward off the 'air-con' cold I can feel coming on. The man at the dispensary greets me with a smile.

'Mr John. What would you like?'

'How did you know my name?'

'You been to Lusong Laku. With Josephine!'

Small town. Everyone knows your business. He hands me a jumbo-sized bottle of vitamins – compliments of the government's subsidised medical scheme. When I return to the bazaar, the crowds have started to disperse and I head down to the old longhouse, where I find myself a table at the 'Hock Mee Café Restaurant'. Two spindly legs protruding from under a pair of baggy shorts approach me.

'You want *bir*? *Kopi*?'

'Is the beer cold?'

'I put ice.'

Ice blocks in the beer. But it's better than drinking it warm. Mr Hock has obviously been visited by the Carlsberg Beer promotional team: his place is decked out with bunting, flags, tent cards and wall posters proclaiming Carlsberg the 'Official Beer of the *Gawai*'.

The beer arrives: two bottles. Mr Hock slaps them on the table, pulls up a chair and joins me. I lift mine up and say, 'To the *gawai*.' He responds with a simple, 'OK.' While we drink, he sizes me up – a potential sale looming on the horizon of his mind.

'You want Carlsberg cap? You buy one box of *bir* and I give you cap. My present for you.'

He gets up to fetch a sample cap, which he puts on my head.

'Very nice. For you!'

An official *gawai* cap, just what I've always wanted. But I have no use either for the cap or the case of beer that comes with it, and I tell him so. He looks disappointed. To take the sting out of my refusal, I order another two bottles for us to share. He likes that.

While he gets the beer, I head for the door marked '*tandas*'. Much to my surprise, it's a Western-style toilet, complete with the usage instructions of two self-explanatory signs: the first one (with a big cross through it) shows a person squatting with feet positioned on the seat; the second one (with a tick next to it) demonstrates the proper sit-down method.

Returning to my table, I find that more guests have arrived – a bunch of boisterous Kenyahs who order just about everything on the menu, plus lots of beer to wash it all down.

While Hock's attention is diverted to better things than my solitary beer, I get a chance to enjoy my drink quietly. The building is interesting and still bears the marks of its longhouse origins. Except that it is now two storeys high, with living quarters shifted upstairs to make room for shops on the ground level. Overlooking the river, it sits on a narrow dirt road opposite a quaint Malay *kampong* – a traditional village of colourful wooden houses surrounded by palm trees and tropical gardens. Two women in sarongs walk down the narrow path, carrying large earthenware jars on their heads and swaying their hips slowly to the rhythm of their steps.

I finish my beer (and Mr Hock's, who seems to have forgotten about it and is now busy demonstrating his 'official *gawai* caps' to the new arrivals) and leave money on the table. As I walk out he waves to me, but immediately returns to the more pressing business at hand.

The *kampong* starts just across the road and I decide to take a stroll through it. It's only small and devoid of any sign of life, except for a gibbering monkey chained to a fishing boat in front of one of the houses. He goes quiet as I approach, eyeing me with great interest, only to resume his chatter after I have passed.

And that's it: the end of the road. Keen to explore the rest of the town, I cut through a field behind the houses and end up at Belaga's pride and joy: the airport, a stretch of grass barely bigger than the average school playground. A lone water-buffalo ambles across it, unperturbed by the numerous 'KEEP OFF AIRSTRIP' signs.

I head back past a few scattered buildings behind the bazaar, where a new single-storey concrete building announces itself in neon lights as the 'Belaga Food Court'. Its five restaurants are empty, their owners eyeing me in hopeful anticipation from behind the counters.

When I turn the corner into the main shopping strip, I am confronted by the Carlsberg promotions team.

'Hello, Mister!' The three girls block my way.

'We have a special promotion: free *gawai* T-shirt for you when you buy just one case of beer!'

The T-shirts are rather nice (especially on the girls), featuring a colourful tribal design specially commissioned for this year's festive season, I am told. I am tempted to buy, but explain that I would have little use for a case of beer as I am leaving town on Sunday. The girls persist, trying to convince me that I would have a good time with so much beer.

We argue back and forth in a friendly manner. Finally, one of the girls pulls out a T-shirt from her Carlsberg sportsbag and hands it to me.

'OK, *lah*, you keep it anyway. Our present for you.'

'Thank you. But I can't accept this. You will get into trouble.'

'No, no. Is good business. If *orang putih* wears our T-shirt, everyone else will want one too.'

Now the tables have been turned. I quietly reason that some 'official *gawai* beer' would make a welcome gift when we visit Josephine's family tomorrow. I buy a case. The girls are delighted. Score: Carlsberg ONE, John NIL.

Back at the inn, Josephine is waiting for me. She is wearing a 'Guinness official *gawai* baseball cap'. Now we have two types of beer to share with the relatives.

Knock on the door.

'Get up, sleepy-head. Is nine o'clock already!'

Boy, did I sleep. First night back on a real mattress. And no need to go down to the river to bathe. My Willy Wonka shower contraption is just three easy steps away. I let the water cascade down over my hair, thinking of the day ahead – a couple of visits to nearby longhouses, without cumbersome boots or backpack! This is real indulgence. Clean T-shirt (official limited *gawai* edition). Great shave. I'm raring to go.

The cousins have whipped up some *mee goreng* and a pot of hot coffee is bubbling away on the stove. The 'reception' area looks like a dentist's waiting room, with the family sitting in a row along one wall, Josephine chatting to a couple of young guys on the opposite side.

'Sit down, John. Have some breakfast.'

I join Josephine's team at the opposite wall.

'Hello. You from Australia, ya?' The man on Josephine's left lights up and offers me one of his cigarettes.

'Yes, that's right,' I reply with the obligatory smile.

'You on holidays here?'

'Yes.'

'You seen much of our country?'

I recount some of our travels while Josephine excuses herself and goes to her room. The man and I are enjoying a lively chat about travel, Malaysia, advertising and a host of other subjects. His friend just listens. Josephine reappears.

'We better go now, my cousin is waiting for us.'

And thus ends the little conversation. Josephine has regained her fast pace, hurrying to get down to the jetty where our boat is tied up. Her cousin has brought the family and a few of his cronies.

'Ready?' he says with a big smile. And off we go. We barely reach the middle of the river when Josephine asks, 'What did the police want?'

'The police? What police?'

'The two men who were talking to you.'

Perplexed, I reassure her that I don't have the faintest clue why they were there.

'You don't have any drugs? Problems with your passport?'

'No, not at all.' (Although the passport, which shows my place of birth as Switzerland, may have something to do with it. Perhaps they're still a bit touchy about the Swiss since Bruno Manser gave them the run-around.)

The others have gone quiet and I mentally go over the conversation I had with the Men in Black. But I can't think of anything I said that could have been incriminatory in any way. Suddenly I remember my passport! Considering the mood of my fellow passengers, this may be a bad time to request an about-turn, but I have no choice: by the time we get back tonight, the police station will be closed. To my surprise, however, no one seems annoyed by my forgetfulness. The boat swerves, returns to the jetty and the party-goers cheerfully call after me to hurry up.

'We're wasting good drinking time, *lah!*'

There are no complications when I collect my passport and the officer wishes me, again, an enjoyable trip. We cast off once more, leaving the town in the care of the fantastic dragon-dogs that sit on top of the tombs on the opposite riverbank, keeping a watchful eye on this tiny government outpost. A paunchy man at the back of the boat starts beating a laptop drum and softly begins to hum a tune in a falsetto voice. One by one the others join in and a song gradually evolves, barely audible over the din of the engine. The man next to the drummer decides to take the ambience a little further, by tearing open a carton of beer and distributing cans of Guinness to everyone.

Soon the police incident is forgotten and our merry little party travels on, singing and waving at other boats on their way to partyland. As we progress further up-river, traffic becomes more intense. Everyone, it seems, is out to visit friends and relatives, boats loaded to the gunwales with baskets, cartons of beer and the odd terrified chicken.

Longhouses glide past thick and fast along this stretch of the river. Unlike in other parts of Sarawak, where communities tend to be fifty or even a hundred kilometres apart, the settlements north of Belaga are heavily concentrated in one small area. Josephine volunteers a running commentary along the way.

'This one is Kenyah. That one Kayan. A Sekapan community. Xayan settlement. Queen Elizabeth stayed in this one.' (Is she serious?)

Her family's longhouse appears in the distance and she points it out, excitement clearly evident on her face. To our left, two longboats, each crewed by half-a-dozen women in large conical hats, are hugging the banks, following the shade of over-hanging foliage. Josephine calls out to them with a great deal of animation. They look around in unison and start waving back.

'My aunties,' she explains.

'What, all of them?'

'Don't be silly. Just five of them.'

Our boat slows down and we travel the rest of the way alongside the longhouse ladies.

The well-constructed jetty is a hive of activity and we find it hard to get a parking spot. On the downstream side, several longboats have tied up against each other, forming a large raft that reaches almost midstream. Ahmad, our boatman, skillfully docks against them and we make our way to the jetty, hopping from one hull to another. I notice that the cousins have left the beer back in our boat and offer to go and retrieve it.

'Shh.' The drummer's friend puts a finger against his lips, 'No beer. Dry house,' the meaning of which sinks in when I spot a large wooden crucifix above the entrance.

'Hello, welcome everybody!' Jo's (immediate) family is lined up on the garden path and her father urges us to come in, putting an end to the hugging rituals that go on around me.

'John,' he says, turning to me, 'it's nice to meet you. Our daughter has told us so much about you already.'

'Nothing bad, I hope.' (Standard reply in such situations.)

He sniggers, 'No, only that you keep falling off logs!' He has an outgoing personality and exudes warmth and friendliness. I immediately take to him. 'How long will you stay with us?'

I refer him to his daughter, who gently breaks the news: we have a busy schedule and can only stay a couple of hours. He must be disappointed, but doesn't show it.

'It's OK, it's OK. We understand!' he says with a big smile.

His apartment is enormous. The family must be part of the aristocratic lot. The traditional rattan mats are spread out on the floor, and around them a collection of sofas and chairs covered in bright floral fabrics. Father pulls up an armchair and motions me to sit down, but I prefer to sit on the floor with the others.

In comes grandma, the beginning of a stream of uncles, aunties, cousins, brothers, sisters-in-law and variously-labelled other visitors. They all chat away merrily and simultaneously in Kayan, and I doubt that any one of them knows (or cares) what the other is saying. But they're evidently having a good time.

Overlooking his flock from a large black-velvet painting on the wall is Jesus, smiling good-naturedly. The painting next to him depicts a local interpretation of the nativity scene: three tribal elders decked out in feathers and goat-hair war coats, bearing gifts of jungle produce. Next to the manger, a sarong-clad Virgin Mary, two water-buffalos and a lone tribal hunting dog look on.

Plates of snacks arrive and tea is being poured. But nobody touches any of the offerings until the head of the household has said grace. Animated discussions resume, as does the constant stream of visitors who are wandering in and out of the apartment in no apparent order. Father starts to hum a melody. Aha. The welcome song. But as the others join in and I pick up the odd English word, I quickly come to the realisation that the welcome song is in fact a hymn. Not knowing the words, and not wishing to offend, I just sway along, pretending to be engrossed in the moment. Grandpa seems to be having a good time. As he waves his hands from side to side, I can't help noticing the tattoos on his knuckles. According to my count, he has chalked up five heads.

The clash of beliefs, past and present, is an interesting one. Ostensibly, one could argue that there is an analogy between headhunting and soul hunting: the former is sudden and definitely terminal; the latter is more subtle, gradually wiping out entire cultures over a period of time. Both use different means (one violent, one crafty) to impose personal spiritual beliefs on others. Whether any of us have the moral right to do this is questionable.

Raja Brooke had definite views on the subject: he decreed that the indigenous people of Borneo had a basic human right to preserve their customs and beliefs (headhunting being the notable exception), and slammed a blanket ban on missionaries in his territory. However, as soon as a window of opportunity arose, following the demise of the White Rajas, the floodgates opened with a vengeance and missionaries of even the most obscure religions had a field day with conversions.

Ahmad the boatman nudges me, 'Do you understand any of this?'

I shake my head. Obviously bored by the hymns, he is looking for an escape and offers me a guided tour of the longhouse. We make our excuses, but the folks are too engrossed in their spirituality to notice our exit. Outside, Ahmad takes my hand and we walk past the longhouse sights at breakneck speed.

'This is the veranda. Rice storage huts. Gardens. Ancestral shrine.'

When we reach the small grove of banana trees behind the house, his hurried sightseeing tour suddenly makes sense: well concealed by the large leaves, we find a group of revellers seated around my depleted case of beer.

'Shh, not too much noise.' The drummer hands me a can. 'To the *gawai*!'

The rascals. Obviously the missionaries under-estimated the power of 'Carlsberg's official *gawai* sponsorship'. Slightly inebriated, we return to the house.

'Did you have a good look around? It's a nice longhouse, isn't it?'

Josephine is clearly proud of her ancestral home. And so she should be: it's an expansive riverside sprawl with beautifully cultivated gardens, a majestic, solid house with an abundance of carvings and art, and above all, warm and very hospitable inhabitants.

Morning tea is served on the veranda: marinated fried chicken wings accompanied by Chinese tea. More singing while we eat. This time it's pure Kayan. Funny, this, if it weren't for the holy pictures on the wall one could swear this was as traditional a longhouse as any other along the river. The people are oozing with hospitality. (Please have some more. Are you comfortable? Will you return to visit us? Can I get you a cold drink?)

Josephine is beaming with joy. It must be nice for her to be back home among her own folks. But her self-imposed duties as a guide dictate that we pack in as many longhouses as possible before I leave, and I almost feel as if I am dragging her away from her family. But she insists, 'It's OK. I'll be back tomorrow to spend a few days with them.'

This being the case, I have no objections at all when she suddenly packs us up, ready to move on. (Ahmad and the drummer show visible signs of relief as we all pile back into the boat, amidst shouted well-wishes from the shore.)

Next stop Rumah Aging. Also Christian. But not 'dry', as is apparent the moment we are greeted by a rowdy rabble of young guys who obviously have been at it since early morning. Josephine is immediately surrounded by the gang. And yes, my suspicions that she is related to half of them turns out to be correct.

'Come, we all celebrate, yes?'

They signal us to follow and break into loud cheers when they spot the case of Guinness that Ahmad is extracting from our stash. To the accompanying beat from the paunchy drummer, our little group of pilgrims ascends the hill.

The house itself is similar to Josephine's home, but perhaps not quite as lavishly fitted-out. There is just a touch of one-upmanship, however. I am told that one of its residents is actually a Member of the Sarawak Parliament! *Borak* seems to be flowing. Even the old ladies sitting in a circle next to the wall are sipping away as if they were having a social glass of sherry with the Vicar. They are a very traditional-looking bunch, with tattoos up to their elbows and heavy earrings that have gradually descended over the years. I find myself a spot on the floor.

'*Borak*? Guinness?' The latter sounds a far more enticing proposition. By the time the carton has made the rounds, it's empty. More drumming. This time from the nearby orchard, where a line of dancers is making its way towards us, singing and cavorting like a troupe of clowns in a circus parade coming to town. They treat us like long-lost friends and their exuberant welcome instantly makes us feel at home. The only problem is, as honoured guests we have to lead the charge in a succession of *borak*-downing competitions, which make my knees somewhat wobbly, a fact I discover when the boom of a solitary brass gong signals lunch and I attempt to get up.

The food has been laid out on a patch of grassy riverbank, under the shade of a few palm trees. The line-up at this eat-as-much-as-you-can smorgasbord of jungle fare looks daunting, but jockeying for a prime position is essential lest the last scraps of food disappear before the very eyes of any latecomer. The offerings look good: barbecued chilli chicken pieces, tiny fish baked in coconut shreds, rice laced with pineapples and fried onions, huge mounds of vegetables in all sizes and shapes, wild bananas and – the *pièce de résistance* – a huge pot of monkey stew with ginger, green papaya and slices of starfruit. I forego the latter.

The food disappears in minutes and the crowd gradually disperses, seeking the comfort of a well-earned siesta. We're ready to move on, too, but our departure is delayed by the pleas of 'one more for the road'. The beer has run out, so it's on to *borak*. Just one glass. Then just one more. Fortunately Josephine proves to be a tower of strength and resolutely shepherds us back to the boat.

The engine won't start. Ahmad keeps pulling the cord to produce a few gurgles, but eventually the outboard dies altogether. There's plenty of advice and helpful hints from bystanders, including several offers of *borak* to lubricate the boatman. But Josephine bravely fends them all off, leaving Ahmad to concentrate on his task. Another pull, and the motor springs into life. The shore crew unties the lines and we cast off to yet more adventures. The sun is merciless and the water surface shimmers under the heat. But when the trees start to sway, I am seriously starting to contemplate the possibility that the effect of the *borak* is beginning to take its course.

In the early afternoon heat I fall asleep and don't wake up until the engine stops and we drift towards a mooring log, where a new crew of longhouse braves awaits us. Same routine. Lots of slaps on backs, words of welcome, invitations to retreat to the veranda and partake of some traditional hospitality. The atmosphere here is slightly more sedate. The debris on the floor, the empty cups and plates, the looks on weary faces are tell-tale signs that the frivolities have reached a hiatus and that the residents are taking advantage of the temporary lull to recover over cups of coffee. Jo is catching up with a couple of old school friends. Ahmad looks bored, and the drummer is chatting up someone's wife.

'Where are you going from here?' A young man in Wrangler jeans and wearing a straw cowboy hat is looking for a lift down-river.

'Back to Belaga. Early start tomorrow,' replies Josephine. She looks at me and then gives me the news, gently at first.

'John? How would you like to take a different route back to Kuching?'

'A different route? Like where?'

'There is another way. Inland across the mountains and down to Tubau. It's a beautiful area and you can continue by Express Boat all the way to Bintulu on the coast. From there, direct flights to Kuching.'

This takes a minute to digest.

'What about time? Would that not take longer?'

'About the same as going down the Rajang.' Then she casually unveils part two of the plot, 'Ahmad will take you. He knows all the logging people and will be able to get a lift easily.'

'And what about you?'

Here comes the crunch. 'Oh, I can stay here, with my family. Saves me coming all the way back.'

She cocks her head and smiles pleadingly. That's a sudden change of plan. But I have already learned that schedules can chop and change at the drop of a hat around here. I smile back and say, 'I'm easy. Let's do that.'

The folks around us, who have been following the conversation with rapt attention, debate my decision and wholeheartedly approve of it. Someone produces a jug of *borak*. Just in case we want to seal the deal with a little celebration. Josephine picks up the jug and starts filling glasses. She raises hers and says, 'Here's to our farewell!'

I propose a toast to thank her. She proposes a toast to my safe trip home. And the glasses keep emptying. By the time we're ready to push on, I can feel the boat swaying under my feet. Not an unusual occurrence, except that we're on dry land. The goodbyes are swift and, under the circumstances, relatively painless. A few hugs and thank yous, and we board the boat, ready to resume our longhouse 'pub crawl'. I'm not sure how much more of this I can take.

Dusk has changed the colour spectrum into dark hues and an orange moon is emerging low over the treetops. A fly-past of rather large bats temporarily darkens the sky over us. Every now and then we pass longhouses where the festivities are in full swing, the sound of gongs and drums carrying far across the dark expanse of the river.

'Not long now,' says Ahmad, 'my house is just down there.' A few flickering lights amidst the thick vegetation give away its location. A continuing thumping in the distance has me puzzled. As we get closer my suspicions are confirmed.

'Disco!' yells Ahmad, and the drummer starts to nod his head to the beat. The guy with the cowboy hat is first out of the boat, swaying his hips and doing a passable John Travolta impersonation as he walks up the log. At the top, the settlement appears as two clear-cut cultural divisions. On my right an open shed, complete with generator-operated disco lights, an over-sized boom-box and a mosh-pit full of tribespeople gyrating to the beat. To the left, tradition lives on in the main house, where gongs and drums are beating away to a slower, more measured cadence.

Contrary to my expectations, Ahmad leads me to the 'oldies' area where he introduces me to his mixed family: his mother, a graceful young Malay, and his father, a traditional Kenyah. Our timing is good – dinner is about to be served. I badly need my stomach to be lined with some solid sustenance. The little rice wine gremlins are starting to cause some serious havoc down there. Fish soup. Fried noodles with chicken. Wild chillis. And a tumbler of brandy each.

On a ledge above the wall, a row of heads carefully tied together with lengths of rattan. For a moment I contemplate offering them my brandy. But I don't know whether it's the right thing to do. Perhaps later, when no one is looking.

The food is superb and the people delightful. But the best is yet to come; Ahmad's mum just got up to put the kettle on. Already I am starting to feel better. A lot better. Our drummer has taken up position behind one of the sets of gongs and is enjoying an impromptu jam session with the local band. I walk over to watch him.

'Would you like to try? You have to pay: one drink, *lah*!'

I oblige and fulfil his request with a glass of brandy.

'No, no! You drink also!'

Philosophical question: Comply and play the gongs, or sit on the floor shunned by the rest of the community? I play the gongs. Somehow *Waltzing Matilda* doesn't quite sound the same on these things. I hand the sticks back to the drummer. Some of the ragers from next door join us and take over the dance floor. It's fascinating to see how they can switch from bopping one moment to swaying gracefully the next to the tune of the *sape*.

'How come you're not at the disco?' I ask Ahmad.

'More drink here!' he replies, without batting an eyelid. We sit around, watch the floorshow. But he's getting fidgety.

'Let's go and have a look,' he suggests.

Feeling my second wind coming on, I join him. The place is bumping and jumping to Malay pop, and before we know it both of us have somehow been dragged right into the middle of the action. I'm dancing with two girls. Ahmad is dancing with the cowboy. But there's no set pattern. Partners switch around continuously, and by the time the DJ calls for a break, I've somehow ended up with the same two girls I started with. Now I feel like a drink. Ahmad concurs. We head back to the main house, where someone is performing a wild pig dance. The sweat is dripping from me and I long for a really cold Coke, but all I can get is lukewarm beer.

It's way past midnight when Ahmad suggests we start heading back to Belaga. Josephine's cousins and their friends register strong protests, but Ahmad is the designated driver and that's that. Reluctantly they stagger along behind us. The night is pitch-black. Our drummer friend has volunteered to play navigator, shining a large torch over the water in the hope of spotting any floating logs before we bump into them – or they bump into us. As we near a bend, he stands up to get a better view. Full of *borak*-infused bravado he starts to impersonate an Express Boat skipper about to challenge a colleague to a race, and promptly falls sideways, causing a huge splash as his rotund mass hits the water. Near him, the shine of the navigation light gets weaker and weaker as the torch slowly sinks to the bottom.

Ahmad brings the boat about and cuts the engine. Drunk, very wet, tribesman to starboard. The cousins bring him in while the rest of us lean heavily to the opposite side to maintain the boat's trim. We drift a little while the navigator recovers. Someone hands him a beer. Then the teasing starts and soon turns into a free-for-all. Open season on drummers. Someone fumbles under the stern seat in search for more beer as Ahmad resumes the merry journey. The darkness is total and I admire his skills as he weaves from one channel to another, picking up currents along the way. It occurs to me that it is going to be difficult for him to see oncoming logs without a torch. He doesn't: an almighty thump sends us all flying sideways. The engine cuts out.

Ahmad tries his magic. But no matter how much he pulls the string, the thing won't start.

Everything is still as we drift. A gentle gurgling where the river tries to find its way between some rocks is the only sound disturbing the silence. Although floating down a jungle river in the middle of the night could easily give cause for mild panic, my fellow travellers seem unperturbed.

The drummer is first to break the quiet with a slow, steady beat. The others join with a song and the party resumes.

It's a beautiful night. Above us, a million stars light up the tropical sky. And from deep in the jungle, the Kayan gods keep a watchful eye over a boat of drunken merrymakers drifting down the mighty Rajang. I lean back and close my eyes, wishing the moment could last forever. My dream, however, comes to an abrupt end when faint lights appear in the distance.

'Belaga!' shouts Ahmad. His announcement stops the singing. A few quick instructions and the crew springs into action. Four of them move over to the portside, causing the hull to lean precariously. But the manoeuvre has the desired effect as the boat is suddenly picked up by a fast current that steers us directly towards the lights, only to stop when we reach deeper waters, about a hundred metres from the landing.

Cousin number one takes the plunge and swims furiously, as if chased by a bunch of crocodiles (which, given where we are, is not as improbable as it may sound). He picks up a line from the jetty and throws it to us. Missed. It gently floats past us, barely out of reach. But cousin number two is quick off the mark; she jumps in the water, retrieves the line and passes it to Ahmad. At the other end, her brother starts pulling. Slowly the bow moves around and we begin inching our way back to civilisation.

The town is asleep, the only sound a faint buzzing from the flickering neon tubes at the government compound. Ahmad starts to sing. Cousin tells him to be quiet. I don't watch my step and fall into a monsoon drain. This amuses my companions. With twisted ankle I limp back to the hotel and realise that somewhere along the line I have lost my sandals. Never mind. It's been a good day.

It's nearly three in the morning. As we have to leave around five, it's hardly worth going to bed. The boys are starting to cook – supper or breakfast, whichever comes first. With Josephine gone, I'm the only guest in the place, which means noise restrictions no longer apply. Ahmad puts a tape in the cassette player and we eat to the mournful tunes of a lone *sape*. With about an hour left before our scheduled departure, I have a long, leisurely shower and change into clean clothes in order to look halfway respectable when I arrive in Kuching.

Fully packed and ready to go, we just have time for an early morning wake-up coffee. It's still dark when we arrive at the jetty, but already a crowd has gathered, waiting for the arrival of the early Express Boat to Sibu. For a moment I have second thoughts about taking the high road over the mountains, but for one last time, I trust Josephine's judgement. Ahmad brings up the boat, we load our gear and cast off, back into the river that saw us drifting about in an inebriated state just a few hours ago. Ashore, our friends are waving to the beat of the drummer.

The trip is only short – some twenty minutes and we arrive at a denuded patch of forest, where the beginning of the logging road ends up as pure mud by the river. So much for my clean clothes. I try to tread as carefully as possible, skirting around the edge of the quagmire. But our Landcruiser sits right in the middle of it and I have no choice but to stomp ahead, immersed halfway up to my knees.

Ahmad knows the driver and negotiates a favourable fare. There are only three elderly Kayan women aboard, so I manage to claim a nice little spot for myself, just behind the driver's cabin. More people arrive. We wait some more. By the time we're ready to hit the road, I count twenty-one people on the back of the truck – the last person precariously perched on the bumper bar, holding on to the tailgate with both hands. A jolt and a bump, and the familiar slips and slides begin as our driver launches us with unbridled enthusiasm into his imaginary cross-country rally.

My fellow passengers are starting to unpack their picnics. I am offered chicken, dried fish, parcels of rice, bananas. The guy hanging from the tailgate hands out cans of beer. But all I want to do is to go to sleep – which I do, all the way across the mountains. When I wake up, we're only half an hour from our destination, the road winding its way through the dense jungle of the lowlands. The food has gone. But my water bottle is full and I nearly empty it, trying to overcome the dry feeling in my throat. I think they call that a hangover.

The trading post of Tubau suddenly materialises out of the middle of the jungle. Tailgate-man jumps off even before we come to a sliding halt near the Express Boat jetty, clutching a beer in one hand, a plastic shopping bag in the other. Slowly the rest of us disembark, stretching limbs in all directions in an attempt to untie the knots in our bodies. Blood circulation restored to acceptable levels, we walk down to the small wooden bazaar.

chapter fourteen

kuching

Tubau is a sleepy little place that seems to exist in a time warp: a single dusty street, lined on one side with rickety shophouses. And that's it. At the far end of the covered wooden walkway, the one and only restaurant. The entire complement of passengers heads towards it, looking like a newly-arrived Japanese tour group. The only thing missing is a flag-waving guide up front.

With half an hour to kill before the arrival of our Express Boat, we indulge in a late lunch of stir-fried venison and fresh fish from the coast. A nice change from chicken and wild boar. The heat is intense and nothing stirs on the street, the scene reminiscent of a wild-west town at high noon.

Our boat arrives early and, as one, the group scrambles aboard. Most passengers head straight for the air-conditioned comfort below deck, but Ahmad and I opt for a comfortable spot up on the roof. A blast from the ship's horn, engines thrust into reverse – and we're off, dodging two heavily-laden Chinese *tongkangs* that are making their way towards the jetty, ready to unload their cargo of fresh provisions from Bintulu.

'A busy little river,' I remark, as we zip past huge timber barges, *tongkangs* with sacks of rice neatly stacked on their decks and longboats bringing jungle produce to Tubau.

'Yes, the Kemena River is the lifeline between the coast and inland settlements. Probably their only link with the outside world.'

The vegetation is dense, but in a pretty sort of way. There's none of the wild, overgrown tangle that reaches out from banks. Instead, neat little settlements are lining the river. Some are traditional longhouses with well-tended gardens and shrubs lining the paths up the hill. Others are Malay villages, their colourful timber houses built high up on stilts and partially hidden by stands of palm trees.

'These are mainly Melanau longhouses,' explains Ahmad. 'Coastal people. Used to be pirates. Now they mainly fish and trade.'

Their longhouses are mostly constructed with modern materials, but gigantic, carved poles, painted in the wildest of colours, proudly display their ancestral tradition. In looks and size, they are not unlike North American totem poles.

'This one here is Iban,' Ahmad points to a large settlement.

They're a long way away from their tribal heartland, it seems, but Ahmad tells me that many of the Iban tribes migrated towards the coast early last century, joining the flourishing pirate trade that yielded not only material rewards, but also much-coveted heads. As my mind wanders back to the wonderful hospitality-filled days I enjoyed as guest of the Iban, the skies open up, sending both Ahmad and I into a wild spin trying to find our ponchos. The pelting rain offers a welcome relief from the oppressive heat, but is only short-lived.

Within minutes, patches of blue sky appear once more and the sun resumes its relentless frying of my bare arms and legs.

One hour to go. Increasingly, Malay villages are starting to replace longhouses along the banks. River traffic increases to a degree where traffic lights could become a seriously viable proposition – something that crosses my mind as our speeding boat just misses a rice barge while trying to avoid an oncoming Express Boat. But the skippers seem unperturbed, tooting and waving as they pass each other.

Suddenly, we veer to the left and head for the mêlée of craft vying for space around the Bintulu landing. Traffic! Cars! I can hardly believe my eyes. Although the sum total of Bintulu numbers hardly more than a few blocks of concrete buildings, this is truly the big smoke after having become accustomed to jungle shelters and longhouse life. Slightly dazed, I step ashore, taking in the wonders of the modern world. Ahmad hails a taxi, which comes to a screeching halt in front of us.

'Airport!' he says. The driver requires no further prompting, leaving a cloud of dust behind as he takes off in wild pursuit of Bintulu Grand Prix honours. The airport is only two traffic lights away (the only traffic lights in town), and we arrive just as I finish manoeuvring my backpack into a position where my legs are relatively comfortable.

Enormous queues everywhere. When we finally make it to the front and look up to the man behind the elevated check-in counter, the news is not good.

'All flights full. You want stand-by?'

'What are the chances? I have an international connection to catch from Kuching.'

'It is holidays, *lah*. Everything full. Have extra flights scheduled already.' He throws his arms in the air in a gesture of despair. I go on stand-by and ask him to try his best. He smiles in resignation and says, 'OK, *lah*, I try,' nodding his head as if to say 'fat chance'.

Ahmad looks around for something to do. 'There!' He's found the restaurant. We order coffee and silently watch the hubbub around us. Under the *teksi* sign a queue of newly arrived passengers has formed. Four-wheel drive vehicles, with foreign oil company logos brightly painted on their doors, flit in and out of traffic, carrying safari-suited executives from Europe to urgent meetings.

The feeling that Bintulu is a boomtown that has recently been catapulted into the big time is inescapable. When Malaysia's biggest reserves of natural gas where discovered just offshore, the old fishing village turned into Las Vegas overnight – complete with neon lights, cinemas, a modern shopping complex and plush company offices in bland office buildings.

A garbled announcement over the PA. I head to the counter full of hope.

'Not yet. Go have more coffee.'

I do as I am told. On the way back I notice a large sign near the departure gate:

Notice. The following items and dangerous weapons must not be carried into the aircraft cabin: all types of pistol, shotgun, rifle, scissors, spear, knife, trident, blowpipe, dart, arrow, parang, sickle, chainsaw, ammunition and explosives. By Order – Director General of Civil Aviation, Malaysia.

You wouldn't find that kind of sign at Heathrow or JFK. I take a shot of it and return to our table. Understandably, Ahmad seems bored.

'Why don't you leave me here and go and see your family?' I suggest, 'I'll be all right.'

'Oh no, I get into trouble with Josephine. She told me I must wait until you are on the plane. Part of the deal,' he smiles.

Trying to reason with him proves fruitless. We order more coffee. After two more attempts at hassling the guy behind the counter, my luck turns and my name is called. I race up to the check-in area.

'Please hurry. The plane is leaving now.'

I quickly re-classify my backpack as hand luggage. A hurried goodbye to Ahmad and I'm out on the steaming tarmac, ready to climb up the metal stairs towards a cabin crew reception committee wearing perpetual plastic smiles.

The flight to Kuching is just a hop, skip and a jump. By the time I have skimmed through the inflight magazine, the aircraft has started its descent towards the capital of Sarawak, its wings shuddering and rocking as we pass through the black of a tropical storm, nose pointed towards a wet runway that glistens in the rain. The humidity is oppressive, but by the time I'm in the taxi the sky has cleared and the city is bathed in a soft yellow light.

'Holiday Inn, *terima kasih!*'

The driver looks me over through his rear mirror, but refrains from commenting on my muddy appearance. I don't care; Indy's back in town and looks forward to some creature comforts. The wide tree-lined boulevards that lead into town end abruptly in a maze of little streets overflowing with exotic merchandise.

India Street, with noisy spice merchants promoting their wares, colourful *saris* swaying in the breeze, tables of shiny brassware, and all sorts of pots and pans destined for kitchens filled with a thousand fragrances. Around the corner, affording glimpses of the exquisite Moorish-style mosque, an enticing shopper's paradise for the devout Muslim: shop after shop brimming with prayer rugs, caps, beautiful framed verses from the Koran and all kinds of memorabilia from Mecca.

The driver pulls in at a gas station on the other side of a large bustling square adjoining the markets, where bunches of bananas and all manner of produce dangle from the low canvas awnings of their stalls.

'Market,' says the driver. 'Bus station. Shops. Restaurants.' He points out the areas as he speaks. 'The centre of Kuching. You want sightseeing? I take you. One hour. Forty ringgit.'

I decline and we drive on through narrow streets that bear witness to the town's strong Chinese influence. The signs above shops and doorways have me fascinated: 'Ah Choo- Herbal Medicines', 'Hop Kee – Specialist in Ear, Nose and Throat. Also Haemorrhoids' (I hope he sterilises his instruments), and then one for the boys, 'Fuk Yue – Tailor'.

We emerge from the confusion of narrow streets into a wide open square lined with trees and dominated by Raja Charles Brooke's Courthouse. It's a magnificent building, surrounded by massive stone columns that cast welcome shade over the tiled walkways. Opposite us, the Sarawak

River, flowing placidly along a pleasant promenade filled
with Kuching's multi-cultural mix of people, out for a late
afternoon stroll. The Raja's residence, the *Astana*, sits
majestically on a hill across the river, like a white pearl in
an exotic garden. My final destination is straight ahead of
us.

'Welcome to the Holiday Inn.' An eager bellboy takes my
backpack. 'Any more luggage, Sir?'

'No, that's all, thank you. But I left some baggage in
storage before I left, would you mind taking that up to my
room?'

I hand him my claim ticket and he disappears into the
tiny baggage room off the lobby. While I check in, I discover
that small clumps of dried mud are falling off me, forming
circles around my boots on the plush green carpet. I pretend
not to notice. But the concierge does. He looks me up and
down in a way only a concierge can, and discretely instructs
a bellboy to remove any trace of me ever having been there.
I smile and thank him. He inclines his head and smiles back.

The ride in the lift seems to take forever. But the man
tinkling away on his piano somewhere above me is keeping
me company. I'm eager to have a shower, make some calls
back home, and above all get changed into a fresh set of
clothes. Finally, the doors open and I find my room at the
end of the hallway.

Traditional room inspection: bathroom with little soaps,
shampoos, shoe-polish kit and shower cap; toilet paper with
tip neatly folded into a triangle; mini-bar stocked up. I turn
down the air-con, call home, have a shower and get changed
into a clean set of clothes. A quick wipe of the steamed-up

bathroom mirror tells me that I am presentable once more. Room key, money, credit cards. I slam the door behind me.

At the lifts, I find two elderly couples waiting. From Idaho it seems, judging by their baseball caps. The women are wearing 'I've stayed with Headhunters at Batang Ai' T-shirts. They've obviously taken the trip up the nearby Skrang River where many longhouses have set themselves up for the tourist trade, putting on cultural shows, selling *borak* at three ringgit a pop and offering overnight stays in Westernised *biliks*, complete with running hot water and flushing toilets. When the guests have departed, the locals usually change back into jeans and put their traditional clothes away until the next tour group arrives.

'Hi there, just arrived in town?' The man with camcorder and booming voice asks.

'Yes.'

'Hot, ain't it?' His portly wife fans herself with a tourist map. Trying to liven-up the conversation, I remark on the girls' T-shirts.

'I see you've been to Batang Ai.'

'Oh yes, just come back. You been there?'

'Er, no. I've heard of it.'

'Well, let me tell you what, you wanna go. The real thing. Headhunters and all. They put on a welcoming ceremony for us and a war dance – and that was something else. Wasn't it, George?'

George nods.

'And they showed him how to use a blowpipe, didn't they George?'

George nods again, 'Oh, yeah, weird experience that was.'

The lift arrives, announcing itself with flashing lights above the door.

'Great shopping, too,' the second woman extends her wrist towards me, 'bought that bracelet. A real bargain. Handmade. Ain't it pretty?'

'You simply gotta go there. They run tours from the hotel, you know. Tell the man, George.'

'Yep. Gotta do it.'

I thank them for their advice and promise I would look into it. At the far end of the lobby I can hear the hiss of an espresso machine. My pace quickens.

Bibliography

References

1.   Munan, H. (1990), *Iban Stories*, Kuala Lumpur: Penerbit Fajar Bakti Sdn.Bhd.
2.   Linklater, A. (1990), *Wild People*, London: John Murray
3.   Davis, W. (1990), *Penan: Voice for the Borneo Rainforest*, Kuala Lumpur: S. Abdul Majeed & Co.
4.   Ibid., Foreword by Dr David Suzuki
5.   Manser, B. (1996), *Voices from the Rainforest*, Petaling Jaya: INSAN
6.   Khaidir, A. (1994), *Save the Penans*, Kuala Lumpur: Berita Publishing
7.   Harrisson, T. (1990), *An Account of the Oxford University Expedition of 1932, Borneo Jungle*, Singapore: Oxford University Press
8.   International Rivers Network (1995), A Review of the Environmental Impact Assessment of the Bakun Hydroelectric Project, Berkeley CA: IRN
9.   Hartley, C.H. (1992), The Sea Dyaks and Other Races of Sarawak – Heads I Win: Contributions to The Sarawak Gazette, 1888–1930, Kuala Lumpur: Dewan Bahasa dan Pustaka

Further Reading

– (1992), *The Sea Dyaks and other Races of Borneo – Reprints 1888–1930*, Kuala Lumpur: Dewan Bahasa dan Pustaka

Barclay, J. (1988), *A Stroll through Borneo*, Wellington: January Books

Bisch, J. (1961), *Ulu – The World's End*, London: Allen & Unwin

Geddes, W.R. (1991), *Nine Dayak Nights: The Story of a Dayak Folk Hero*, Singapore: Oxford University Press

Gullick, J.M. (1995) *Adventures and Encounters – Europeans in South-East Asia*, Kuala Lumpur: Oxford University Press

Hose, C. (1986) *Field-Book of a Jungle-Wallah – Shore, River and Forest Life in Sarawak*, Singapore: Oxford University Press

Kedit, P.M. (1993), *Iban Bejalai*, Kuala Lumpur: Sarawak Literary Society

Kedit, P.M. (1982), *An Ecological Survey of the Penan*, Kuching: Sarawak Museum

King, V.T. (1992), *The Best of Borneo Travel*, Singapore: Oxford University Press

King, V.T. (1994), *World Within: The Ethnic Groups of Borneo*, Kuala Lumpur: S. Abdul Majeed & Co

Krohn, W.O. (1991), *In Borneo Jungles: Among the Dyak Headhunters*, Singapore: Oxford University Press

Lo, J. (1986), *Glimpses from Sarawak's Past*, Kuching: Agas Sdn.Bhd.

MacDonald, D. (1992), *Expedition to Borneo*, Kuala Lumpur: S. Abdul Majeed & Co.

MacDonald, M. (1956), *Borneo People*, London: Jonathan Cape

MacKinnon, J. (1975), *The World's Wild Places: Borneo*, Amsterdam: Time-Life Books

Morrison, H. (1982), *Sarawak*, Singapore: Times Books International

Munan, H. (1989), *Sarawak Crafts – Methods, Materials and Motifs*, Singapore: Oxford University Press

O'Hanlon, R. (1987), *Into the Heart of Borneo*, New York: Vintage Departures, Random House

Rain, N. (1992), *Penan: Borneo's Hunters & Gatherers*, Kuala Lumpur: S. Abdul Majeed & Co

Sarawak Gazette; various contributors.

Sutlive, H.Jr. (1992) *The Iban of Sarawak – Chronicle of a Vanishing World*, Kuala Lumpur: S. Abdul Majeed & Co

Tettoni, L.I. (1996), *Sarawak Style*, Singapore: Times Editions

Wright, L. (1983), *Vanishing Worlds – The Iban of Borneo*, New York: John Weatherhill

glossary of Translations

adat	tribal laws
astana	official government residence
babi	wild pig
bagus	good, fine
bejalai	test of manhood
bekela	leaves used as sandpaper
bilik	longhouse apartment
borak	intoxicating drink made from fermented rice, same as tuak
dipden	slaves
durian a	tropical fruit
gatimang	plant used as an antidote to poisoned darts
gawai niau	end of mourning celebration
gawai	traditional celebration
hipuy	common people
ikan bilis	dried fish
ipoh	tree from which poison is extracted
jong	dream bracelet
jumpa lagi	farewell
kampei	cheers!
kampong	traditional village
kanjar dodo	war dance
kedai kopi	coffee shop
kopi susu	sweet coffee
lamin	jungle shelter made from saplings and palm fronds
maaf	sorry
makan or makai	food, to eat
maren	the ruling class
mee goreng	fried noodles
minum	drink
nasi kampong	a fried rice dish
nimang	war song
nipah	type of palm
nyagang	species of tree from which blowpipes are made

Oia Aheng	story of the creation of the world
orang putih	white man
orang ulu	a person from upriver tribal areas
pade	brother
padi	seeds
pandong	altar for headhunting ceremony
panyin	common people
parang	sword, machette
Phengulu	chief of all longhouses in one area
pua-kumbu	woven mat
rendang	beef dish
ruai	main veranda
sago	type of palm
salong	funeral plinth
sape	a string instrument
selabit	carrying basket
selamat malam	good evening. good night
Selamat jalan	farewell, have a pleasant journey
Selamat petang	good afternoon
Selemat pagi	good morning
sumpitan	blowpipe for poisoned darts
tajeun	poison from tree sap
tamu	trading day
tandas	toilet
taro	a root vegetable
terima kasih	thank you
teksi	taxi
toh	spirits
tong kang	Chinese cargo boats
tuai burong	the longhouse chief-birdwatcher
tuai rumah	headman
tuak	intoxicating drink made from rice
ular	snake
ulu	upriver tribal areas
wayang	shadow puppet show